The Capitalist Class:
An International Study

The Capitalist Class:
An International
Study

Edited by

Tom Bottomore and Robert J. Brym

NEW YORK UNIVERSITY PRESS
Washington Square, New York

First published in the U.S.A. in 1989 by
NEW YORK UNIVERSITY PRESS
Washington Square
New York, NY 10003

Library of Congress Cataloging-in-Publication Data
The Capitalist class: an international study/edited by Tom Bottomore
and Robert J. Brym.
p. cm.
Bibliography: p.
Includes index.
ISBN 0-8147-1110-3   ISBN 0-8147-1111-1 (pbk.)
1. Social classes—Case Studies.   2. Elite (Social sciences)—Case
studies.   3. Capitalists and financiers—Case studies.   4. Middle
classes—Case studies.   5. Capitalism—Case studies.   I. Bottomore.
T. B.   II. Brym, Robert J., 1951-
HT609.C28   1989   88-31523
305.5'54—dc19   CIP

Contents

1 The Capitalist Class

Tom Bottomore

I

When social scientists, and still more political journalists, nowadays refer to the 'demise' of class in the advanced capitalist societies they may have several different phenomena in mind. One is the contraction (in absolute or relative size) of the industrial working class, and the supposed decline, in various senses, of the traditional labour movement in its trade union, cooperative and political forms. A second is the related growth of the middle classes, the consequences of which have often been represented as the emergence (more or less imminent, or already partially accomplished) of 'middle-class societies' in which class differences become blurred, and the conflicts between a dominant class and a subordinate class no longer have the salience or the political importance which they had in the nineteenth century and the first half of the twentieth century. A third phenomenon is the change, strongly asserted by some and contested by others, in the composition and nature of the dominant class, or dominant groups, in advanced capitalist societies; a change that has been debated in terms of a shift in the locus of power from the owners to the controllers of productive resources, and of a movement towards a new type of post-industrial, technocratic or 'programmed' society (Touraine 1969). Finally, there are the consequences for the class structure, and especially for class relations, of rapid and sustained economic growth after 1945, the achievement (and maintenance until the mid-1970s) of full employment, and the expansion of welfare services; all of which produced much higher and steadily improving levels of living for the great majority of the population in these societies (Bottomore 1975: ch. 8).

These changes, however, have been interpreted in diverse ways, and most of the interpretations have concentrated on the situation of the working class and the middle classes, while paying much less attention to the dominant class, or to the class structure as a whole. The various and conflicting views on the rise of the middle classes have been critically surveyed by Abercrombie and Urry (1983), but their work also goes on to advance a more general claim; namely, that a profound transformation of the class structure has been taking place in the capitalist societies of the late twentieth century with the growth of a 'service class' which is 'taking on ... the functions of capital, namely, conceptualisation, control and reproduction' (p. 153), and increasingly dominates the deskilled white-collar workers and a diminished working class. Their argument resembles that of Touraine (1969: 51) to the effect that while property was 'the criterion of membership in the former dominant classes, the new dominant class is defined by knowledge and a certain level of education', although they do not go quite so far in dismissing the element of property ownership in class domination.

A distinctive feature of such studies is that in analysing the class structure as a whole they are obliged to consider the nature of the dominant class (instead of ignoring its existence and dealing in isolation with the working class or middle classes), and at the same time to recognise the existence in some form of a conflict between a dominant class and subordinate classes, no matter how those classes are constituted. In this respect they have affinities with some earlier attempts to move away from, and so far as possible replace, a Marxist theory of class structure; and notably with the theory of elites. The essential concept in the latter theory, originally developed in somewhat different ways by Pareto and Mosca, is that of a 'governing elite' or 'political class' which is not – or not exclusively – constituted on the basis of ownership of productive resources, but as a result of directly political struggles in which a minority of 'superior individuals' establish themselves as the rulers of society (Bottomore 1964; Albertoni 1987).

According to this conception the major conflicts in society (to which Pareto attributed great importance, regarding the idea of class struggle as Marx's fundamental contribution to social theory) take place between the elite and the masses, and between elites which are competing for supreme power.

The elite concept has played an important part in later social theory: in Max Weber's (and Michels') emphasis on the 'charismatic leader' and his critical view of mass democracy; in Schumpeter's account of the role of the entrepreneur in the development of capitalism and his redefinition of democracy (following Weber) as 'competition for leadership'; and in various studies of the relation between elites and classes which aimed to separate clearly the economic and political spheres. C. Wright Mills (1956) rejected the concept of 'ruling class' which he described as a 'short-cut theory' asserting that 'an economic class rules politically [which] may or may not at times be true', but in general 'does not allow enough autonomy to the political order and its agents, and says nothing about the military as such'. Instead, he proposed the term 'power elite' to describe the coalescence of three elites – political leaders, big business executives and military chiefs – into a unified ruling group in American society. In a similar fashion Aron (1950) posed the question of classes and elites in terms of the relation between social differentiation and political hierarchy in modern societies, and argued that the 'abolition of classes' in the sense of abolishing private ownership of the means of production would not resolve the problems of social differentiation, formation of elites, and inequalities of political power.

II

The chapters in this book examine directly the capitalist class in seven leading industrial countries, and in a concluding chapter the international connections of capital. In the course of their studies the contributors also raise more general questions about the composition of the capitalist class, its place in the class structure, and the changes that have taken place in the postwar period. The purpose of my introduction is to analyse more fully these wider issues. We may begin by distinguishing two broad problem areas in such a theoretical analysis: first, how is the capitalist class to be defined and located in the class structure; and secondly, in what sense and degree can the capitalist class be shown to be a dominant or ruling class?

The capitalist class (or bourgeoisie) can be defined, in Marxist terms, as a constituent element in the class structure of a society based upon the capitalist mode of production. This distinctive class structure comprises the owners of the major productive resources (or as Marx expressed it, 'the owners of the system of production'), the industrial workers who sell their labour power to these owners, and diverse 'middle strata' (including small producers and white-collar workers of varying levels of skill). The basic conditions of a capitalist economy were more comprehensively stated (in a form broadly consonant with Marx's conception and clearly derived from it) by Max Weber (1923: 208–9): rational capital accounting as the norm for all large industrial undertakings, which involves the appropriation of all physical means of production as disposable property of autonomous private industrial enterprises, freedom of the market, rational technology and mechanization, calculable law, free labour (i.e. the existence of persons who are legally in the position and also economically compelled to sell their labour on the market without restriction), and finally the commercialization of economic life.

But Weber, like Schumpeter, emphasized as the defining characteristic of capitalism 'the method of enterprise' and the role of the entrepreneur (Weber 1923: 207), whereas in Marx's conception the crucial feature is the private ownership of productive resources and the specific form of the social labour process which produces commodities (Bottomore 1985: 6–10). Marx distinguished between industrial capital (the essential feature of capitalism), merchant capital and money capital, and in later Marxist writing money capital was given increasing prominence, particularly by Hilferding (1910) in his conception of 'finance capital'. In the later stages of capitalism, therefore, the capitalist class came to be viewed as comprising the private owners of industrial, merchant and money capital; and the role of the banks in the process of capitalist development was more strongly emphasized, along with the growth of joint-stock companies or corporations, which Marx himself briefly analysed in their early stages as a phenomenon of transition from capitalism to socialism.[1]

The development of giant corporations, especially multinational corporations, has proceeded apace in the second half of the twentieth century. At the same time the role of the providers of money capital, now comprising insurance companies, which have at their disposal large pension funds, and trust companies, as well as the banks, has been enhanced, and there has also been increasing state intervention in the economy, notwithstanding the efforts in a few countries to return to what is regarded as a more *laissez-faire*, 'free market' type of economy. In general, therefore, the economic system of the advanced capitalist countries can appropriately be described as 'organized capitalism' and we need to consider the nature and composition of the capitalist class in this system.[2]

A long-standing debate, which has been re-animated in recent years, concerns the so-called 'managerial revolution' in which, it is claimed, the dominant position of the owners of capital has been taken over by managers and technical experts who are now responsible in the large corporations for all major decisions affecting the production process. This claim raises a variety of questions. It is obvious that the major productive enterprises in a modern capitalist economy are not for the most part owned by individual capitalist entrepreneurs, although the decline of individual and family ownership has sometimes been exaggerated (see Chapter 3 on France and Chapter 5 on Italy below; and on Canada, Ornstein 1988), but it does not in any case follow that the juridical ownership of corporate enterprises is fragmented among numerous small shareholders who have surrendered control to non-owning managers. On the contrary, studies of modern corporations have shown that although there is diffusion of share ownership a few large shareholders are normally able to exert effective control, and that the top managers themselves are usually substantial shareholders.[3] It is necessary, further, to make a distinction between the *juridical* and the *economic* ownership of capital. Hegedüs (1976: 93–105), in his analysis of property relations, distinguishes between juridical ownership and effective 'possession', the latter being 'the manifestation of property relations as an essential relation' which enables individuals or groups of individuals to 'direct people's activities as the executors of productive labour', to dispose 'over the means of production and the structure of production', and 'to use, appropriate or at least distribute the surplus product'.

Thus in two respects it can be claimed that an identifiable group of individuals, comprising the large shareholders and the top managers and directors (who may also be shareholders), controls the process of production in a capitalist economy; and this directly challenges the view expounded by Touraine, Abercrombie and Urry, and others, that a 'new class', which is not constituted by property relations as juridical owners or effective possessors of productive resources, has replaced the former capitalist class. At the same time it is evident that the capitalist class has been transformed over the past century by the rise to economic dominance of the large corporation, so that the structure of ownership or possession has become more impersonal that it used to be in the days of the individual capitalist entrepreneur. But as Scott (1979: 175–6) has shown in a very thorough study, this

has not resulted in a loss of power by wealthy persons. . . . Wealthy families hold shares in a large number of companies and they form a pool from which corporate managers are recruited, though these managers may not come from families having a substantial ownership stake in the companies which they run. The propertied class has interests throughout the corporate system and is able to ensure its continuity over time through the monopolization of social and cultural assets as well as the monopolization of wealth. Those who head the major corporations and the constellations of interests which control them are increasingly characterized by the possession of some kind of educational diploma, and so the educational system becomes a crucial mechanism in ensuring class domination of the economy.

It is in relation to the last point that the idea of a 'service class' is important, and even then it has to be seen as a group which is by no means distinct from the capitalist class, but on the contrary forms part of it.

If the argument that a new 'service class', unrelated to property ownership, is becoming or has become the dominant class, must be rejected, so too must those more general elite theories which assert that in every society an organized minority, constituted on various social bases other than property ownership, dominates the unorganized majority.[4] Critics of Mills' (1956) concept of the 'power elite' observed that he did not show how the three separate elites which he identified are formed into a single elite, that contrary to his own thesis property ownership was treated as the ultimate source of power, and that Mills' social elite (or 'high society') is constituted by an upper class 'based upon large corporate wealth that is looked after by male members of the intermarrying families that are its basis' (Domhoff 1970: 56, 60-70). In recent studies of elites the idea of substituting elite theory for class theory seems to have been largely abandoned, and the central preoccupation has become the relation between democracy and political leadership, and more generally the role of political leaders in diverse types of modern society (Albertoni 1987: 145-64). This change of emphasis is connectd with new conceptions of democratic participation, and with the extent of state intervention in, or direction of, the economy in socialist as well as capitalist societies, and in the postwar welfare states which can perhaps be seen as occupying a 'halfway house'. I shall return to these questions later.

The thesis that a clearly delineated capitalist class[5] exists as a component part of the class structure in societies based upon the capitalist mode of production has not yet, in my view, been seriously undermined by the varous criticisms directed against it, or replaced by any convincing alternative conception, and it has therefore to be retained as an essential part of any viable theory of classes. It is from this standpoint that the following chapters analyse in detail the main features of the capitalist class in the leading capitalist countries.

III

We have now to consider in the light of the evidence that these chapters provide how the capitalist class is located in the class structure, what changes it has undergone in recent times, and in what sense it has remained a dominant or ruling class. There can be no doubt that over the postwar period as a whole the capitalist class in the West and in Japan was generally able to maintain and even strengthen its position in the class structure, notwithstanding the considerable changes that have taken place in economic and social life. Chapter 5 on Italy, for example, notes that 'the recent history of the Italian capitalist class provides an interesting case of reacquisition of business power and influence', while Chapter 9, in the course of an historical study of the formation of an international capitalist class, examines the role of the Marshall Plan in re-establishing capitalist control of the West European economies under American leadership in the context of the Cold War. On the other hand, Chapter 7 on Canada shows the consequences of increasing working-class power between 1945 and 1981, as well as the effects of the subsequent capitalist reaction; and there have certainly been periods of growing working-class power elsewhere, especially in the immediate postwar years, as I argue below.

Diverse historical and cultural contexts have affected the development of the capitalist class in different countries, as the following chapters reveal, but there are also major universal factors which have largely determined its course. One of these, discussed earlier, is the rapid growth of large corporations which have acquired a dominant position in national economies and in international capitalism. This has involved a more impersonal type of ownership, which is still based, however, upon family wealth; and also an increasingly close connection between productive enterprises and financial institutions (see the discussion of interlocking directorates in Chapter 8 on the United States and in Chapter 9 below; and also Scott 1986). The question of the domination of industrial companies by the banks, as formulated by Hilferding, has been vigorously debated (Coakley and Harris 1983: ch. 8), and the situation undoubtedly differs from one country to another; but at the very least, significant alliances between the banks and industry can be identified.

The position of the capitalist class in the class structure has been affected by changes in other social classes. In the immediate postwar period long-established working-class parties were very strong in many West European countries, and their policies, which included a considerable expansion of the social services and the nationalization of basic industrial enterprises (and in a few cases also financial institutions), placed constraints upon the capitalist class. The greatly enhanced role of the state in the economy[6] limited to some extent the accumulation process of private capital, while facilitating it in other respects; and these societies could no longer be regarded as *purely* capitalist, even though the dominance of capital was not fundamentally challenged. By the 1960s they were frequently described as 'mixed economies', and they fitted reasonably well the category of 'organized capitalism' which both Hilferding and Schumpeter regarded as a transitional stage between capitalism and socialism. But the transition was soon arrested (as Schumpeter had suggested might happen) at a stage which came to be described as 'corporatism', broadly conceived by some social thinkers as a more or less enduring form of society in which a powerful state, in cooperation with the corporations and the trade unions, determines economic policy and regulates social life.[7] Since the 1970s, however, there has been a trend towards a 'restoration of capitalism' in a more *laissez-faire* form, through the restriction of public spending and the reprivatisation of nationalized industries; a trend that has emerged most strongly in Britain where government expenditure has slowly declined from 50 per cent to some 42 per cent of GDP, and will no doubt decline further.

One change which has greatly facilitated this trend is the diminishing social and political strength of the working class in most of the advanced capitalist countries, vividly illustrated by the decline of such occupations as coalmining and steelmaking which formed the core of the traditional labour movement. Overall, manual workers now account for less than 50 per cent of the employed population.[8] In manufacturing industry, increasingly automated, new occupations have developed which have no historical links with the labour movement.[9] At the same time there has been a great expansion of service occupations, but these are extremely varied and cannot be assigned as a whole to a particular class. Many are very low paid, more or less manual occupations; others may be regarded as constituting a 'service class', but this is more differentiated than Abercrombie and Urry (1983) suggest, and alternative analyses have been given by Poulantzas (1975) and Wright (1975).

Only a small segment of it, comprising the top managers and directors of companies (who may or may not be professionally qualified as accountants, graduates of business schools, technical experts, and so on), actually performs the 'functions of capital' in the sense of directly determining the use of capital and controlling the labour process. A much larger segment simply executes, at various levels of responsibility, the decisions of the possessors of capital. Beyond the confines of the service class in the sphere of production, trade and finance, there is a range of white-collar occupations, including those in the public services, whose members are not directly involved in capitalist production and express diverse and vacillating attitudes to capitalism as a form of society.

The strength of the capitalist class during much of the postwar period rests in part, therefore, upon the relative weakness of opposing, or potentially opposing classes, which has resulted not only from changes in class structure, but also from a certain loss of confidence in, or disillusionment with, the idea of a socialist alternative to capitalism, following the experience of authoritarian socialist regimes in Eastern Europe and the often limited achievements of socialist or social democratic governments when they have been in power in capitalist countries.[10] It is important, however, that we should consider also the inherent strength of the capitalist class, which is a major element in its dominance and its capacity to rule.

The capitalist class is dominant economically, politically and culturally. The foundation of its dominance is the ownership of the major productive resources of society, which bestows the power to shape and direct the whole social labour process. The corresponding subordination of other classes is primarily determined by this situation, which Marx summarized as 'the dull compulsion of economic relations'. This economic dominance is the main source, sometimes in indirect and complex ways, of a general social dominance; that is to say, the aquisition of social privileges and the permeation of social life and institutions generally with a capitalist ethos, or the values of the capitalist class. It is also the source of a cultural dominance through the legal institutions, the educational system and the mass media. But this general dominance is neither monolithic nor unchallenged.[11] Social and cultural dominance does not flow automatically from economic power, and the latter may itself be restricted by the actions of government; in particular by social and fiscal policies designed to redistribute wealth and income, and by the nationalization or socialization of major sectors of production. The dominance of the capitalist class, which may be seen as being always to a certain extent precarious in the advanced countries, needs to be maintained and assured by political power. We have therefore to enquire whether, and in what manner, the capitalist class is a 'ruling class'. This question has several degrees of complexity.

First, do capitalists act collectively as a class in the exercise of political power? The problem posed here has a more general reference to classes as 'collective actors', and it has been the subject of much recent controversy. Some critics, for the most part exponents of 'rational choice' theories, have maintained, following the earlier arguments for methodological individualism, that only individual human beings can be actors; others, while upholding the notion of collective actors who, like individuals, are capable of reaching decisions and acting accordingly, argue that classes do not belong to this category.[12] This is too large and general an issue to pursue here, and I shall only state my view that the arguments against a conception of classes as collective actors are not conclusive.[13] At the same time these arguments highlight the fact that collective actors are very complex entities, and that classes in particular are extremely variable – both historically and as between different classes – in their capacity to act collectively. In the present context the important point is that the capitalist class is in general a more effective collective actor than are other classes. One reason for this is that it forms something close to an 'organized minority', in which there is a relatively high degree of social and political interaction among the members, through family connections, associations deriving from a distinctive educational experience, interlocking directorates, business associations, pressure groups, and so on. A second reason is that the capitalist class disposes over ample resources, both economic and cultural, for coordinating action and implementing decisions.

But as I observed earlier, this does not mean that the capitalist class is completely unified or that its power is unassailable. There may be significant divisions within it (sectoral, regional, ethnic) as some of the following chapters show (see especially Chapter 5 on Italy); its actions may be confused and unsure; its power is always limited in some degree by the actions of other classes, and may be substantially curtailed, or even destroyed, in particular historical circumstances, such as the upheavals of war or economic depression. But over the postwar period as a whole it seems clear that the capitalist class in the leading capitalist countries has effectively maintained its position as a ruling class, and in some cases has enhanced its power, notably during the past decade. We have first to examine the evidence for this claim, and then further, to provide some explanation of the phenomenon.

A dominant class exercises its rule through political institutions – government, administration, judiciary – whose higher personnel must represent the class, unifying so far as possible its actions and reinforcing its control over the process of social reproduction. In the case of the capitalist class this means ensuring the reproduction of capitalist relations of production and hence the private accumulation of capital, and at the same time the reproduction of political and cultural institutions which are favourable to its rule. These conditions are most obviously secured when government, administration and the judiciary are safely in the hands of people who themselves belong to the capitalist class, or in some other way are wholly committed to it. Hence the importance of studying the social origins and class affiliations of the leading members of the principal state institutions; and all such studies have shown that over the long term the capitalist class has succeeded in retaining its dominant position. In most countries, even where there have been periods of rule by labour or social democratic parties, the capitalist class has been able to resist any profound structural changes which would fundamentally alter the balance of political power,[14] and in some countries (above all in Britain) over the past decade it has launched a vigorous counter-offensive which can properly be described as a 'class struggle from above' (Miliband 1987).

But it is not only by studying the class character of the state in terms of those people who occupy its 'commanding heights' that the rule of the capitalist class can be demonstrated.[15] We can also judge the degree of its success in maintaining a ruling, and generally dominant, position in society by observing the effects of its actions on the social structure and the reproduction of social relations. One important effect is the maintenance of great inequalities in the distribution of wealth and income, especially in Britain, which has possibly, in the words of Atkinson (1974: 23), 'the doubtful distinction of leading the international inequality league'. Although it is difficult to measure, in particular, the distribution of wealth, and there is a marked lack of fundamental research in this field,[16] the evidence for Britain suggests that in the postwar period up to the mid-1960s there was a gradual diminution of inequality (Field 1983), thereafter a period of little change, and since the late 1970s an increasing inequality of income and almost certainly of wealth. Although these trends are not exactly paralleled in other leading capitalist countries it is clear that the capitalist class overall has been remarkably successful in defending its wealth. From another aspect this is also evident in the continued predominance of large corporations in the ecomony, only tempered by a limited nationalization of some basic industries (which did not radically change the balance of economic power and is now being countered by policies of reprivatization), again with considerable variations between countries. Capitalist relations of production and control of the social labour process have thus been broadly sustained throughout the postwar period, and along with this a general social and cultural dominance, notwithstanding the occasional vigour of political movements that aimed to bring about a radical reconstruction of the economy and society.

We need to consider, therefore, just how the capitalist class has been able to remain in power. The problem can be stated, and has frequently been stated in one form or another, in the following way: how is it that in democratic societies a small minority can effectively dominate and rule? Or as de Tocqueville in the mid-nineteenth century expressed the idea from the other side: 'it is contradictory that the people should be at the same time impoverished and sovereign'. Of course, the capitalist class has not always ruled democratically, as the experience of fascism in Europe and the existence of miscellaneous dictatorships throughout the world at the present time remind us. But the leading capitalist countries today are democratic societies, even if they are not strongly committed to the greatest possible extension of democracy, and it is in this situation that the continued dominance of the capitalist class has to be explained.

Some elements of an explanation were suggested earlier: the character of the capitalist class as an 'organized minority', the effects of changes in the class structure, and the doubts about socialism as an alternative form of society. But to these we should add the effects of generally rising standards of living from 1945 to the 1970s, brought about by rapid economic growth, full employment, a great expansion of social services, and a modest redistribution of income. Contrary to Schumpeter's (1942) argument that capitalism would be destroyed by its economic success, which in his view was bringing about social and cultural conditions inimical to its own survival, it seems probable that this success, when it is accompanied by changes in the occupational structure and by somewhat more egalitarian social policies, does reinforce the dominance of the capitalist class (Bottomore 1984: ch. 8). Conversely, its dominance, and its capacity to rule, are threatened by economic recession, growing inequality, mass unemployment, increasing poverty, and widening social divisions; that is, by new circumstances such as those that have developed in the 1980s.

The present domination by the capitalist class, therefore, is still no more than a particular historical condition which is susceptible to change over shorter or longer periods; and social scientists are well advised to set their studies in the context of a long-term view of the development of modern capitalism. That is precisely what is done in the following chapters, whose authors show in considerable detail the historical trends in different countries, as well as the international connections which have so far made it difficult for any single country alone to implement a radical alternative to existing economic and social policies. This volume, we hope, will encourage further and continuing studies of the capitalist class, its course of development and its modes of rule. It is after all of the highest importance that we should know as accurately as possible what interests are at work in our societies, and where the present dominant forces are taking us.

NOTES

1. In *Capital*, vol. 3, ch. 27, Marx observed that the joint-stock company 'is the abolition of the capitalist mode of production within capitalist production itself, a self-transcending contradiction which is *prima facie* only a phase of transition to a new form of production ... the capitalist joint-stock companies, just as much as the cooperative factories, have to be seen as transitional forms between the capitalist mode of production and the associated one, only that the opposition is transcended negatively in the one and positively in the other'. This idea was further developed by Hilferding (1927) in his conception of 'organized capitalism' as a 'planned and consciously directed economy', and it played a major part in Schumpeter's analysis of the decline of capitalism, according to which 'the economic process tends to socialize *itself*' (Schumpeter 1942: 219; see also Bottomore 1985: 66–8).
2. See note 1. Virtually the same conception has been expounded by Marxist economists in the USSR and the German Democratic Republic in the theory of 'state monopoly capitalism', but with a different political emphasis (Hardach and Karras 1978: 63–8; Bottomore 1985: 68–9). The latter concept is preferred by some theorists because it emphasizes the important role of the state in the recent development of capitalism.
3. See the entry 'Joint-stock company' in Bottomore (1983).
4. It deserves notice that Mosca, and still more Michels, anticipated to some extent the thesis of the 'service class' by attributing the dominance of the organized minority to their possession of educational qualifications.
5. By this I do not mean that the boundaries of the class can easily be drawn in a definitive way, but that such a class, despite its partly indeterminate boundaries, can be conceptually distinguished and located in a real structure of classes. Social classes, like other entities with which the social sciences have to deal, always have somewhat blurred edges.
6. Indicated by the increasing proportion of GDP spent by government. In Britain, for example, government expenditure amounted to about 10 per cent of GDP before the First World War, just over 20 per cent of GDP in the 1930s, and 50 per cent of GDP in the mid-1970s; and there was a similar trend in other capitalist countries.
7. See Panitch (1980). But 'corporatism' seems to differ little from 'organized capitalism' except in so far as it virtually eliminates any idea

of a transition to socialism; and the same phenomena are in fact analysed by Habermas (1973: 33–40) using the latter concept.

8. The change has been described in a somewhat exaggerated way by Gorz (1980). For a more general account of the French labour movement see Touraine (1987).

9. Nevertheless, some of these occupations could be regarded as elements of a 'new working class'; see Mallet (1963), and for a critical review of this conception Mann (1973).

10. These observations raise complex issues which cannot be explored further in the present context. I have discussed them in greater detail in a forthcoming book (Bottomore 1989). But it may be noted here that the concepts of 'effective possession' and the 'service class', or closely related concepts, have also been used in critical studies of the emergence of a new class structure in the East European socialist societies (Hegedüs 1976; Konrád and Szelényi 1979).

11. Schumpeter (1942) thought that the decline of capitalism would result in part from the decay of capitalist values brought about by social criticism and the widely diffused critical attitude fostered by capitalism itself; and many social theorists in the 1960s envisaged a movement towards a more socialist form of society inspired by a 'cultural revolution'.

12. See the discussion by Hindess (1987), and his more general study of rational models (1988).

13. I have developed this argument more fully in an essay on class interests and class consciousness which is to be published in a volume of collected essays.

14. There are, of course, significant differences between countries, and in some of the smaller countries such as Sweden and Austria the political power of the capitalist class has been more severely restricted. But it still cannot be said that these countries have advanced very far towards socialism as a radically different type of economy and society; their regimes are best described as advanced forms of 'welfare capitalism' and the 'mixed economy'.

15. See on this question the debate between Miliband and Poulantzas, in Miliband (1983: ch. 2) and Poulantzas (1969, 1976); also Alford and Friedland (1985).

16. In Britain a Royal Commission on the Distribution of Income and Wealth was established by the Labour government in 1974 and published several useful reports before being disbanded by the Conservative government in 1979.

REFERENCES

Abercrombie, Nicholas and Urry, John (1983) *Capital, Labour and the Middle Classes* (London: Allen & Unwin).

Albertoni, Ettore A. (1987) *Mosca and the Theory of Elitism* (Oxford: Basil Blackwell).

Alford, Robert R. and Friedland, Roger (1985) *Powers of Theory: Capitalism, the State and Democracy* (Cambridge: Cambridge University Press).

Aron, Raymond (1950) 'Social structure and the ruling class', *British Journal of Sociology*, I (1) pp. 1–16 and I (2) pp. 126–43.

Atkinson, A. B. (1974) *Unequal Shares: Wealth in Britain* (Harmondsworth: Penguin Books).

Bottomore, Tom (1966 [1964]) *Elites and Society* (Harmondsworth: Penguin Books).

Bottomore, Tom (1975) *Sociology as Social Criticism* (London: Allen & Unwin).

Bottomore, Tom (ed.) (1983) *A Dictionary of Marxist Thought* (Oxford: Basil Blackwell).

Bottomore, Tom (1984) *Sociology and Socialism* (Brighton: Wheatsheaf Books).

Bottomore, Tom (1985) *Theories of Modern Capitalism* (London: Allen & Unwin).

Bottomore, Tom (1989) *The Socialist Economy: Theory and Practice* (Brighton: Wheatsheaf Books).

Coakley, J. and Harris, L. (1983) *The City of Capital* (Oxford: Basil Blackwell).

Domhoff, G. William (1970) *The Higher Circles: The Governing Class in America* (New York: Random House).

Field, Frank (ed.) (1983) *The Wealth Report 2* (London: Routledge & Kegan Paul).

Gorz, André (1982 [1980]) *Farewell to the Working Class* (London: Pluto Press).

Hardach, G. and Karras, D. (1978) *A Short History of Socialist Economic Thought* (London: Edward Arnold).

Habermas, Jürgen (1973) *Legitimation Crisis* (London: Heinemann, 1976).

Hegedüs, András (1976) *Socialism and Bureaucracy* (London: Allison & Busby).

Hilferding, Rudolf (1910) *Finance Capital* (London: Routledge & Kegan Paul, 1981).

Hilferding, Rudolf (1927) 'The organized economy', in Bottomore, Tom and Goode, Patrick (eds), *Readings in Marxist Sociology* (Oxford: Clarendon Press, 1978).

Hindess, Barry (1987) *Politics and Class Analysis* (Oxford: Basil Blackwell).

Hindess, Barry (1988) *Choice and Rationality in Social Theory* (London: Allen & Unwin).

Konrád, G. and Szelényi, I. (1979) *The Intellectuals on the Road to Class Power* (Brighton: Harvester Press).

Mallet, Serge (1963) *The New Working Class* (Nottingham: Spokesman Books, 1975).

Mann, Michael (1973) *Consciousness and Action among the Western*

Working Class (London: Macmillan).
Miliband, Ralph (1983) *Class Power and State Power* (London: New Left Books).
Miliband, Ralph (1987) 'Class struggle from above', in Outhwaite, William and Mulkay, Michael (eds), *Social Theory and Social Criticism* (Oxford: Basil Blackwell).
Mills, C. Wright (1956) *The Power Elite* (New York: Oxford University Press).
Ornstein, Michael D. (1988) 'Social class and economic inequality', in Tepperman, L. and Curtis, J. (eds), *Understanding Canadian Society* (Toronto: McGraw-Hill Ryerson).
Panitch, L. (1980) 'Recent theorizations of corporatism', *British Journal of Sociology*, 31.
Poulantzas, Nicos (1969) 'The problem of the capitalist state', *New Left Review*, 58, November–December.
Poulantzas, Nicos (1975) *Classes in Contemporary Capitalism* (London: New Left Books).
Poulantzas, Nicos (1976) 'The capitalist state: a reply to Miliband and Laclau', *New Left Review*, 95, January–February.
Schumpeter, Joseph A. (1942) *Capitalism, Socialism and Democracy* (London: Allen & Unwin, 6th edn, 1987).
Scott, John (1979) *Corporations, Classes and Capitalism* (London: Hutchinson).
Scott, John (1986) *Capitalist Property and Financial Power* (Brighton: Wheatsheaf Books).
Touraine, Alain (1969) *The Post-Industrial Society* (New York: Random House, 1971).
Touraine, Alain (1987) 'The rise and fall of the French labour movement', in Outhwaite, William and Mulkay, Michael (eds), *Social Theory and Social Criticism* (Oxford: Basil Blackwell).
Weber, Max (1923) *General Economic History* (New York: Collier Books, 1961).
Wright, Erik Olin (1978) *Class, Crisis and the State* (London: New Left Books).

2 Britain

David Coates

I

It is conventional in liberal academic circles to dismiss both the notion and the applicability of the concept of a 'ruling class', and to see its contemporary use as a legacy of over-simplistic theoretical systems and outdated bodies of evidence and belief. And it must be conceded that the underlying image associated with the idea of a ruling class *is* a very simple one: to paraphrase C. Wright Mills, that since class is an economic concept and ruling a political one, to put them together is to imply that those who dominate economically also rule politically (Mill 1956: 277). Mills thought all that too much to pack into one term, and chose another – he preferred to talk of a 'power elite'; and many others since have agreed – at least with his unease, if not with his alternative. Liberal scholars have pointed to the quite enormous set of tasks involved in establishing the existence of a ruling class. Giddens, for example, has argued that to show a particular class to be a ruling one, 'it is necessary to specify the modes in which its economic hegemony is translated into political domination; which means examining, among other things, processes of recruitment to elite positions in the major institutional spheres, the relations between economic, political and other elites, and the use of effective power to further definite class interests' (Stanworth and Giddens 1974: xi). How can that be done successfully, we are asked, in the face of the complexity of modern social divisions? Perhaps it could be done for the past: to demonstrate the dominance of landed interests in feudal

Europe, or of industrial interests in the nineteenth-century heyday of early capitalism. But hasn't any nineteenth-century dominance of a capitalist owning class been eroded by the rise of a professional managerial stratum? Hasn't the closed social universe of aristocratic privilege been undermined by the meritocratic requirements of complex industrial systems? And hasn't the tight political control once exercised by the socially privileged and economically powerful been eroded by the rise of democratic institutions? There is inequality, we are told. There is even an Establishment. But what there is not any longer in Britain is a ruling class in any meaningful sense of that term.

All that may seem initially extremely plausible, and yet I want to argue the reverse: that in spite of all these complexities, Britain does still possess a ruling class, and one of considerable longevity and power. I want too to concede that to make such an argument is to accept all that the term implies. For Britain has a ruling class on the most rigorous, as well as on the most generous, understanding of that term. If by a ruling class all we mean is 'a group which provides the majority of those who occupy positions of power, and who in their turn can materially assist their sons to reach similar positions' (Guttsman 1968: 357) then Britain definitely possesses such a class. If by a ruling class we mean, in addition, that the basis of elite privilege rests on the ownership and control of capital – a dependency on capital, moreover, which gives the elite both a set of common interests in its accumulation and the resources to press those interests effectively on governments of any political persuasion – then again we have a ruling class in contemporary Britain. And to go further, to the point at which by a ruling class we also mean a class capable of persuading the vast majority of the people for most of the time that its privileges are inevitable and legitimate, and that its interests are those of the nation as a whole – if, that is, by a ruling class we mean one with truly hegemonic power, then again Britain possesses such a class. It has been the case down the centuries in Britain that three things have gone closely together: the control of dominant economic resources, the monopoly of social privilege, and the capacity to direct the state. If these three things had not gone together, it would never have been legitimate to talk of the existence in Britain of a class which ruled. When scholars now record changes in the content of, and relationship between, the socially, economically and politically dominant in this society, what they record is not the destruction of the ruling class as such, but rather its perpetual reconstitution – its transformation from one kind of ruling class to another. It is with that process of reconstitution, and with the resulting character of the contemporary ruling class in Britain, that the rest of this chapter will be concerned.

II

The controlling institutions of economic life in contemporary Britain are large industrial firms and major banks. The traditional centrality of land to economic production was a casualty of the nineteenth-century rise of industrial capitalism in Britain; and the orginal form which that capitalism took (of small industrial companies) has in its turn been the casualty of trends towards monopoly and finance which have characterized all industrial capitalisms since 1914. Of course, land and the class which owns it does not vanish when replaced in dominance, as small firms do when out-competed by monopolies (and indeed even the small company sector of British industry continues to reproduce itself, in spite of the monopoly growth of its stronger sections and the bankruptcies of its weaker ones). But the ownership of land in Britain was always monopolized by a few, and that remains the case; and the contribution of small firms to industrial production (just like that of small farms to agricultural output) is now lower in Britain than in other major industrial capitalisms. Economic activity in contemporary Britain is dominated by a remarkably limited number of firms. They in their turn are closely interlinked to an equally impressively monopolized banking sector; and both industry and finance in their monopoly forms are dominated by firms that operate on an international scale. If anyone is to qualify for ruling-class status by virtue of economic power, it can only be those who now control these enormous industrial and financial multinational conglomerates.

Let me indicate the information which can begin to sub-stantiate those sweeping assertions. It is true, for example, that as late as 1971 there were 1.25 million small firms in Britain, contributing nearly 20 per cent of GNP and employing six million people. But by then their industrial activity was drowned by that of their large equivalents. Whereas in 1914 it took 2000 companies to produce half of the economy's total manufacturing output, by 1970 it took only 140. In 20 of the 22 industrial sectors then listed by the Department of Employ-ment, six firms or less were responsible for half the sector's output; so that by the mid-1970s it seems likely that the top 100 companies in Britain contributed 62 per cent of the total turn-over and earned 69 per cent of the profits of the top 1000 companies, and that 50 of those very big firms probably between them provided 48 per cent of the output, 49 per cent of the investment and 56 per cent of the profits of the top 1000 companies as a whole (Marsh and Locksley 1983: 35). In fact, 'a mere 87 giant enterprises were responsible [in 1976] for over half of British exports' (Harris 1985: 12).

Degrees of concentration are equally significant in the banking and finance sector. In fact, the very name by which that sector is generally known in Britain – 'the City' – with its image of a 'square mile' of banks and discount houses packed into the old centre of London, is one indication of the concentration of ownership and resources in this key part of the British economy. The 'square mile' has, in reality, a much wider circumference. Clearing banks based in London have local branches in every high street. The rapidly growing building societies still keep their headquarters in the provinces; and the foreign banks based in the City have their head offices, of course, abroad. Yet the actual square mile does 'remain the centre around which the whole financial system revolves' (Coakley and Harris 1983: 3); and within that system large institutions now dominate financial life. In the last twenty years, the clearing banks have amalgamated down into the Big 4, and have been joined as significant actors by rapidly growing building societies, insurance companies and pension funds. Among the banks one, Barclays, is by far the biggest: its 1981 assets took up £48.8 billion of the banks' total assets of £331.7 billion. Among the building societies, the Halifax stands in a similar position of prominence. In 1981, it had assets of £11.9 billion out of the £62.3 billion held by the societies in total; while among pension funds the Prudential has assets of £10.9 billion, and so on. Collectively these large financial concerns now control resources of a quite staggering magnitude. In 1981, for example, 'City institutions [had] at their disposal the massive treasury of some £562 billion, or just over £10,000 per head of the 1981 British Population ...£562 billion is roughly double the 1981 annual domestic product (as measured by GDP) of the U.K. or more than 28 times that of the Third World country Columbia.' Though City institutions 'do not own most of that £562 billion, the fact remains that, within some constraints, they exercise the power to dispose of it as they please' (Coakley and Harris 1983: 4); and as Table 2.1 shows, it is the banks which are in possession of the bulk of that £562 billion.

Table 2.1: Division of the £562 billion December 1981

	£(billion)	%
Banks	331.7	59.8
Insurance companies	74.3	13.0
Building societies	62.3	11.0
Pension funds	63.8	10.9
Trusts	16.1	2.8
Others	13.8	2.5
Total	562.0	100.0

Source: J. Coakley and L. Harris (1983), *The City of Capital* (Oxford, Basil Blackwell), p. 5.

We need to recognize too that there is an international dimension to this concentration of ownership and resources in manufacturing and finance. In fact there are several, for 'the British economy has an unusually high proportion of multinational corporations, and the 1960s and 1970s saw a considerable expansion both of such foreign capital in Britain and of British firms with operations abroad' (Harris 1985: 11). In the manufacturing sector, a growth in company size beyond a certain point seems invariably to be accompanied by the arrival of world-wide concerns. The bigger the firm, the less is

it dependent simply on UK markets for its outlets, and the
more is it likely to own plant and equipment abroad. Table 2.2
shows just how far that internationalization has gone, with 21
of the biggest 50 companies in the UK now more concerned
with operating abroad than at home: indeed for a least two of
the 50 companies, only the headquarters remain in the UK,
production has moved entirely abroad, and sales are wholly in
foreign markets.

*Table 2.2: United Kingdom/overseas involvement of industrial and
commercial companies*

Analysis by asset size involved	50 largest %	The rest (1450) %
Proportion of total assets of 1500 companies surveyed	48.5	51.5
Operating wholly in UK	7.4	40.2
Operating mainly in UK	50.4	48.1
Operating mainly overseas	38.2	10.7
Operating wholly overseas	4.0	0.9

Source: J. Hughes (1981), *Britain in Crisis* (London: Spokesman), p. 29.

The financial sector is, if anything, even more international
in its scale of operations. If we take Barclays again as a prime
example, we find that in 1981 39 per cent of its profits came
from banking abroad, in a year in which some 427 overseas
banking companies already had offices in the City of London.
Through these banking outlets £10.6 billion of UK private
investment went abroad in 1980 as exchange controls were
lifted by the incoming Conservative government. Since only
£3.3 billion came in from overseas investors in the same 12
months, we have some indication in those figures of how
internationally diversified now are the interests and profit
sources of major holders of private capital in the UK (see
Coakley and Harris 1983: 7, 45). In fact, long before exchange
controls were eased, the UK had established itself as a major
exporter of capital. In 1966 UK banks and manufacturing
companies were the source of 'almost 18 per cent of world total
accumulated assets of foreign direct investment ... second only
to the United States (61 per cent), and well ahead of France,
Canada, Germany, Japan and Sweden' (Hodges 1974: 21).

Yet at the same time, the UK economy was also a major recipient of foreign-generated investment, and possessed a significant number of foreign-owned companies in its key growth areas. As early as 1965, foreign-owned companies were responsible for over 6 per cent of the UK GNP, and 23 per cent of its exports, and were particularly heavily concentrated in 'technology-based industries (pharmaceutical products, machinery, scientific instruments, telecommunications, electronics) and industries with a high income-elasticity of demand (vehicles, rubber, domestic electrical appliances)' (Hodges 1974: 26). By 1981 foreign-owned firms had come to be responsible for 18.6 per cent of net manufacturing output in the UK and 14.9 per cent of industrial employment (Fine and Harris 1985: 107). The bulk of the foreign investment placed in the UK originated abroad in very large companies: in 1965 '69 large foreign-owned firms, with investments over £5 million, controlled 63 per cent of the total value of foreign direct investment in the UK, while the remaining 37 per cent was controlled by 862 firms' (Hodges 1974: 30). Many of these firms were American: 68.8 per cent of all foreign-owned firms in Britain were US-owned in 1971, and that figure was still 53.4 per cent a decade later (Fine and Harris 1985: 107). So when we assess the character of the ruling class in Britain, we need to bear in mind both the existence within the UK of large firms with extensive overseas concerns and the presence within the UK economy of large companies owned and controlled from abroad.

But before we begin to do that, we need one final feature of the system of industrial and financial ownership on which the class structure in Britain ultimately rests; and that is the relationship between industry and finance itself. Historically, the gap between the two in Britain was, in comparative terms, unusually wide. Nineteenth-century British industry, through its very success, helped to spawn a banking system which was disproportionately involved in the development of its overseas competitors. Until as late as 1914 northern-based firms invariably expanded on their internally-generated funds, and generally required no major injection of bank capital; so that the banking system, increasingly London-focused, came in consequence to be preoccupied with the export of capital and the raising of foreign loans. It had, quite literally, nothing else to do. The characteristic fusion of banks and industry to which Lenin, among others, attached such significance in his analysis of imperialism – and which was such a feature of early capitalist industrialization in Germany and the United States – was notable for its absence in the economy of the nineteenth century's most successful imperialism. But history has now brought Britain and Lenin closer together, at least on this. For it is clear that the gap between industrial and financial capital in Britain has diminished significantly of late, and that the big banks and large industrial concerns are now closely interrelated. This is indicated partly by the scale of share ownership of industrial companies by big City institutions. In 1979 financial institutions owned 58 per cent of all UK listed ordinary shares (the pension funds held 17 per cent, insurance companies 16 per cent, investment trusts 10 per cent and the banks the bulk of the rest). By then just four major banks, seven insurance companies and nine merchant banks between them had a controlling interest in ten of Britain's top 50 manufacturing companies; and the linkages now go deeper than just the holding of shares. Bankers sit on the boards of industrial companies in increasing numbers, and play a growing role. Both merchant and commercial banks seem now to sit at the centre of integrated blocks of companies, linked together by personnel and investment sources in loose coalitions around the banks as 'hegemonic controllers' (Scott 1986: 117). John Scott has described the contemporary situation as follows (Scott 1982: 143–4):

Each of the banks brings together a relatively distinct set of interests to form a bank-centred sphere of influence. These spheres – currently centred on Barclays Bank, Lloyds Bank, Midland Bank and National Westminster Bank – overlap with one another and their membership shifts over time, but at any particular moment they have a great significance in relation to the allocation of capital, the recruitment of business leaders and the flow of information. Share and loan capital comes from the insurance companies, pension funds, unit trusts and investment trusts, and capital is generally mobilised and syndicated by the merchant banks with whom those 'institutions' are associated. The clearing banks, aided by the merchant banks, oversee the allocation of this capital and help in the provision of personnel for the institutions and the enterprises in which the institutions are involved. The clearing banks co-ordinate the constellation of interests which are involved in the control of the majority of the larger enterprises, and the smaller merchant banks act as brokers between the institutions and the various spheres of influence.

All that that suggests, of course, is the concentration of economic power within British society in the hands of just a limited number of large economic institutions: in the main financial institutions of the City and the large industrial concerns. If such a concentration is to be an element in the constitution of a ruling class, it has to be intimately connected to the pattern of social privilege which surrounds it; and it is. Two features of that privilege stand out immediately as significant here: the persistence of vast inequalities of wealth, and the highly restricted nature of the social circles which are trawled to fill the majority of senior positions in the key private economic institutions. There is a distinct upper class in Britain, a class whose privileges derive both directly and indirectly from the unequal ownership of capital, and a class which takes enormous pains to control entry into its own ranks.

The figures on the distribution of wealth are clear enough. Wealth has been redistributed to a degree this century, but in the main that redistribution has 'not been between the rich and the poor but between successive generations of the same family and between husbands and wives' (Urry, in Coates 1985: 60). That is, it has largely been a redistribution *between* the rich. So 'while the share of personal wealth held by the top 1 per cent of wealth holders fell from about 60 per cent to 30 per cent' from 1923 to 1972, 'the next 4 per cent increased their share from about one-fifth to one quarter, while the next 5 per cent doubled their share ...and the next 10 per cent tripled theirs' (ibid.: 60). Urry's figures are shown in Table 2.3.

Table 2.3: *Share of total personal wealth, England and Wales 1923–72*

	Top 1%	Next 4%	Next 5%	Next 5%
1923	60.9	21.1	7.1	5.1
1972	31.7	24.3	14.4	14.5

Source: John Urry (1985), 'The class structure', in D. Coates, G. Johnston and R. Bush (eds), *A Socialist Anatomy of Britain* (Oxford, Polity Press), pp. 60–1.

Equally significant as measures of social privilege are the indicators of restricted social access to senior economic positions. Social mobility as a whole is still extremely limited in British society. That has been made plain by the recent Oxford studies of *upward* mobility which found, in a seven-class study, 'that those born in classes 6 and 7 remained more than three times less likely, and those born in classes 3, 4 and 5, more than twice as unlikely, to end up in classes 1 and 2 as those who had been born into the top two classes'. These relative inequalities 'remained in fact quite consistent over the whole period of the survey (1918–72)' (Goldthorpe 1980: 201) suggesting that overall 'in most institutions ... there has been a broadening of the social base of entrants to lower positions of leadership but little change at the top'. (Salaman and Thompson 1978: 283). At the top, now as before, a propertied class remains firmly in control. Similar impressions are created by looking *down*, focusing not on mobility but on elite recruitment. For from where do senior figures in significant private institutions come? In the most general sense, the answer to that question is that they come from 'the same place'. Very large industrial and financial concerns continue to recruit the bulk of their board members from a narrow segment of the population. With the exception of the

Table 2.4:   The social origins and educational backgrounds of company chairmen

	Working-class (%)	Middle-class (%)	Upper-class (%)	Unknown (%)	Public school (%)
Clearing banks	—	3	74	23	86
Merchant banks	—	—	89	11	76
Misc. manufacture	1	13	59	27	54
Breweries	2	11	75	12	76
Iron and steel	2	11	55	32	70
Railways	—	11	86	3	70
Shipping	—	10	67	23	62
Oil	—	13	47	40	57
Retail	—	32	21	47	21
Mean	1	10	66	23	Total 65

Source: P. Stanworth and A. Giddens (1974), *Elites and Power in British Society:* (Cambridge: Cambridge University Press), pp. 83, 84.

remaining family-controlled firms, most company chairmen show a remarkably consistent set of upper-class origins and public school education.

In senior positions in the British economy, aristocratic elements remain significantly over-represented relative to their numbers in the population as a whole; and nowhere is that more obvious than in finance and banking. Eschewing trade (only 67 per cent of directors of retail companies appear to have been privately educated, and few had aristocratic connections) leading English aristocrats have clung to banking and land whilst sending others of their families off to the army, the judiciary and to a lesser extent, the church. Amazingly, the compilers of Table 2.4 were unable to locate 'among the chairmen of the merchant banks' even 'one case of an individual emanating from a background outside the upper class' (Stanworth and Giddens 1974: 83). Other studies found that, as late as 1959, 'a third of all [army] officers of the rank of Lieutenant-General and above had aristocratic or gentry connections'; and that as late as 1970, '70 per cent of all English diocesan bishops could be said to be recruited from upper middle-class backgrounds, and as many as 34.9 per cent of them have kinship connections with the landed peerage' (ibid.: 201). Indeed, the easiest way of showing how socially restricted is the recruitment of senior figures in British public and private life is to consider the question of schooling. Doing that makes it obvious that, if you want to get to the top, the trick is first to pick your parents with care, and then have them send you to one of the major public schools. Table 2.5 documents this heavy preponderance of public school-educated people in senior positions in British society.

It would be wrong to create the impression that the upper echelons of British life are entirely closed to new blood. On the contrary, the English upper class has long been open at the bottom to the controlled absorption of chosen individuals. In this century this controlled openness to new members has tended to take the form of the enrichment of a very limited number of senior managerial figures, whose rise up the bureaucratized hierarchies of private capital has been rewarded by vast salaries, the gift of shares and entry into the exclusive social world of those born rich and well-connected.

Table 2.5   The educational background of elite groups
(i) *The public school background*

	Total	Percentage from public schools
14 year olds in England and Wales (1967)	642,977	2.6
Conservative MPs (1970)	330	64.4
Conservative Cabinet (1970)	18	77.7
Royal Navy (Rear-Admirals and above, 1970)	76	88.9
Army (Major-Generals and above, 1970)	117	86.1
RAF (Air Vice-Marshals and above, 1971)	85	62.5
Ambassadors (1971)	80	82.5
High Court and Appeal Court judges (1971)	91	80.2
Church of England bishops (1971)	133	67.4
Directors of forty major industrial firms (1971)	261	67.8
Directors of clearing banks (1971)	99	79.9
Directors of merchant banks (1971)	106	77.4
Directors of major insurance companies (1971)	118	83.1
Governors and directors of the Bank of England (1971)	18	55.5

Source: T. Noble (1975), *Modern Britain: Structure and Change* (London, Batsford), p. 314.

(ii) *Grammar school education in eight elite groups*

	1939 (%)	1950 (%)	1960 (%)	1970–1 (%)
Civil service (under-secretary and above)	6.6	25.5	25.8	31.4
Ambassadors	0.0	11.8	9.5	12.0
High Court and Appeal Court judges	5.0	6.1	10.3	9.5
Royal Navy (Rear-Admirals and above)	19.0	6.3	5.0	12.9
Army (Major-Generals and above)	4.6	10.2	4.2	8.3
RAF (Air Vice-Marshals and above)	0.0	5.5	8.6	23.5
Church of England (assistant bishops and above)	4.5	11.5	15.1	17.9
Directors of clearing banks	3.9	5.8	10.1	9.0

Source: Ibid., p. 320.

But it has been a process of absorption, not of replacement. The much cited 'managerial revolution' that was supposed to have swept away the capitalist class in fact stopped well short of transforming property relationships, class patterns and associated attitudes and culture at the very top of British society. The British ruling class has been, and remains, a very exclusive club. Boardrooms have opened, to a limited degree, to the gifted or fortunate few from the middle ranks of the class structure; but there is 'little evidence that the elite has opened to men (and certainly not to women) whose origins are to be found in the working or lower middle classes' (ibid.: 220). It has opened, moreover, only on terms of exclusivity which the initiates have been only too keen to meet. The test of membership has been the willingness of the newly arrived to socialize themselves into existing attitudes and practices, and to transmit both those values and their privileges to their offspring. The public schools and to a lesser degree, Oxbridge, have acted, and continue to act, as the crucial mechanisms[1] for the production of those values, and for the transmission of that privilege. The result has been the consolidation of a self-confident, coherent and remarkably self-conscious Establishment, a whole network of privileged and interconnected people consolidated around a set of important institutions and productive of a climate of values, opinions and preoccupations that constitute the common sense of an entire ruling class.

What has to be grasped too is the linkage between this pattern of social privilege and the existence of monopoly institutions in the economy. Such a linkage is central to the character, interests and longevity of ruling-class power in Britain. For what we are seeing in Britain is 'the monopoly of privilege by the privileged within the monopolies' (Coates 1984: 108). At the core of the propertied class stand the owners and controllers of the big industrial and financial concerns. 'The privileges and wealth of the whole of the upper class depend on the activities of these core members who run the large business enterprises. This core consists of three interrelated groups: entrepreneurial capitalists, internal capitalists and finance capitalists' (Scott, in Coates 1985: 40). John Scott has argued convincingly that entrepreneurial capitalists are declining in number in Britain, but that a least 48 of the top

250 companies are still controlled by family-based enterprises of a recognizably nineteenth-century kind (particularly in retailing, food and drink, construction and leisure – the names of Cadbury, Colman, Wills, and Marks and Spencer spring to mind). More common however are what Scott calls internal capitalists: 'bureaucratic executives who owe their privileges to their position within the administrative hierarchy of a particular enterprise rather than to any shares they may own in that company. As the class as a whole diversifies its wealth, the role of internal capitalist becomes the characteristic business career open to members of the upper class – though it is also', as we have seen, 'a channel of social mobility into the upper class from below' (ibid.: 41). These internal capitalists then share power in industry and finance with a tiny group of finance capitalists who link companies through their occupation of a multiplicity of directorships. These 'controlling co-ordinators of money capital' (Scott and Griff 1984: 24) – a remarkably small group of perhaps 200–400 people – lock industry and finance together in a maze of interconnected boardrooms. Because so far 'in Britain there have been few studies of interlock, and there has been almost no attempt to map out the structure of the network in a systematic way', the maze cannot yet be catalogued in any comprehensive fashion. But if it cannot yet be catalogued, it can still be illustrated, in the kind of layout produced in Figure 2.1, which John Scott created to capture the set of linkages resulting from 57 directorships held by just eleven men in 1976.

As family firms have given way in centrality to bureaucratically managed and complicatedly interlinked big corporate structures, capital has become highly mobile, no longer tied to individual firms but only to accumulation as a whole. The days are gone when large capitalists had all their eggs in one basket, dependent for their very survival on the viability of a particular firm. That is still the lot of small capital, but it is no longer the fate of the richest among us, for the propertied class has been the beneficiary of those very changes (the separation of ownership and control, the arrival of the professional manager, and the rise of the big financial institution) which liberal scholarship has often hailed as corrosive of the class inequalities of early capitalism. Such

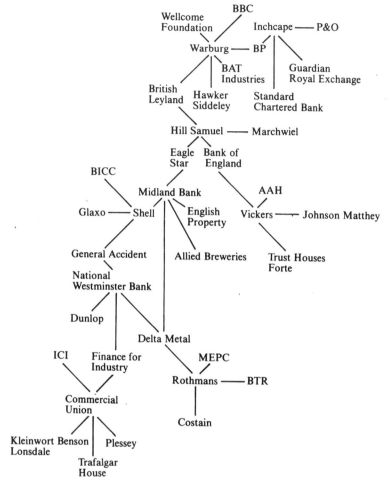

Figure 2.1: Top company links, 1976

Reproduced from J. Scott (1985), 'The British upper class', in D. Coates, G. Johnston and R. Bush (eds), *A Socialist Anatomy of Britain* (Oxford: Polity Press), p. 45.

developments, important as they are, have not dissolved capitalism's owning class. What they have done is to inflict upon capital 'a managerial reorganization' from which 'the privileged class of propertied families' have emerged stronger precisely because their survival is now 'increasingly autonomous from particular proprietary interests', even though 'its members continue to monopolise positions of strategic control in modern capitalist economies' (Scott, in Giddens and Mackenzie 1982: 229)

The particular form which the internationalization of capital has taken in our epoch then adds its own contribution to this freeing of capital's dependence on individual capitalist concerns, to enable at least the richest among us to live off the accumulation process of the world economy as a whole. When we looked earlier at who owns large firms in Britain, we found that a significant percentage of industry here is owned by foreign firms and individuals, and that the profits which flow to large British firms contain within them significant foreign earnings. For the networks of ownership over which key British-based capitalists preside stretch out far beyond the boundaries of the United Kingdom, and part of the space which they have left behind in British industry has been colonized by key capitalists from elsewhere. And in this way the basis of privilege in this society has come to depend, even more directly than it did in earlier periods of imperialist domination, on the existence of inequality on a world scale; and some of the inequality over which the privileged preside here helps to sustain ruling classes far away, in the United States, in Japan and elsewhere.

So some of the wealth created in the UK goes abroad, to sustain the life-style of privileged members of other societies. But the bulk of it does not. It stays here, and is supplemented by profits repatriated by British firms from processes of capital accumulation going on abroad under their control. That wealth is then used to sustain, not simply further rounds of capital accumulation, but also (through rentier incomes, inflated managerial salaries and professional fees) the lifestyle of the many more people – the perhaps 100,000 or so individuals – who surround these key indigenous capitalists, and who are linked to them by kinship, education, social bonds and a shared culture. Here we find perhaps 1–2 per cent of the population, differentially dependent on finance, industry, rents or the professions, but commonly dependent for their privileges on the maintenance and success of the monopolies, and on the preservation of highly unequal rights and rewards between top management and the rest. These people constitute a class of the socially privileged, a class whose privileges derive from the possession within them and their families of large amounts of private capital and private property. These people are what I have called, in this section, an upper class.

It is possible both to chart and to specify the constituent elements of this dominant owning class, for it is a class with its own history and its own institutions. Like all classes, the upper class in Britain is shaped by its past. Its constituent elements now, and the values they espouse, reflect long patterns of class alignment and associated social change. In particular, and unlike other European capitalist classes, the British ruling class has a recent past which is largely free of major traumatic upheaval. The pre-capitalist aristocracy of feudal Europe (whose equivalents were swept away so brutally in France in 1789, in Russia in 1917, and in a different way in Germany and Japan in 1945) in Britain accommodated itself without revolution to the rising tide of industrial capital. Aristocratic wealth, originally created through the ownership of land, moved inexorably in the last quarter of the nineteenth century into commerce and finance. Since successful industrial capital in Britain often made the reverse movement into finance and even land, what emerged in Britian by 1914 was a genuine *fusion* of old and new elements into one propertied class – into a plutocracy.

Initially that plutocracy contained the vestiges of an earlier regionalism since its very creation represented the subordination of *northern* industrial interests to *southern* commercial ones. But otherwise it was remarkably free of religious, ethnic or larger geographical differences; and consolidated itself precisely by its ability to fuse its disparate elements into a class unified socially by a standard mode of language, accent and dress, and by the possession of a common set of values and attitudes. The plutocracy then used private inheritance and public schools to transmit its privileges and life-style between generations, and steadily distanced itself from dependence on particular firms, industries or even whole economies, so guaranteeing its own continued prosperity as local economic performance faltered. It faltered, of course, precisely because the plutocracy systematically privileged finance over industry, and the maintenance of Empire over national industrial reconstruction (Coates and Hillard 1986: passim). But the price of this economic decline was paid by lower classes in Britain (in the form of unemployment, lower living standards and depleted welfare services) and not by their social superiors. The international investments and entrenched income differentials of the plutocracy protected them and their children from the full impact of the economic decline over which they presided.

Instead of slipping *down* as the economy slipped down, the children of each generation of the plutocracy slipped instead *out* and *up*: out, to occupy key positions in the state, the universities, the media and the churches; and up, through marriage, to strengthen the economic base of a social system still presided over by monarchy and aristocracy. Open at the bottom to talent, and at the top to birth and rank, the propertied class consolidated itself economically and socially at the very moment when democratic pressures were extending the franchise, consolidating the labour movement, and calling for greater social equality and reform. Indeed, here is one of the great paradoxes of recent British history: that the rise of political democracy and the consolidation of upper-class power should have gone on together, and should have done so with only the most limited signs of the tensions and contradictions endemic in such a paradoxical union. Democratic pressures should have stopped this socially privileged class from consolidating itself as a ruling one. They did not. Instead, the plutocracy which emerged from the late nineteenth-century fusion of old and new propertied classes in Britain successfully absorbed and contained these democratic pressures. Quite how it did that, and why therefore it does deserve to be thought of as a ruling class, is the subject of the final section of this chapter.

IV

There is no escaping the political power of the privileged in contemporary Britain. Their continued existence as a recognizable social group, in spite of a century or more of radical and socialist initiatives to remove them, is itself a testimony to that power: an indication of the upper class's capacity to dull to insignificance any attempts to erode their privileges and their capacity to reproduce themselves. The continuation (and indeed intensification) of private monopoly power in key economic areas is evidence too of the political potency of the privileged. City institutions in particular have a stranglehold on the freedom of manoeuvre of all governments – Conservative no less than Labour – for which the trade union movement would gladly give much. The rapid export of capital, sharp alterations in ruling rates of interest, and speculative movements against sterling, have disciplined recalcitrant governments at crisis points with steadfast regularity in the postwar years; and big multinational companies have proved elusive to the intermittent attempts of Labour governments to control them. Private capital simply possesses enormous economic resources: the power to invest and disinvest, the capacity to create or destroy jobs, the ability to fund parties and propaganda, and a generalized legitimacy which derives from two centuries of popular exposure to dominant pro-capitalist ideologies of property, markets and profit. In addition, private capital sits on top of, and survives by riding, processes of competitive accumulation on a world scale which dictate the interests of local capitalist classes just as firmly as they structure the constraints experienced by governments; and governments in their turn, desperately seeking prosperity for their electorates and taxable revenues for their own programmes, regularly approach multinational industrial and financial concerns in the guise of supplicant rather than of governor. In the pursuit of their own requirements as politicians, governments in Britain regularly find it necessary to create the conditions which private capital requires, and those include the avoidance of any disruption to the continued enjoyment of social privilege by the capitalist rich and of industrial power by their economic core.

The political potency of private capital is always at its most visible when Labour governments are in office, because then the radicalism of the Labour Left exists to challenge the imperatives imposed on governments by private capital and to threaten the social privileges demanded by the capitalist rich. The fate of the 1974–9 Labour government is particularly significant here because of the sharpness of the clash between the privileged and the radical. That Labour government came into office committed to achieving 'a fundamental and irreversible shift in the balance of power and wealth in favour of working people and their families' (Coates 1980: 3). Though internally divided, and more radical in the main in its rhetoric than in its intentions, the new cabinet was none the less determined to generate economic growth and full employment by the development of a corporatist relationship between itself, private industry and organized labour. But it quickly found that it could not achieve its objectives, and certainly could not do so by a corporatist route. Greater levels of private capital accumulation were on offer, from private firms, only if the social and economic conditions created by the Labour government were right: and those conditions involved such major items as wage controls, tax cuts and the protection of managerial privileges. Yet union cooperation was available only on the basis of the state planning of industry, extensive welfare provision and industrial democracy; and wage restraint by union members could not be guaranteed indefinitely even then. In such a context management were always, and unions became, progressively more wary of government intentions; and cooperation (never very fulsome on the side of private business) rapidly drained away. And without extensive managerial support, investment remained low and competitiveness deficient, while an increasingly beset trade union leadership found it progressively more difficult to restrain rank-and-file militancy in the face of the persistence of large-scale inequality and poverty.

Caught between these two incompatible forces, the Labour government eventually and reluctantly broke to the more powerful: and that was capital. Throughout its period in office, the Labour government was systematically exposed to the criticisms of its radicalism from media which were predominantly privately owned and politically conservative, and met their full fury on the issue of industrial democracy, when the Confederation of British Industry orchestrated a public outcry of quite hysterical proportions. Yet even in quieter times, the Labour government had to operate within financial limits set for it by capital movements, runs on sterling and shifts in interest rates initiated by hostile international financial agencies; and like many radical governments, when defeated by balance of payments problems, the loan it raised from the International Monetary Fund was given only on the condition that any vestigial radicalism was abandoned. Under these pressures the Labour government retreated from its proposals on industrial democracy, and sacked its left-wing ministers who sought tight planning agreements with private industry. It cut welfare provision, allowed unemployment to rise, and imposed wage restraints; and when it did attempt to control American-owned car firms who were threatening (in Chrysler's case) to shut down factories or (in Ford's) to pay wage rises above the permitted norm, it eventually had to bale Chrysler out only to see them sell their UK assets secretly to Peugeot Citröen, and it eventually had to surrender to Ford to prevent them moving all their new investment to Spain. Indeed, the Labour government did more than fail to control the multinationals. It actually prepared the ground for the return to office of a Conservative government more sympathetic to the requirements of private capital. For it spent its middle years in office educating its trade union supporters in the need to move from Keynesianism to monetarism, before falling victim to the anger of those disappointed supporters, first in the 1978–9 strike wave (the 'winter of discontent') and then in the electoral defeat which followed.

In arguing in this way, that the Labour government of 1974–9 fell victim to the power of organized capital, I do not want to suggest any simple conspiracy theory, or to give credence to what, in the literature on the state, is often its academic equivalent – namely the 'instrumentalist' view of state power – which has the state as the tame agent/instrument of the requirements of an all-dominant capitalist class.[2] The relationship between the state and private capital is altogether more complex, more mediated and more problematic than that. It seems more sensible to argue that the state operates within constraints established by the economic requirements and social privileges of the capitalist class, and is locked into the reproduction of those privileges, and the servicing of those requirements, in a number of complex ways.

The most obvious way is through the linkages of personnel and funds. There is a significant overlap in personnel at the top of the hierarchies of the state and private capital. The original Thatcher cabinet, for example, for all its new brand of self-made Tory, still had 'four-fifths of its members drawn from public schools, with one-third from Eton and Winchester alone' (Scott, in Coates 1985: 50). Senior levels of the civil service show that linkage too, though to a lesser extent, with 69 per cent of top civil servants as late as 1970 having an Oxbridge background, and 62 per cent a public school one too (ibid.: p. 48). The Conservative Party is funded heavily by private capitalist concerns. Thatcher, as John Ross puts it, has her friends. They pay and they benefit. Apparently, 'three sections of the British economy (finance and property companies, food, drink and tobacco firms, construction companies) have steadily been accounting for a larger and larger proportion of Conservative Party company donations' (Ross 1983: 37) and now provide 45–55 per cent of those funds. Other sectors (notably engineering and general manufacturing industry) have been progressively cutting back on money to the Party. What Ross found, for the first Thatcher government (1979–83), at least was a remarkably direct connection between 'those who paid' and 'those who gained' (ibid.: p. 41). For 'what is clear is that if the financing of the Conservative Party does not reflect accurately the shape of the British economy as a whole, it does reflect with quite astonishing accuracy the levels of profits and changes in production which took place under the first Thatcher government' (ibid.: pp. 41–2). Of course correlations do not establish causes, and we shall have to wait for the memoirs to see just how, and to what degree, funding shaped policy; but as the theoreticians of the state build ever more sophisticated versions of state–capital interplays, they would do well not to forget the old adage that 'he who pays the piper calls the tune'.

Moreover the state in Britain is still surrounded by a veritable Establishment of the 'great and the good' who people its advisory committees, sit on its Royal Commissions, and appear at its cocktail parties. This informal web of socially connected and strategically placed individuals encircle the state, and are 'concerned less with the actual exercise of power than with the established bodies of prevailing opinion which powerfully, and not always openly, influence its exercise' (Fairlie, in Scott 1982: 159). Linked together through institutions like the Conservative Party, the public schools, Oxbridge and the London clubs, the Establishment is in essence an 'old boy network, a system of social contacts which stem from family and education' (Scott 1982: 159). Though the Establishment is now less all-pervasive than it was in an earlier age of more limited government and a more aristocratic social elite, this informal mechanism for orchestrating and articulating upper-class opionion remains politically immensely potent, creating an ambiance of accepted opinion and belief within which government is pursued and privilege protected. Henry Fairlie may only have coined the term 'Establishment' in 1955, but what he said then has a timeless quality to it, and captures an important and still contemporary truth. It was his view that the Establishment (Fairlie 1955:1)

in this country is today more powerful than ever before. By the 'Establishment' I do not mean only the centres of official power – though they are certainly part of it – but rather the whole matrix of official and social relations within which power is exercised. The exercise of power in Britain (more specifically, in England) cannot be understood unless it is recognised that it is exercised socially. Anyone who has at any point been close to the exercise of power will know what I mean when I say that the 'Establishment' can be seen at work in the activities of, not only the Prime Minister, the Archbishop of Canterbury and the Earl Marshal, but of such lesser mortals as the chairman of the Arts Council, the Director-General of the BBC, and even the editor of *The Times Literary Supplement*, not to mention divinities like Lady Violet Bonham Carter.

Yet if this was all there was to upper-class political power, breaking it, though difficult, would at least be relatively straightforward – a matter of replacing the Conservative Party, changing the civil service, picking new friends and dismissing the great and the good. But sadly there is more to it than that, as Labour governments have all too often discovered. For what radical governments in Britain face is not just an upper class of a particularly well-organized kind. What they actually face is a power bloc of truly hegemonic proportions.

Both the notion of 'bloc' and of 'hegemony' are vital here. Political power is not, and has not been, an easy thing for the British ruling class to retain, as democratic forces realeased by the contradictions of the first industrial capitalism have grown in scale and confidence. A landed ruling class facing a scattered feudal peasantry could rely, ultimately, on the church and its own force to maintain itself in power. A capitalist ruling class facing an emerging proletariat invariably needed more. Power in Britain since the onset of the industrial revolution has had to be *organized*, and successive governments have come to play a crucial and relatively autonomous role in that organization. The challenge of Chartism, for example, was contained in the end partly by the judicious use and threat of force (think of all those army barracks in the cotton towns of Lancashire). It was also contained, however, and its programme incrementally implemented, through the creation of a bloc of classes – of Whig landlords, northern industrialists and skilled sections of the emerging trade unions – under the banner of Gladstonian Liberalism and the programme of *laissez-faire*. The English ruling class survived the first shock of industrialization by persuading leading sections of the working class to vote *with* their employers: and this was an achievement of truly epochal proportions.

Then, at the end of the century, as the economic conditions underpinning that bloc began visibly to disintegrate under the impact of international competition, a much less secure bloc of classes was consolidated – with financial and colonial-industrial interests at its core, and with a more limited penetration into organized labour – under new Conservative policies first of Empire and ultimately of protectionism. In each case, subordinate classes were incorporated into the dominant order by the granting of genuine concessions as well as by the orchestrating of a definite ideological package which asserted common interests between the privileged and the rest. Those concessions had to be at their greatest when the proletariat were at their most politically radical, particularly in and around 1945. The postwar settlement of full employment and welfare provision established then, initially under Labour Party leadership and later under the Conservatives, consolidated a bloc of classes which united industrial capital and organized labour within a shared framework of Keynesianism (from 1945) and corporatism (in the 1960s). The significance of Thatcherite politics for the continuation of existing patterns of privilege and power lies precisely here, in the Conservative Party's attempts – as Keynesian corporatism collapsed in the 1970s – to forge a different alliance of classes behind a new ideological project – this time protecting ruling-class privilege by allying dominant elites to a remobilized middle class, and to sections of organized labour addressed not primarily as workers but as consumers, houseowners, share-buyers and law-abiding and self-sustaining individual citizens. Keynesianism may have lost its role as the common sense of an age, and trade unionism may now find itself excluded from the corridors of power; but the more nakedly unequal universe of Thatcherite Britain should not obscure the earlier role of Keynesian corporatism in sustaining ruling-class hegemony in a period of capitalist prosperity.

The British ruling class is politically dominant only in this hegemonic way. It maintains itself through the private ownership of big capital, and protects itself economically by progressively transforming its core institutions into rentier ones dependent only on accumulation wherever it is successful. It reproduces itself through private education and the transmission of wealth between generations; and it protects itself socially by its own exclusivity, low public profile, and astute public orchestration of the pre-capitalist institutions of monarchy and aristocracy. In these ways its economic base and social status are carefully preserved; and so too is its political domination. The British ruling class continues to protect itself politically by its willingness to support successive national projects (first Liberalism, then Imperialism, then Keynesianism and now the social market philosophy of a revamped Conservatism) that indicate with which subordinate classes it should ally and at what level of material and social concesssions the radicalism of subordinate classes can be blocked. Looked at in this way, British society possesses not simply a ruling class, but in truth a ruling class of immense political sophistication and power. Socialists in our readership would do well not to underestimate it. In the battle between classes it has so far taken all the honours.

NOTES

1. They are, of course, reproducers of inequality rather than its prime cause. As Perkin put it, 'it is not because 90% of the great landowners went to major public schools, and 40% to Oxbridge, that they are great landowners. They went there because their fathers were rich' (H. Perkin, 'The recruitment of elites in British society since 1800', *Journal of Social History*, vol. 12 (1977), p. 229.
2. On this, see D. Coates, *The Context of British Politics* (London: Hutchinson, 1984), chapter 10; and B. Jessop, *The Capitalist State* (Oxford: Martin Robertson, 1982), passim.

REFERENCES

Coakley, J. and Harris, L. (1983) *The City of Capital* (Oxford: Basil Blackwell).

Coates, D. (1980) *Labour in Power?* (London, Longman).

Coates, D. (1984) *The Context of British Politics* (London: Hutchinson).

Coates, D., Johnston, G. and Bush, R. (1985) *A Socialist Anatomy of Britain* (Oxford: Polity Press).

Coates, D. and Hillard, J. (eds) (1986) *The Economic Decline of Modern Britain: the debate between left and right* (Brighton: Wheatsheaf Books).

Fairlie, H. (1955) 'The Establishment', *Spectator*, 23 September.

Fine, B. and Harris, L. (1985) *The Peculiarities of the British Economy* (London: Lawrence and Wishart).

Giddens, A. and MacKenzie, G. (eds), (1982) *Social Class and the Division of Labour* (London: Cambridge University Press).

Goldthorpe, J. H. et al. (1980) *Social Mobility and Class Structure* (Oxford: Oxford University Press).

Guttsman, W.L. (1968) *The British Political Elite* (London: MacGibbon and Kee).

Harris, L. (1985) 'British Capital: Manufacturing, Finance and Multinational Corporations', in D. Coates et al. *A Socialist Anatomy of Britain* (Oxford: Polity Press).

Hodges, M. (1974) *Multinational Corporations and National Government* (Farnborough: Saxon House).

Ingham, G. (1984) *Capitalism Divided? The City and Industry in British Social Development* (London: Macmillan).

Jessop, B. (1982) *The Capitalist State* (Oxford: Martin Robertson).

Marsh, D. and Locksley, G. (1983) 'Capital, the neglected face of power', in D. Marsh (ed.) *Pressure Politics* (London: Junction Books).

Mills, C. Wright (1956) *The Power Elite* (New York: Oxford University Press).

Ross, J. (1983) *Thatcher and Friends* (London: Pluto).

Salaman, G. and Thompson, K. (1978) 'Class structure and the persistence of an elite: the case of army officer selection', *Sociological Review*, vol. 28 (2).

Scott, J. (1979) *Corporations, Classes and Capitalism* (London: Hutchinson)

Scott, J. (1982) *The Upper Classes* (London: Macmillan).

Scott, J. (1986) *Capitalist Property and Financial Power* (Brighton: Wheatsheaf Books).

Scott, J. and Griff, C. (1984) *Directors of Industry* (Oxford: Polity Press).

Stanworth, P. and Giddens, A. (eds) (1974) *Elites and Power in British Society* (London: Cambridge University Press).

3 France

Jane Marceau

Revolutionary in 1789, France two centuries later is unmistakably a bourgeois, capitalist country. It is, moreover, a country where the bourgeoisie has been notably successful both in retaining control of the corporate sector and in consolidating its political influence overall. The majority of owners and controllers of capital have succeeded in holding on to their assets even through periods of considerable economic restructuring, including both enterprise nationalization and a widespread influx of foreign capital sparking a merger movement, sometimes publicly directed. As a recent observer put it,

it is clear ... that between the Fourth and the Fifth Republics ... the French ruling class did not undergo massive internal upheavals: there was simply an alteration in its structures, a change linked to the concentration of enterprises, to the rise to power of senior managers and of Présidents-Dirécteurs-Généraux who have been taking the place, except in small and medium firms, once occupied by 'divine right owners' and an increasing movement from the public sector ... to the private, a movement which reinforces the interpenetration of the two sectors. (Birnbaum et al. 1978: 187)

This conclusion, that the ruling class in France changed in few of its essentials despite massive economic changes after 1945, has been that of almost all writers on contemporary France over the last few decades (Bourdieu et al. 1973; Poulantzas 1974; Marceau 1977; Birnbaum et al. 1978; Bellon 1980). The evidence for the continuing hegemony of the bourgeoisie is diverse, drawn both from theoretical analyses, in the tradition of Althusser or Poulantzas, and from empirical studies linked to a different theoretical approach, such as those of Bourdieu and his colleagues or Birnbaum's own team.

At the centre of sociological discussions about the ruling class, in France as elsewhere, are analyses of the capitalist class. Who owns and controls the major enterprises of France, the backbone of the economic system and the focus of much government policy? Has the personnel in charge changed? Geographically and socially where do they come from? How are they educated? How do they relate to the state, to the intellectual and other fields of power? Do all fractions of the business class have the same interests? If not, who mediates? How does the system hold together? What are the implications for both private and public power of the changes in the structure of the productive system in France since 1945 and especially of the growth of strong industrial and financial groups, some brought under public ownership after the political shift of 1981?

This chapter brings together recent literature on the capitalist class in France which addresses these issues and sets it in the context of the broad economic changes which have taken place both in France and much of Europe since 1945. Debates about the power and structure of the capitalist class in France have much the same concerns as those elsewhere: in France they are given a special slant because of other elements of both the social and educational and politico-administrative systems.

Who, then, forms part of the capitalist class? The capitalist class is here taken as the central section of the broader class, the bourgeoisie, which also contains closely allied groups whose members include the 'reigning' personnel in the political sphere, leading members of the intelligentsia and a 'service' section formed by the legal and other liberal professions. The core of the capitalist class is composed of the business fractions of the bourgeoisie. 'Capitalists' in the widest sense include all individuals owning economically productive capital – whether in the physical plant and equipment and business goodwill of the enterprise or in the shares, bonds and debentures which are the units of property in limited companies. Many owners of productive capital, however, own only small quantities: the businesses they own are small or they hold only insignificant shares in larger firms. While these capitalists constitute the petty bourgeoisie and continue to be extremely numerous in France, they *individually* have little economic power and less social and political influence. Despite the fact that small enterprises, employing less that ten people, constitute well over 90 per cent of all French firms and together employ around 40 per cent of the labour force, they have little clout, even collectively.[1] In contrast, the 1 per cent of enterprises which employ more than 1000 workers and produce 40 per cent or so of GNP have very considerable social, economic and political power. It is the owners and controllers of these firms, now mostly linked together in groups, and of the holding companies which head them who constitute the core of the capitalist class in France. It is with these enterprises and their rulers, therefore, that this chapter is essentially concerned.

Speaking of the core of the capitalist class in this way does not, of course, mean that the group is totally unified. Within the class as a whole there exist several fractions and even within the core there are different segments. The central members of the segments formed around major enterprises, however, constitute the centre of a system of social organization and power which has, as John Scott (1982) remarks when talking of Britain, a 'massive tail' of more junior managers, professionals and technicians whose material and social conditions depend on the actions of the core. It is members of the core who allocate economic resources between alternative uses and it is their decisions which determine the overall success of the whole group. Their interests may clash in some areas but they are similar to the degree that makes a largely common political strategic approach possible.

The core of the capitalist class also seems to many observers to consist of a series of units held together by kinship and personal links which provide the ties which unite groups across fraction boundaries as well as uniting individuals within the inner group and which enable the core membership to cohere over the generations. This core is described by Carré as an *élite familiale* which is 'composed of men who, as creators or successors, have organised or maintained a system which ensures their perpetuation. The patrimony on which their power is founded is first and above all the enterprises and banks whose capital they hold' (Carré 1978: 21).

Similarly, according to Morin (1976), the *bourgeoisie capitaliste* can be characterized as the class which holds full economic power. It is thus the class which not only has the power to take the profits from economic activity but also that which 'holds the power of allocation and the power of management of the means of production. In brief, it is the class which combines *simultaneously* these three powers *and* which exploits paid workers' (Morin 1976: 13). This definition excludes the petty bourgeoisie from full membership of the capitalist class but, in contrast, *includes* directors of companies because, as Morin says, they share fully in the power of allocation and management of the means of production. Moreover, although directors do not always hold formal ownership, they almost always have the power to share in profits. Directors, therefore, in Morin's view are 'indubitably and integrally a part of the capitalist bourgeoisie' (1976: 13). Bourdieu and his colleagues take the same view. They see the *patronat* as including not only the owners of business but also the members of the *Conseil d'Administration* of any particular enterprise, its directors, and the top management team. They thus speak of the business bourgeoisie as including not only owners but also the *cadres dirigeants* (controlling managers) of French enterprises (Bourdieu et al. 1973).

How then is this group structured, and what is its social image? The sections below describe the changes which took place in the patrimony of the capitalist class in France between 1945 and the 1980s and the corresponding changes which took place in the social and political 'presentation' of the business bourgeoisie. The fundamental economic change, from 'family' to 'technocratic' or 'organizational' capitalism, which took place in the second half of the twentieth century has been common to many countries and everywhere generated much sociological debate about the implications of the changes both for the control of enterprises and hence of the economy and for the social position of those more clearly recognizable as 'capitalists' in an earlier age. Two aspects of the French situation, which set the capitalist class in France somewhat apart from its peers in many other parts of the world, are the focus of this chapter. The first is the continued social, educational and political homogeneity of the capitalist class despite the massive changes to which it has been subject over recent decades. The second is the very particular role which the state, both through the policy directions pursued and through personal links channelled through the public administration and public enterprise, plays in determining the direction of business decisions. Through incessant, far-reaching and coordinated intervention in the economy, the state in France plays a major part in shaping the structure of capital and hence of the capitalist class. These two themes – family and social homogeneity, and the close links between the controllers of private capital and the state – run through the discussion below.

STRUCTURE OF CAPITAL IN FRANCE

It has frequently been shown that industrialization on a massive scale came late to France which well into the twentieth century remained a country of small enterprises in both industry and agriculture (Dupeux 1964; Carré et al. 1972; Marceau 1977). The period of postwar reconstruction, followed in the 1950s and 1960s by two decades of expansion, saw many changes in the productive structure and the investment of capital. By the end of the period to 1970 France was recognizably a 'modern' economy, dominated by large firms in central and expanding sectors. In this process the state played a vital role and the petty bourgeoisie, both rural and urban, lost ground. The role of the state, then ruled by a left-wing coalition, in the immediate postwar period in shaping this new economy was evident in the wave of nationalizations which provided essential capital and infrastructure for a new start for France after 1945. At this time, most of the major banks and insurance companies were taken into public ownership, as were basic industries such as steel, cement, and rail and air transport.

The regular intervention of public authorities continued even after the left-wing parties lost political power. First it was seen in the long series of national 'indicative' plans which were designed to centralize information and stimulate markets.

Later, concern with the national interest in the face of fast changing technology and the massive capital inflow from the United States of the late 1950s and early 1960s pushed the government to become an active agent in the merger movement designed to create 'national champions' in high technology and sensitive industries such as electronics and petro-chemicals (Michalet, in Vernon 1974).

The action of the state in collaboration with business during these decades laid the groundwork for an aspect of the structure of capital in France in the 1970s and 1980s which, although existing elsewhere, is particularly striking in France. This is the dominance of the economy by a considerable number of extremely powerful industrial, commercial and banking groups. By 1970, stimulated to regroup by the mergers involved in the creation of the 'national champions' and by the need for constant negotiation with the state as well as the new market opportunities provided by an expanding economy, all of the 200 biggest industrial firms and the 40 biggest financial institutions were at the head of important groups and controlled the financial coordination of many sub-units. At the financial centre of these groups, in the mother or holding companies, are taken the major strategic decisions about investment, expansion through further asset acquisition and production directions, which, enforced through an intricate network of share holdings, form the framework of daily decisions in far-flung enterprises. Groupings such as these allow new linkages between family capitalists as well as the tapping of new resources.

Many of these largely sectoral groups are linked into *groupes financiers* led by the two major banking groups, Paribas and the Banque de Suez, which each coordinate the activities of hundreds of companies, including some of France's biggest enterprises (Allard et al. 1978) in many areas of the economy. They thus dominate much business decision-making. In turn, the small number of central business coordinators enormously increases the chances of the views of business leaders being heard by the state. These groups became increasingly dominant in the economy throughout the 1970s – hence their position as prime candidates for nationalization in 1981. Before nationalization, groups such as St Gobain-Pont-à-Mousson, Péchiney-Ugine-Kuhlmann, the Compagnie Générale d'Electricité (CGE), and Thomson each had more than 100,000 employees and were involved in takeovers totalling tens of billions of French francs each year. Groups in the exceptionally powerful 'ensemble Paribas' employed 650,000 in 1978.

The importance of public policy intervention in the private decisions of these groups can be seen in the proliferation of close personal links with senior members of critical areas of the state apparatus. *Pantouflage*, the movement of senior public officials into controlling positions in the private sector, enormously increased over the period. The choice of top executives had to reflect the centrality of the state as partner, client and interlocutor. Personal cross-sector links became both major channels of communication and negotiation for both sides as well as facilitating the implementation of decisions taken. As business grew closer to the state so the state grew closer to business.

Not all went smoothly, however. The restructuring decades were characterized by sharp conflicts between capital and labour, evident in widespread and prolonged strikes in many areas of the economy. Increasing disaffection as more groups were affected by the 'modernization' process culminated in the events of May 1968 which almost toppled the government. Once the immediate crisis was over, however, the public fright generated by so much direct action in the streets and factories of the country made possible the dominance of a conservative political agenda throughout the 1970s. The decline of the broad-based Conservative Party, the RPR, as the memory of de Gaulle retreated was accompanied by the rise to power in Parliament of the leaders of big business. Work by a group of scholars at the Fondation Nationale des Sciences Politiques showed how the Républicains Indépendents Party led by Valéry Giscard d'Estaing brought together the most traditional Catholic (practising) Parisian fractions of the bourgeoisie with the closest links to the top levels of industry, banking and commerce (Cayrol et al. 1973: 27).

The severe shocks to the economic system caused by the successive oil crises of the 1970s had the same social effects in France as elsewhere. Rising unemployment, factory closures, and an overloaded social security system brought back into prominence basic conflicts between groups located in different parts of the productive system and society. The tensions generated finally swept the Socialist–Communist coalition, the Union de la Gauche led by François Mitterrand, into Presidency and Parliament in 1981. This victory sparked an apparent shift in economic power, since between 1981 and 1983 a new wave of nationalizations brought many of the major financial-industrial groups into public ownership.

The recent history, then, of the capitalist class in France is essentially one of business forging new relationships with the state as the political and economic fortunes of different groups ebbed and flowed. Loss of power by the political Left in the late 1940s, allied to the very success of the reconstruction policies practised, muted the intervention of the state to a mode of incessant regulation rather than direct control. Over the decades of the presidencies of de Gaulle, Pompidou and Giscard d'Estaing the private capitalist class grew in importance to the economy and grew increasingly close to the state in determining the industrial policies which assisted the economic growth on which continued political dominance seemed to depend through the creation of some kind of consensus (some of the side-effects of the increasing influence of industrial and financial interests were seen most graphically in a series of political scandals during the last years of the Pompidou and Giscard d'Estaing presidencies, including the 'Affaire Boulin' which, after eight years reappeared in the press in late 1987). The change of political leadership in 1981 with the advent to power of the Left coalition and President Mitterrand, ushered in a new era of direct intervention in the economy but one which seems to have achieved little. The end of the left-wing government and the election to Parliament in 1986 of the party headed by Jacques Chirac heralded a further change. De-nationalization returned to the agenda, a return again called into question by the re-election of President Mitterrand and the formation of a left-wing government in mid-1988.

Opinions differ on the impact of the 1980s nationalizations on the French capitalist class. It seems clear that some enterprises, such as the Rothschild Bank, changed their name but little else. Others, such as Thomson, went their own way, taking directions contrary to the government's intentions. The people chosen to run the newly nationalized companies, while their earlier careers had been different, hardly changed the social and educational composition of the *dirigeants* of French industry and finance. Failing to rally new men from the ranks of the unions and junior managers,

the socialists finally had to give in and govern with the existing elites ... The solution found was the association of 'old crabs and young turks' ... [which was] based on the rapid realisation that the state could not find new top management teams from within the socialists' own ranks, that recourse to people from public service departments could only be limited and that the internal reform of the enterprise which could have allowed the promotion of union leaders was not possible. ... It was ... essentially in the seedbed of the *grands corps* that the Left in power dug to find new *dirigeants* when it did not simply keep on the old ones. ... It kept the principle of cooptation at the top. ...The elite coopted remained homogeneous as before, [since] keeping on the old top team was the most frequent solution. (Cohen, in Birnbaum 1985: 255, 257)

Although only five of the heads of the 12 enterprises newly nationalized remained in place for the whole four years to 1985, their replacements came from the same background, both in social origins and education, and in the careers they had pursued in the state administration, as Bauer (in Birnbaum 1985: 277) points out.

OWNERSHIP AND ENTERPRISE: FAMILY OR TECHNOCRATIC CONTROL?

Who then constitute the capitalist class in France in view of the considerable changes in the economic structure of the country? In particular, how have capitalist families fared? As elsewhere, much debate in France has centred on the issues of the ownership and control of major private enterprises. It is clear from official statistics that the capitalist class as a whole has been losing members, although many of those 'lost' were the owners of small firms. It is also clear that in some of the older industrial sectors, notably textiles, many of the old families no longer held sway by the end of the postwar restructuring period. The Mottes, Tiberghiens, Desurmonts and Masurels, among many, had to give way to the creators of major new groups, run by such men as the Frères Willot. While the capitalist families as such have not disappeared, many of their sons have had to look elsewhere for suitable careers and join the salaried bourgeoisie (Marceau 1989).

In some sectors, however, families managed to retain their hold on the major companies created by earlier generations. Morin (1974) shows that half of the 200 biggest French companies were still family-controlled in the early 1970s while of the 20 biggest, six were family-controlled, the family continuing to hold either a majority (in 38 per cent of cases) or a minority (in 62 per cent) of the shares. In 1975, almost half (42 per cent) of the 250 biggest enterprises in France were 'under family control' which means that 'the families owned a proportion of the capital sufficient to control company policies' (Carré 1978: 26). Seventy-five units in Carré's sample were holding companies belonging to 85 families: the latter were all to be found in the top ten in each relevant industry sector and were dominant in retailing, clothing, food and drink, wood, leather and shoes, and publishing. In other sectors, notably mining, paper, aeronautics, automobiles, tyres, rubber and chemicals, they shared the top places with other private enterprises or with the state. In the mid-1970s, the biggest family-controlled firm among the 250 largest enterprises employed 40,000 people in metropolitan France and the smallest 8000. In total, says Carré, family-controlled firms provided a livelihood for five million workers, almost a quarter of the total labour force. The list included companies and families with household names such as Schlumberger, Schneider, Michelin, Dassault, Peugeot, Gillet (Pricel & Rhône-Poulenc) and de Wendel; they hold a very large place in the fortunes of the national economy and their firms stand alongside the other major industrial groups of France such as Denain-N-E Lonwy, Saint Gobain-Pont-à-Mousson, BSN-Gervais-Danone and Thomson-Brandt.

These industrial groups in turn became closely linked to the banking sector, both joint-stock and privately owned. Indeed some industrial groups absorbed or created banks while in other cases industrial companies became linked to a group topped by a major financial house, such as Paribas or the Banque de Suez as we saw above. In this connection Bellon (1980) points to the many links between industrial companies and financial institutions, many of them family-owned. They include Marine Wendel (Banque Demachy), Michelin (the private Banque Industrielle et Immobilière), PUK and the CFRC (Crédit Chimique), CGE (Electrobanque) and Peugeot (Financière de Banque). It thus seems that in France, in the 1970s, the industrial and financial sectors were firmly linked, with the 'attached' banks providing companies with credit for expansion in the way initially developed during the industrialization period of the nineteenth century and with new outlets for the use of family capital.

Because of these linkages, the question of 'family' or 'technocratic' control of major segments of the economy loses much of its sense. In these industrial-financial groupings, links developed or continued between family capital and companies 'technocratically' or 'managerially' controlled. There have, for instance, been durable links between the Banque de Suez, the Compagnie Dassault and the Air Liquide groups. Similarly, the capital of the Vernes family (Banque Vernes et Commerciale de Paris) was divided into three equal parts and the aid of the Vernes capital allowed the Banque de Suez to acquire in 1972 Lille Bounières et Colombes. To Vernes, too, is linked the Béghin-Say group, created also in 1972. Suez in turn has a durable alliance with the long-standing financial families of Hottinguer and Rothschild. Similarly there exists an old association between the Lazard (bankers), Michelin, Peugeot and Agnelli (FIAT) families (Bellon 1980: 75). Many industrial companies within the groups and between groups are also linked together by family connections. Exchanges of directors and enduring family networks continue in contemporary France to support long-standing alliances (Bellon 1980: 75). The growth of groups has diluted but by no means eradicated the potential economic power of family capital.

Families of the capitalist class may continue to own many large French companies (of which only a very few were nationalized in 1981) but do they effectively control them? Is the French capitalist class one which controls as well as owns? There are, of course, two well-known opposing theses. One suggests that the owners of capital have relinquished their power to enterprise managers who make both daily and strategic decisions. The second contends that even managers holding great responsibility for their enterprises remain fundamentally subject to the decisions of capital owners. To some degree, to judge from evidence not only from France but also from the UK (Scott 1982, Useem 1984) and the USA (Llewellen 1971, Herman 1981), the question is misplaced. It seems quite clear from these studies that top managers both own *and* control, that those who own *also* control. Herman, for example, stresses the similarity of position between the top executives and directors of joint-stock companies and those of their colleagues more normally considered the business bourgeoisie. At the very top, it seems, ownership and control re-merge.

This re-merger can be seen in the extent of capital ownership, resulting both from the 'wealth-creation programmes' (remuneration deals) offered by companies to their top people and the investments of those people themselves, and in the attitudes, values and policies which they espouse. Both Llewellen and Herman for the USA and Useem for the UK indicate the remarkable capital holdings held by directors and top executives, certainly enough to ensure compatibility of outlook on policies for the profitability of the enterprises in their charge.

The evidence on capital-holding by top executives in France is less clear but there is no reason to believe that it is less considerable than elsewhere. The system linking the *dirigeants* of the great enterprises together – similarity of background and education, family links, a career (in part) in a public administration – and the general pattern of wealth-holding in France, in so far as that is known, seems to suggest that the capitalist class includes both owners and daily controllers. Some people are indeed both *cadres supérieurs* and *patrons*, as Birnbaum (1978) shows.

Asking the question, 'who has power in an enterprise?', when describing the 'private government' of France's major industrial groups, Bauer and Cohen (1981) reply that it is those who form the *système dirigeant*. By this they mean the group of actors who draw up and ensure the acceptance of strategic decisions for the firms concerned. These actors define the means of accumulation and development for the group as a whole. This set of controllers includes internal executives as well as outside directors and other advisers brought in from elsewhere. Examining the similarities of background suggests that the ties between all members of this group of actors are close and that they are all indeed clearly full members of the capitalist class.

But what of the families whose enterprises went out of business or were absorbed during the merger phase or whose industrial futures have otherwise changed? Evidence found by Scott in the UK suggests that over time many families sell their businesses and diversify their holdings. Their sons and daughters still belong to the capitalist class, however, because, while they may have joined the salaried segment of the business bourgeoisie, their patrimony, on which their life style and status much depend, is still dependent directly on the effective functioning of the companies in which capital is held. This is the case, too, in France. Families in the textile industry, bought out during mergers and restructuring, seem to have 'invested' their sons in other companies while investing their financial capital in still other enterprises (Bergeron, in Lequin 1983).

In summary, then, the view of events which suggests that in France, as elsewhere in western countries, the capitalist class has undergone many transformations, such that as many companies are 'technocratically' controlled as are family-run, and the state has an ever larger share in enterprise decision-making, greatly oversimplifies reality. Debates about technocratic or family control miss much of the complexity of the relationships underlying the external façade of the national economic structure. Such debates seem to suggest that the 'capitalist class' is linked only to the ownership of business, when the analysis should include examination of the whole group of privileged relationships which extend beyond major enterprises, beyond the whole business bourgeoisie. These relationships reach deep into the senior echelons of the state administration as well as into the other fields of power, which generate the ideas, the inventions, the administrative structures and political arrangements which underlie and co-determine the policies developed and practised by economic actors.

This brings us back to an earlier remark on the role of the state in France. As was said then, it is impossible to conceive of modern French capitalism without the state, not only because 40 per cent of GDP is redistributed by the state but because of the direct role played by public officials and representatives in shaping the economic fabric and in regulating everyday economic activity. Direct personal links join business to politics in France not only through interest but through kinship. Thus, as an example, as Bellon (1980: 21) shows, de Gaulle was linked to the Farjon family (of Baignol and Farjon) by his wife; to the group Banque de l'Union Parisienne through his brother; to the de Wendel family through his son; and to the *direction* of Péchiney through his daughter. In his turn, Giscard d'Estaing was linked to the Banque d'Indochine by both father and grandfather while his brother links him to the groups of IBM and Erickson & Gibbs. Moreover, businessmen who have been in the public administration are far from rare, as we saw above.

THE FAMILIES OF CAPITAL

Many of the capitalist families of contemporary France sprang fully formed from the enterprises created by their ancestors in the nineteenth century. Many names that are household words today have lengthy ancestries. Thus Kuhlmann, Motte, Gillet, de Wendel, Reverschon, Peugeot and Schlumberger first created enterprises well over a century ago, and in many cases considerably more. These families did not grow from their business ventures: rather their enterprises resulted from their wealth. Nineteenth-century French enterprises were created frequently by men of substance whose wealth had origins in banking, commerce or artisan activities. Rags to riches, it seems, was a relatively rare ascension (Kindleberger 1976). The links with high-level and exclusive education began early. In the UK, Kindleberger points out, professionalism in family businesses decreased over time: in France the reverse occurred, the heirs of the founders embracing a scientific education as preparation for their business over the generations. From this stems the importance from the early nineteenth century of the scientific *grandes écoles* as the seedbeds of the leaders of industry and later the public administration and politics as well.

In particular regions, notably in the Nord and Alsace, intermarriage among business families early served to strengthen bonds at both personal and business levels (Bergeron, in Lequin 1983). This tradition carried on into the twentieth century as recent studies have shown (Girard 1964; Lévy-Leboyer 1979; Marceau 1976, 1988). Families have also long played a central part in the production and reproduction of the controllers of French industry in that leadership of the private sector has, of course, always been much more hereditary than that of the public sector. In the mid-1970s still, 68 per cent of all *patrons* were the sons of *patrons* (Birnbaum et al. 1978: 95); and although there has recently been a great increase in the number of *cadres supérieurs'* sons becoming *patrons*, this still largely constitutes recruitment from within the business class. Indeed, at least between 1939 and 1973, the number of *patrons* from privileged backgrounds actually *increased* from 80 to 83 per cent (Lévy-Leboyer 1979: 142).

Many studies have shown the very limited social recruitment of the capitalist class in France in the mid to late twentieth century. Thus, a study by Delefortrie-Soubeyroux in the late 1950s indicated that a very large proportion (two-fifths of those providing information) of a sample of 2000 senior business executives, were raised in families headed by business owners or top managers. A further 47 per cent came from the upper class, including military, administrative, professional and management families. In contrast, only 9 per cent came from shopkeeper backgrounds, and 4 per cent from those of farm, artisan and manual workers. The picture changed little over the period of economic expansion. A decade later, a study by Hall and de Bettignies (1968) in the late 1960s found identical recruitment among the *Présidents-Directeurs-Généraux* (PDG) of the 50 largest French companies. For a similar period, Monjardet (1972), taking only the 100 largest enterprises, including publicly-owned firms, found that three-fifths of the PDG were the sons of businessmen – business owners, merchants, brokers and bankers. Between a quarter and a third were from other bourgeois families while only a tiny 0.03 per cent were from farm and primary school teacher families, and none at all were the sons of manual or white-collar workers. The larger the company, indeed, the higher the social origins of their controllers and the more exclusively was recruitment to top positions from families already established in the business world.

Later again, Birnbaum and his colleagues (1978) found that nearly half the PDG of large firms were the sons of business-owners and top managers. Few, they found, who started their professional lives as *patrons* ever held any other occupation (only 10 per cent in 1974). Many business owner sons became *cadres supérieurs* but only while waiting to obtain *patron* positions, often in the same businesses. Birnbaum and his team observe that:

sons of *patrons* who became technocrats [managers in firms they did not own] do not for that reason have less power ... The dominant class simply reconverted. The social distances have been maintained ... many senior managers are simply *patrons* in fiscal disguise or the sons of *patrons*. They represent the new private ruling class, some with a direct relationship to property (since 50% of *cadres supérieurs* are members of the Boards of Directors), some under the indirect control of capital. (1978: 42)

A study of younger managers completed half a decade later suggests that over the next generation at least little will change in recruitment to the capitalist class. The study of French students and alumni of the international business school, INSEAD, at Fontainebleau, showed that very high propor-tions were from business backgrounds. Nearly 40 per cent of the students entering the Institute between 1959 and 1977 came from families headed by fathers who were business owners or independents, who were PDG, Chairmen of the Board, Directeurs Généraux, Managing Directors, General Managers or *Directeurs*. A further 8 per cent had fathers who were senior managers while another 14 per cent came from families whose heads were in business, in other management or in professional positions. In contrast, only 16.5 per cent came from public-sector backgrounds and 17 per cent from all other occupations together. (In some other European countries, it should be noted, the predominantly *patronat* background of students was even more pronounced, notably in Belgium and Holland.

See Marceau, 1988.) If, as seems likely, these young men head important businesses later in their careers there will be very little change in the personnel of the capitalist class in France, at least over the next few decades.

Most of the people controlling enterprises in France, then, come from families already well established in the business world. To just what degree they are established and how strong is the lineage is suggested by the study of INSEAD students and alumni referred to earlier. Thus, if 20 per cent of the respondents' fathers were business-owners and a further 18 per cent top and senior managers, their grandfathers were almost equally entrenched in business. A quarter of all paternal grandfathers were *patrons* with a further 7.5 per cent senior managers while 17 per cent and 13 per cent of maternal ones were in these categories. Social homogamy ensured the continuation and consolidation of the tradition: 23.5 per cent of respondents had mothers from *patronat* families while 21 per cent of mothers had *cadres supérieurs* fathers. Similarly in the grandparents' generation: 24 per cent of paternal and 13.5 per cent of maternal grandfathers married wives from the *patronat* and 9 per cent and 16 per cent respectively chose wives from the families of the *cadres supérieurs* of business.

In total, the homogamy of the business class has been very great: even greater is that of the upper class as a whole. Thus 70 per cent of fathers in the INSEAD study were from the upper class (including public servants, members of the liberal professions, military officers and senior 'intellectuals'), as were 53 per cent and 63.5 per cent of paternal and maternal grandfathers and 71 per cent of mothers, 56.5 per cent and 59.5 per cent of paternal and maternal grandmothers. In their own generation respondents followed a similar pattern: almost half of their wives were from families headed by *patrons* and *cadres supérieurs*, as were nearly a third of their wives' grandparents, and most of the others were from other sections of the upper class. Data on the extended families, including the uncles, cousins, siblings and their spouses of members of the sample, show a similar very strong homogamy: 36 per cent of brothers, 28 per cent of sisters' husbands, 41 per cent of uncles and 47 per cent of male cousins held senior business positions. A further 20 per cent on average held more junior ones but as many were still young at the time of the survey the proportion joining the capitalist class later in their careers is likely to grow quite considerably.

The social homogamy so clear in most respondents' marriages arises from the structuring of opportunities for meeting appropriate spouses. Marriages in this milieu are no longer arranged but neither are they left to 'luck': rather they arise from meetings in situations so structured by social and family circumstances that the field of competition for partners is severely limited. The great majority had met their spouses at friends' houses or through the family-organized *rallyes* of the French upper class, at dinner parties or private receptions (Marceau 1989).

The social standing of the parties to the marriage is confirmed by the long guest lists (13 per cent of respondents had more than 1000 guests) at wedding receptions, while the 'dowries' brought by the wives, and which include real estate and other capital, ensure that the young couple will be able to live in suitable style (Marceau 1989). The usefulness of the capital generated by such marriages is clear: not only does it provide social capital, *entrée* to many new and appropriate circles, but it also concentrates economic capital in a few hands (Lévy-Leboyer 1979; Marceau 1989).

If the personnel of the capitalist class have remained socially, in origins and education, much the same in France over recent generations, it none the less seems that changes in some attitudes and outlook have occurred. Compromised by wartime collaboration with the enemy, the *patronat* after 1945 needed to refurbish its image. Jean Reynaud long ago observed that the rise of opposing social forces led the leaders of big business to seek new methods of action, more publicly defensible, and to turn to arguments about technical efficiency (1967). Many business organizations as well as the heads of individual enterprises felt the need to emphasize the modernity of their structures and their contribution to broadly-defined national goals. Symbolic of this mood as it developed through the 1960s was the change of name by the employer group Centre des Jeunes Patrons to Centre des Jeunes Dirigeants d'Entreprise and its public recruitment of eminent management intellectuals.

Observing these changes in rhetoric, and others in management and lifestyle, which seemed to go hand-in-hand with changes in enterprise control, bringing to prominence a salaried rather than a possessory business bourgeoisie in the decades after 1945, Bourdieu and his colleagues showed how the traditional *patron* had been engaged in modernizing his image. They pointed to the change from the *personal* mode of domination typical of family capitalism to a *structural* mode of domination in which the new *patrons* specialized in external public relations and internal human relations, learning a 'soft' management style from business school edicts. Qualities sought of leaders became aptitude for discussion and negotiation, knowledge of foreign languages and polite and subtle manners, the opposite of the 'character', the energy, directness and military style which characterized the older *patron de combat* (Bourdieu et al. 1973: 80–1). In a new economic age, focused on marketing rather than engineering, new social models rose to prominence. Businessmen and politicians alike spoke of progress, modernization, social evolution, partnership, the inevitability of change, in pressing their views. So publicly dominant did technocratic language become that Bourdicu and Boltanski were moved in 1976 to issue an 'Encyclopédie de la Technocratie'. A public process of social differentiation led by younger business men was well underway. They distanced themselves from past images by espousing the rhetoric of technocracy and the 'new bourgeois' lifestyle, associated at work with internationalism – the executive with the briefcase at the airport – and at home with 'light' food, 'modern' furniture and a passion for films rather than opera. The 'young wolves' had replaced the 'old lions' in the board rooms of French capitalism. Or so it seemed, at least, until the harsher economic environment of the late 1970s and 1980s, when older values, associated with the traditional *patron*, re-emerged in France as elsewhere.

BECOMING A CAPITALIST: EDUCATION AND CAREER

Capitalists in France, it would seem, are both born and made. The proportion born into the business bourgeoisie continues to be very high and few sons from business families seem to consider seriously any other career (Marceau 1989). The pressures from families, both immediate and extended, that push younger members to conform to tradition are powerful, and the social and financial rewards for such conformity are considerable. Moreover, once on the business track, few leave in mid-career (Birnbaum et al. 1978).

In France, however, top businessmen and *patrons* clearly do have to be 'made' as well. The top educational establishments play the central role in preparation for the path to the top. Business will always offer opportunities for people with talent but who lack formal education and those born into businesses may not 'need' education to succeed as others do. In France, however, the capitalist class, in contradistinction to the *patronat* as a whole, has long espoused the need for top-level scientific and technical education. By the middle of the nineteenth century, many top businessmen had degrees from the top Parisian *grandes écoles* – Polytéchnique, Mines or Centrale – while later other schools in Paris and the provinces began to cater for the increased demand. It is these schools which are both the *écoles du pouvoir* and the gatekeepers of power still in the late twentieth century. It is through them that the complicated interrelationships so important in France between the capitalist class and the state are woven and perpetuated. They are thus central to the distribution of top personnel and the development of top careers in both private and public sectors. The intense competition for entry to the schools ensures that those selected are highly prized in the managerial labour market. Intellectual selectivity is largely matched by social selectivity, their student populations being socially the reverse of the nation.

All the studies quoted earlier on family origins also indicate the importance to careers of passage through the *grandes écoles* and the position of these schools is too well known to need much elaboration here. Suffice it to say that, for example,

Monjardet (1972) found in the 1960s that 38 per cent of PDG of the top 100 companies were graduates of the Ecole Polytechnique. The predominance of the Polytechnique was largely confirmed by Hall and de Bettignies (1968), by the Union des Industries Métallurgiques et Minières (1970) for a range of other companies, by Bourdieu and his team (1973) and Birnbaum and his colleagues in their respective studies of the *patronat* (1978) and by Bauer and Cohen studying the 'private government' of top enterprises (1981).

How then do those born into the capitalist class make their way to the top? Clearly for the sons of family-owned enterprises entering these firms there is relatively little problem providing they show a modicum of talent, often tested by *stages* in other enterprises. For others, however, there may be a thornier road. Unfortunately, there are few studies of careers in French business. Most commentators have contented themselves with counting the diplomas held by those currently at the top. Available evidence suggests the existence of three major paths to senior business positions, one almost by default. Two of these may be called the 'loyalist' and the 'challenge success' routes and involve only the private sector. The third, the 'catapult', links public and private together.

'Loyalist' careers involve slow movement up through the ranks of a given company, or possibly two firms, a young manager gradually showing his talents and being rewarded by promotion to the next rung. While some of those who choose this route will reach the top (there is no clear French evidence on this), especially if they are products of the very best *grandes écoles*, it is not the route chosen by the most dynamic from the business bourgeoisie. Rather, my study of INSEAD alumni suggests, the most ambitious and those from business backgrounds are more likely to choose the 'challenge success' route to the top, a path which involves risk-taking and jumping between functions, enterprises, even countries, in the search for visibility for one's success in the challenges posed by companies. Success on this route is measured by innovation and by 'good management' but essentially by the 'bottom line', the profits which can be clearly seen to be due to an individual's efforts. The ambitious young manager, putting his faith in his technical expertise, his contacts and his flair, thus seeks out the risky and the visible: the deals which show profits, the clients introduced to a bank, the moribund divisions or subsidiaries made profitable, the new markets developed. This route involves many changes of direction, many new starts, many moves closer to the centres of enterprise power. It involves risks but, if successful, provides the highest rewards.

The final way to the top relies on the link between the state and private enterprise and the increasingly common *pantouflage*, the move from a top public to an equivalent private position sector, traditionally the prerogative of graduates from the best *grandes écoles* and the most senior ranks of the public administration, notably those whose paths have led through ministerial *cabinets*. Many members of the top management teams of France's biggest enterprises when recruited to senior positions, therefore, have very little experience of the problems facing private enterprise, although they may well come from capitalist families (Bauer and Cohen 1981). Their value to the enterprise resides essentially in their possession of the skills necessary for negotiations with every major company's principal 'client', the state.

Useem in his study of the recruitment of the top management team in the UK, and Herman in his research in the USA, both concluded that the criteria of choice for the top management team of a major enterprise were radically different from those applying lower down the organizational hierarchy. Obeying the same logic, but in a situation where the state is a crucial partner, the same division appears in France. From their study of a sample of major French industrial groups in the late 1970s, Bauer and Cohen show how different is selection for the leading posts from the procedure used for the choice of the ordinary *cadres* below. At the very top many of the men selected to control major businesses in France come from the *grands corps* of the central administration. As Bauer and Cohen explain:

The qualities sought [of candidates] from outside are precisely those which cannot become manifest on the inside of the industrial group because of the extreme division of labour and the dispersion of responsibilities. The skills sought among outsiders are those that the *système dirigeant* monopolises, the control of the resources of the state and above all the know-how-power (*savoir pouvoir*), the skills of negotiation, of the elaboration of strategic plans and of their translation into practice. ... (1981: 200)

For aspirants not from the public sector, these observers suggest that it may take 15–20 years to get to the top. That period is one of triple apprenticeship. Chosen initially on the basis of a first 'triple selection' – education (*grande école*), social background and the right experience (public sector) – once inside the enterprise candidates must pass the three tests of the apprenticeships. They have to acquire the *savoirs* (skills) of 'industry power, predatory power and organizational power'. The first apprenticeship lies in strategic training. Senior managers aiming for the top need to learn about the history of the success or failure of group projects so as to assess the realism of current plans. They need to learn about double accounting, fulfilling legal requirements while also 'losing' profits. Second, they need to learn to sit on boards of directors, to develop a vague discourse to satisfy small shareholders and to play on the multiple interests that link shareholders and the group. Third, they need to learn to be a *chef* and must show leadership qualities during a brief test 'on the ground'. Once in place, these men (and they are almost all men) will use their technical expertise and their contacts with the state and other enterprises to put together, as in an example given by Bauer and Cohen, a team of men who speak the same language and who share a common vision of the management of that type of enterprise and its market. Constantly involved in complex politico-financial dealings, industrial groups in France need leaders who master both public and private sectors. In this way, French enterprises mirror the British as described by Useem (1984) who select top men on the basis of their links with government, although in France these links are much closer, their capacity for negotiation with other enterprises and their accurate scanning of developments on the business horizon, both public and private, developed through membership of industry organizations and through holding positions as outside directors in other companies.

In these choices, the selection to the top of people both from similar positions in other enterprises and with experience of public office, sons of the business fractions of the bourgeoisie are likely to be especially well placed. The social mechanisms governing selection to the most prestigious educational institutions, to high administrative rank and to suitable 'jumping off' points in business all suggest that the capitalist class in France will long remain well in control of its destinies.

CONCLUSION

Shaken somewhat by the wave of nationalizations of 1981, which in the end did little more than change the leading personnel, and only some of those, the capitalist class in France seems set to continue to build on the gains accruing from the economic restructuring of the 1960s and 1970s. Its members will continue to guide their enterprises into new markets, particularly the international ones developed under the auspices of the Common Market. The government in turn, more or less directly, will continue to shape and influence major strategic business decisions, ensuring that national interests hold sway where that is crucial, that research investments are made and that the national political agenda is at least in part absorbed by private Boards of Directors. Recent experience suggests that a state controlled by the Left may be unable even to find alternative directors for the enterprises it wishes to take over, failing to attract either unions or junior managers to posts made available under its aegis (Bauer, in Birnbaum 1985). Further nationalizations would seem unlikely, at least in the foreseeable future. Macroeconomic policy will continue to rely on fiscal instruments and on the government's long-standing investment control powers, such as those vested in the Caisse des Dépôts et des Consignations. Failure under the Mitterrand presidency to allocate sufficient resources to rectify the ailing central planning mechanism has ensured that the coordination of public and private decisions will continue to be made through personal links as much as through government intervention and regulation. The interpenetration of careers in French capitalist enterprises and the state administration will ensure that the system operates reasonably smoothly. Recent political choices seen in the return to power of the Right in 1986 and the uncertain majority of the Left in 1988 suggest that labour's issues, such as the internal reform of the enterprise, are largely off the public agenda.

The changes in economic structure in the last few decades have only increased concentration in a few hands of the reins of social and economic power and largely left unaltered major aspects of enterprise policy, notably those governing relations with labour, despite gains made by trade unions in the immediate post-war period. As Bauer and Cohen conclude:

whether the small number of *dirigeants* are owners or salaried makes no difference to their strategic choices; the cleavages cut across these categories. Family capital has no industrial policies which it can set against those of banking, state or foreign capital. These few men who rule France's important industrial groups have made themselves into private governments who control in detail the development of present activities, who monopolise the preparation, decisions and realisation of the huge operations of diversification and disinvestment undertaken and who allocate the work of their armies of experts, engineers and managers ... These groups are controlled by a coopted oligarchy ... [The fact that property-owning is no longer necessary for access to the *système dirigeant* does *not* mean a widening of the dominant class to include all knowledge holders ...] This is oligarchic capitalism. Technocracy is limited by the oligarchic exercise of power. (1981: 174–5, 230)

Their words are echoed by Birnbaum and his colleagues when talking of the links between the capitalist class and the ruling class as a whole in France, links which are personal, financial, educational and political.

At the end of this study, we can confirm that the leading categories of the dominant class do indeed form a ruling class. Recruiting its members within the same social space, in the heart of the same social class, the French ruling class appears to be an ensemble, closed in on itself, crystallised; almost no actors drawn from other social classes succeed in penetrating its frontiers. Its sons possess social characteristics identical to those of their fathers: they simply change, in some cases, their professions and sectors. (1978: 187)

The controlling oligarchy is closely knit and socially and politically homogeneous. Many of its members even live in close proximity. While there are regional sub-groups, as can be seen in studies not only of family capital but also of interlocking directorates (Stokman, Ziegler and Scott 1985) economic power, with political power, remains concentrated in Paris. Leading industrialists, financiers and public servants alike choose to reside in Paris; the 16th *arrondissement* in particular bears the stamp of the social homogeneity of its inhabitants. Residential style and propinquity become the physical manifestation of the continuing homogeneity, economic power and social dominance of the capitalist class as a whole in late twentieth-century France.

NOTE

1. There have, of course, been exceptions. The Poujadist movement brought together small capitalists such as shopkeepers and peasants in the 1950s but was shortlived. Perhaps at present the 'nationalist' movement led by Le Pen has a similar social base.

REFERENCES

Allard, P., Beaud, M., Bellon, B., Lévy, A. M. and Liénart, S. (1978) *Dictionnaire des Groupes Industriels et Financiers en France* (Paris: Le Seuil).

Bauer, M. and Cohen, E. (1981) *Qui Gouverne les Groupes Industriels?* (Paris: Le Seuil).

Bellon, P. (1980) *Le Pouvoir Financier et l'Industrie en France* (Paris: Le Seuil).

Bergeron, L. (1983) 'La tradition du textile', in Lequin, Y. (ed.) *Histoire des Français XIXe et XXe Siècles, Tome 2 La Société* (Paris: A. Colin).

Birnbaum, P. (ed.) (1985) *Les Elites Socialistes au Pouvoir 1981–1985* (Paris: Presses Universitaires de France).

Birnbaum, P., Barucq, C., Bellaiche, M. and Marie, A. (1978) *La Classe Dirigeante française* (Paris: Presses Universitaires de France).

Bourdieu, P., Boltanski, L. and de Saint Martin, M. (1973) 'Les stratégies de reconversion', *Social Science Information*, 12: 61–113.

Carré, B. (1978) *Le Pouvoir de l'Elite Familiale* (Paris: Presses Universitaires de France).

Carré, J. J., Dubois, P. and Malinvaud, E. (1972) *La Croissance française* (Paris: Le Seuil).

Cayrol, R., Parodi, J-C. and Ysmal, C. (1973) *Les Députés français* (Paris: A. Colin and the Fondation Nationale des Sciences Politiques).

Cohen, E. (1985) 'L'Etat socialiste en industrie: volontarisme politique et changement socio-économique', in Birnbaum, P. (ed.) *Les Elites Socialistes au Pouvoir 1981–1985* (Paris: Presses Universitaires de France).

Cohen, E. and Bauer, M. (1987) *Les Grandes Manoeuvres Industrielles* (Paris: Belfond).

Delefortrie-Soubeyroux, N. (1961) *Les Dirigeants de l'Industrie française* (Paris: A. Colin).

Dupeux, G. (1964) *La Société française 1789–1960* (Paris: A. Colin).

Girard, A. (1964) *Le Choix du Conjoint* (Paris: Presses Universitaires de France).

Hall, D. and de Bettignies, H. C. (1968) 'The French business elite', *European Business*, 19: 1–10.

Herman, E. (1981, paperback edn 1982) *Corporate Control, Corporate Power* (New York: Cambridge University Press).

Kindleberger, C. (1976) 'Technical education and the French entrepreneur', in Carter, E., Forster, R. and Moody, J. (eds) *Enterprises and Entrepreneurs in Nineteenth and Twentieth-Century France* (Baltimore: Johns Hopkins University Press).

Lévy-Leboyer, M., (ed.) (1979) *Le Patronat de la Seconde Industrialisation* (Paris: Les Editions Ouvrières).

Lewellen, W. (1971) *The Ownership Income of Management* (New York: National Bureau of Economic Research and Columbia University Press).

Marceau, J. (1976) 'Role division and social cohesion: the case of some young French upper class families', in Allen, S. and Barker, D. (eds.) *Dependence and Exploitation in Work and Marriage* (Harlow: Longman).

Marceau, J. (1977) *Class and Status in France: Economic Change and Social Immobility* (Oxford: Oxford University Press).

Marceau, J. (1989) *A Family Business? The Making of an International Business Elite* (Cambridge: Cambridge University Press).

Michalet, C. (1974), in Vernon, R. (ed.) *Big Business and the State* (London: Macmillan).

Monjardet, D. (1972) 'Carrière des dirigeants et contrôle de l'entreprise', *Sociologie du Travail*, 13 (2): 131–44.

Morin, F. (1974) *La Structure Financière du Capitalisme Français* (Paris: Calmann-Lévy).

Poulantzas, N. (1974) *Les Classes sociales dans le Capitalisme aujourd'hui* (Paris: Le Seuil).

Scott, J. (1982) *The Upper Classes* (London: Macmillan).

Stokman, F., Ziegler, R. and Scott, J. (eds) (1985) *Networks of Corporate Power* (Cambridge: Polity Press).

Union des Industries Métallurgiques et Minières (1970) *Ingénieurs et Cadres* (Paris: UIMM).

Useem, M. (1984) *The Inner Circle* (New York: Oxford University Press).

4 Federal Republic of Germany

Willfried Spohn and Y. Michal Bodemann

INTRODUCTION

There is in mainstream German sociology today an abundant
literature on employers, managers, the business elite and the
upper middle class in general, as well as an established body of
research on German social structure. However, few contemporary German sociologists still find the concept of a capitalist
class in West Germany useful.[1] Social historians reacting
against the largely ahistorical approaches of sociologists have
made some important contributions to the study of the social
evolution of employers, industrialists or the *Bürgertum*, but
they also shun the term 'capitalist class'.[2] In the few instances
where Marxist writers in West Germany have used the concept
of a capitalist class, they have done so rather abstractly,
referring to economic structures in general or writing in terms
of a global critique of capitalism. The capitalist class as an
empirical collective actor is virtually non-existent in this
literature as well.[3]

The West German capitalist class therefore appears difficult
to identify. A number of reasons for this come to mind. First,
there is no stratum of capitalists in West Germany that is a
self-conscious, socially cohesive ruling group. Wealth, by and
large, is not displayed ostentatiously; top capitalists tend
towards anonymity and may see themselves simply as the best
examples of the German virtues of hard work and diligence.
Second, there is little similarity between the sharp class
antagonisms of Imperial Germany and the relatively stable
contemporary West German social structure, and this explains

characterizations of West Germany such as Schelsky's (1965) 'levelled middle-class society' (Mooser 1984).

Third, workers and employers no longer think they live in a class-divided society, even though the notions of 'they at the top' and 'we at the bottom' still prevail. The antagonistic relations between capitalists and proletarians notwithstanding, the idea of a 'social partnership' between employers and employees prevails and there has emerged a general consensus based on political democracy and the welfare state (Popitz 1957; Dahrendorf 1965). West German workers do not think of themselves as a class, and West German capitalists probably do not either. It is therefore not entirely surprising that the disappearance of the language of class in West German society is reflected in the disappearance of class in West German sociology. This holds true even though at the twilight of the German 'economic miracle' and in the crises of the late 1960s, the language of class was revived by the neo-Marxist student movement. The way, however, in which this language was then used did not represent more than a memory of past class struggles, like a 'venerable disguise' that no longer fits (Marx 1969: 115).

The following survey of the capitalist class in the Federal Republic in comparative perspective is based on four key assumptions. First, we assume that advanced industrial societies should be characterized as capitalist or capitalistically structured societies when capital valorization and accumulation on the basis of wage labour still constitute the central organizing principle of society (Giddens 1973: Bottomore 1979, 1985). The dual structure of capital and wage labour is essential even though by itself its underlying antagonisms and conflicts do not determine how in any given historical epoch it is socially, culturally and politically articulated.[4]

Second, we assume that the term *capitalists* includes both owners of the means of production and their managerial functionaries (Jaeggi 1973; Giddens 1974; Wienold 1986). Moreover, capitalists and managers are distinguished in terms of economic sectors, wealth and power, and they constitute different fractions of capital such as industrialists and bankers, big and small capitalists or economic elites versus non-elites.

Third, we assume that the capitalist class should be viewed

in the context of and distinguished from *Bürger* ('burghers') a category that refers to both members of the capitalist class and various strata of the middle class who define themselves as *Bürger* without being properly linked to the sphere of capitalist production (Kocka 1986, 1987). Fourth, we assume that the capitalist class is not only characterized by its specific class position, but as a social group is also defined by its specific social, cultural and political characteristics. This assumption implies a holistic approach to class that has been shown to be particularly fruitful in the analysis of working-class formation.[5]

In the light of these assumptions, we shall look at the German capitalist class first in terms of its economic conditions; second, in terms of its social composition; and third, in terms of its political-cultural constitution. This necessitates joining together heterogeneous material from economic and social history, sociology and political science. However, before we address these different levels of capitalist class formation systematically, we shall briefly sketch the main features of its historical development and its formation in the context of the peculiarities of modernization in Germany since the mid-nineteenth century. This historical review will help us understand the peculiar restructuring of the capitalist class in the Federal Republic today, as well as the continuities and discontinuities of capitalist class formation in the course of German history (Conze and Lepsius 1983).

CAPITALIST CLASS AND THE PECULIARITIES OF GERMAN HISTORY

In contrast to the relatively steady and continuous development of western capitalist-industrial societies during the twentieth century, the founding of the Federal Republic of Germany constitutes a radical break in relation to its prehistory, and this had a decisive influence on the structure of its capitalist class. The victory of the Allies over Nazism, the occupation and dismemberment of the German Reich, especially the loss of the eastern provinces and the integration of the Soviet zone into the Soviet hemisphere and of the western zone into the Western Alliance, as well as the establishment of state socialism in the GDR and the reconstruction of capitalism in the Federal Republic – all these events enormously altered the societal context of the capitalist class in West Germany. It is true, of course, that 1945 was not a *Stunde Null*, a 'Zero Hour', as is commonly assumed. Indeed, much of the social and institutional structure, deeply rooted in German history, had survived. Nevertheless, there were some important discontinuities which resulted in a clear restructuring or 'remaking' of the West German capitalist class. Let us now examine these continuities and discontinuities in class formation and summarize the main features of capitalist class formation from the unification of Germany in the nineteenth century to the collapse of German fascism.

Ever since Barrington Moore's classic study of the social origins of dictatorship and democracy (Moore 1969), the German path to modernization has been widely characterized as conservative. This characterization is based on the fact that the Prussian gentry, the *Junker* class, managed to preserve its hegemonic power until well into the twentieth century. This class was able to shape the path of German modernization because of the failure of a bourgeois revolution in Germany. Indeed, the *Junker* class played a dominant role first in the suppression of the revolution of 1848, then in the 'revolution from above' until German unification, and later in the Bonapartist semi-constitutional political system of Imperial Germany, the conservative rollback of the Weimar Republic and lastly, the establishment of National Socialism.[6] This explanation has been widely accepted as a frame of reference for the thesis of the German *Sonderweg* proposed by the new German social and economic history (Puhle 1972; Kocka 1973; Wehler 1974; Winkler 1979).

Barrington Moore, however, fails to deal with the question whether, and if so how, the emerging industrial bourgeoisie itself may have contributed to the conservatism of German modernization (Skocpol 1973; Wiener 1976). In West Germany, quite similarly, advocates of the German *Sonderweg* thesis such as Hans-Ulrich Wehler and Jürgen Kocka have stressed the important role of the surviving pre-capitalist and absolutist-bureaucratic forces contributing to the weakness of the German bourgeoisie; Geoff Eley and David Blackbourn, their Anglo-Saxon critics, on the other hand, have pointed to the active contribution of the bourgeoisie itself in the German path of modernization (Blackbourn and Eley 1984, 1980; and from there Wehler 1981).

The German case can in fact not be explained solely by the discrepancy between its economic and its political modernization, because on account of their economic interests, the industrial capitalist class itself favoured, or at least accepted, non-liberal forms of domination. This can be shown for a number of instances. In 1848 the emerging capitalist class settled for a compromise with the economically liberal but politically conservative late absolutist state (Landes 1969; Sheehan 1978; Nipperdey 1983). The national unification of Germany in 1871 secured Germany's economic dominance in continental Europe but the democratization of its political system was neglected.[7] Weimar democracy was only half-heartedly tolerated by the German bourgeoisie; its dissolution by Nazism they actively supported, passively accepted, but rarely vigorously opposed.[8] We therefore suggest that the conservatism of the German path of capitalist development and modernization was not only due to the Prussian *Junker* class and the state bureaucracy against the class interests of the industrial bourgeoisie; the capitalist class itself played an active role in this path to modernization. The reason for this must be sought primarily in the conditions of German capitalist industrialization. In contrast to the relatively even and organic industrial development in Britain as the first industrial nation, industrialization in Germany was uneven, largely due to the domination of England in the world market (Landes 1969; Kemp 1969; Costas 1980; Borchardt 1985; Kaelble 1983b). German industrialization was therefore characterized by features which today we would describe as the 'development of underdevelopment': the growing discrepancies between developing industrial and backward pre-industrial and agrarian sectors and the important role of the large banks and especially the Prussian and the other quasi-absolutist German states in the process of industrialization (Gerschenkron 1963; Landes 1969). English competition necessitated state leadership in policies pertaining to industrial development and modernization. The capitalist class had no reason to oppose these state policies as long as they were carried out by Prussia as the hegemonic power in Germany.

After the unification of Germany, the advantages of backwardness (Gerschenkron 1963) became apparent, and gradually German capital was able to overtake its British competitor. At the same time, however, it is characteristic of German industrialization that the components of the development of underdevelopment were being further reproduced. This was especially true for Imperial Germany, but it held true until the rise of Nazism. The dualism between a highly developed industrial sector on the one hand and a backward pre-industrial agrarian sector on the other continued. Moreover, the neo-mercantilist protective tariff system, introduced after 1878 in reaction to the declining competitiveness of the *Junker* economy, had a particularly important function in securing for the capitalist class the growing domestic market. Big capital cartelized and monopolized the home market at the expense of small capital.

Furthermore, the large banks continued to support big capital and its expansion strategies; and the Imperial state also continued to intervene with a variety of measures in order to strengthen the competitiveness of German heavy industry. All this resulted in a peculiar pattern of international growth which in contrast and in opposition to British liberal 'informal' imperialism was shaped by methods of formal colonialism overseas, by military expansion within continental Europe, and by protective controls in the world market. Germany's highly developed industrial capitalism thus reproduced specific economic structures which were rooted in the original backward situation of the German economy. Therefore, all the characteristics features of German capitalism which have been conceptualized as 'organized capitalism', 'finance capitalism', 'monopoly capitalism' or 'imperialism' did not represent a generally higher stage of capitalism, but rather an historical configuration of the development of underdevelopment within an already existing hegemonic world market (Spohn 1977).

In the context of this type of industrialization and until the rise of fascism, the bourgeoisie was largely amalgamated with the imperial state. At the economic level, we find the emergence and consolidation of the various factions of capital. On one side, the agrarian capital of the *Junker* class with its declining economic power due to growing agrarian competition from overseas; on the other side, the steadily growing industrial sectors with ever greater concentration and centralization of capital: heavy industry, mechanical engineering, railroads, chemical and industrial production. While this sector achieved ever greater significance, the mass of small capital in the more traditional spheres of production found itself under increasing economic pressure and dependency. This constellation produced a cooperative relationship between big agrarian and big industrial interests – albeit slowly tilting towards the latter – which converged in nationalist protectionism, monopolistic cartelization and formal imperialist expansionism.[9]

At the societal level, the conservatism of German modernization preserved traditional social structures and perpetuated the peculiar hierarchical order of quasi-feudal estates. Conservatism expressed itself mostly in the social dominance and exlusiveness of the *Junker* class – the nobility of the civil service and of the military – and other classes were influenced by it. Germany's uneven pattern of industrialization only accentuated social inequalities and class barriers. This resulted in the cultural adaptation of the German bourgeoisie to the values of the nobility. At the same time, the bourgeoisie was rejected by the nobility. The parallel closure of the bourgeoisie to the lower middle and working classes, in turn, proved to be of great consequence to the social history of these groups.[10]

Finally, at the political level of capitalist class formation, we find a strengthening of authoritarian, militarist and nationalist-imperialist traits, over time. At the same time, we find ever-weaker anti-authoritarian, democratic and republican orientations. This hardening conservatism could be attributed to a number of other factors. First was the continuing patriarchal attitude at the plant or workshop level which resisted trade union representation of workers' interests. Second, the bourgeoisie found itself increasingly beleaguered by the rising mass parties, especially the Catholic *Zentrum* (Centre Party) and by Social Democracy. This clearly weakened the liberal parties as the bourgeoisie's political representatives. It seemed therefore more attractive to capital to represent its interests directly via the newly established industrial organizations. Third, the growing pressure towards greater constitutional democracy on the part of the trade unions, Social Democracy, the *Zentrum* party and left-wing liberalism brought the bourgeoisie at best to a superficial acceptance of these social forces as opposed to a genuine compromise.[11]

This pattern was even perpetuated in the Weimar Republic whose democratic institutions capital supported only very ambivalently. Once these institutions were paralysed, it took the rising tide of Nazism for granted, although only segments of the bourgeoisie like the owners of heavy industry in the Rhine and Ruhr districts actively supported the totalitarian regime. While it would be wrong, therefore, to view National Socialism as the *ultima ratio* of the pattern of capitalist class formation just sketched, the integration of this class into the fascist dictatorship brought its contours into sharp relief, temporarily at least. Nationalist autarky, monopolistic cartelization and militarist expansionism were now driven to their extremes. Although German fascism helped smash traditional social barriers, politically – and after the destruction of the autonomy of the working-class movement – it created a repressive-patriarchal industrial regime and a fascist-corporatist absorption of working-class interests.[12] Only the fall of the Nazi dicatorship in 1945 terminated the German conservative path to modernization.

THE ECONOMIC RESTRUCTURING OF THE CAPITALIST CLASS IN THE FEDERAL REPUBLIC OF GERMANY

The defeat of Nazi Germany and the occupation policies of the victorious Allies ruptured existing economic and political structures so decisively that a conservative modernizing route could no longer be pursued. The loss of the eastern agrarian provinces, the flight of the East German population, the division of East and West Germany and the gradual development of two different social systems in the GDR and the Federal Republic – all this had a number of important consequences. First, the *Junker* class as the main pillar of conservative modernization was wiped out. They were broken politically by the Nazis, especially following the attempt on Hitler's life on 20 July 1944; and with the end of the war they lost their agrarian base in the territories east of the Elbe. Second, the capitalist class was now confined to West Germany; it was cut off from its traditional markets in Eastern Europe and became integrated into the western world market which blocked the traditional German pattern of capital reproduction.

The continuation of an authoritarian regime along the path of conservative modernization also became outdated for a number of other reasons. Despite significant counter-tendencies, the Nazi elite did by and large lose its power, and a significant number of opponents of Nazism returned from exile. The political parameters were also changed by a decided opposition against any new dictatorship and the reluctantly accepted imposition of liberal democracy by the Western Allies which in turn led to the foundation of the Bonn democracy as an alternative to the Communist regime in the East.[13]

At the time of the foundation of the Federal Republic, then, it was mostly the structural conditions of the capitalist class that were different – not the pattern of class formation. On the contrary, the social composition of the bourgeoisie showed a marked continuity from Nazi Germany to the postwar period (Zapf 1965; Berghahn 1985). This was due to the fact that denazification only hit – and only very temporarily and superficially – that part of the economic elite that had been manifestly allied with the Nazi regime. The other segments of capital, especially the second rank of the economic elite, were not subjected to most of these measures and soon assumed their old positions, mostly because their economic, legal and technical expertise were very much in demand. And together with these foot soldiers of the Nazi economy, their peculiar social, political and cultural class attitudes and beliefs returned as well. Here as elsewhere we find that Nazism at the level of the state had been destroyed while it survived, partly even intact, in large segments of the civil society.

The bourgeoisie – and especially their traditional power centre in the industries of the Rhine and the Ruhr – naturally sought to influence the economic and political development in accordance with their conservative values. This undoubtedly had an impact on the shape of West German society; but in the long run, the radically new postwar conditions which were so clearly at odds with the earlier trajectory of German modernization, gradually brought about certain changes to the traditional German pattern of capitalist class formation.

Apart from these ruptures in the political and social structure during the war years and the early postwar period, the real basis for the remaking of the capitalist class lay in the reconstruction of German capitalism and especially its integration into the western world market. The reconstruction of capitalism was, of course, a necessary precondition for the reproduction of the capitalist class. However, it was mainly the further development and the different trajectory of capitalist industrialization after the war that changed the economic conditions of capitalist class formation. Therefore we shall now sketch some structural components of capitalist-industrial development in the Federal Republic and then document the consequences this had for the new economic structure of the capitalist class.

Recent West German economic history is usually divided into three phases: reconstruction, from 1945 until the foundation of the FRG in 1949, the boom phase, from the early 1950s until the mid-1960s, and the phase of normalization and adaptation to the general development of western capitalism.[14] The immediate postwar period, it is usually argued, prepared the main preconditions for the following rapid process of capitalist growth. This is only partially true, however: German industrial capacity had been enormously expanded by the Nazi war economy and only marginally destroyed by Allied bombing and the subsequent dismantling of industrial installations. Moreover, the West German labour force potential was considerably enlarged by the huge stream of fugitives from the eastern provinces of Germany. Finally, there was the long postponement of consumer demand in consequence of shortages, destruction and starvation in the years after the war.

All that was needed, then, was a push by the Marshall Plan and currency reform to put the wheels of capitalist reproduction into full motion.

The forces of economic growth that were held back in the first postwar period were able to unfold fully in the 1950s and 1960s. To the Federal Republic, this presented itself as an 'economic miracle', the *Wirtschaftswunder*, that contributed much to the internal stability of West German society. The *Wirtschaftswunder* was fuelled by huge investments in many economic sectors which, like the transport system, the consumer goods industry and the construction industry had previously been either neglected or destroyed. It was fuelled, moreover, by the chemical, electrical and mechanical engineering industries that, in order to survive, had to regain their competitiveness in the world market; growing domestic and international demand during that time was a significant factor in this regard as well. Finally, it should not be forgotton that the constant flow of mostly skilled labour from the GDR to West Germany considerably enlarged the capacities of industrial production there.

These extraordinary conditions of industrial growth, however, could only be preserved until the mid-1960s. The recession in 1966–77 represented a transition to the normal cyclical course of capitalist growth although even the following years continued to be characterized by above-average growth rates, as well as by a continuing influx of foreign workers. With the crisis in the world market in 1973–4 the West German economy followed the general trend towards massive rationalization, technological innovation, structural adaptation and rising unemployment. These trends have been, *grosso modo*, characteristic for all advanced industrial societies since then.

Along with this process of economic growth we find fundamental economic and social transformations in West Germany. These transformations involve the relative weight of the economic sectors: the relative proportions of the industrial branches; the processes of concentration and centralization of capital; and the integration of West Germany's economy into the world market. While it is true that these changes occurred in all western advanced industrial societies, they constituted, for West Germany, a decisive break with its traditional pattern of industrialization and thus distinctively shaped the economic conditions of the capitalist class.

As far as the relative weight of the economic sector is concerned, we can see first of all how that balance has shifted from the turn of the century until today (Table 4.1). For example, during the first half of the twentieth century, employment in the primary sector gradually lost its traditional importance; in the secondary sector it remained more or less stable, and in the tertiary sector it increased slowly. But the decisive shift came with the development of the West German economy after the war (Abelshauser 1983: 120; Petzina 1977: 173). For Germany, this change meant thorough-going industrialization, urbanization on a large scale, the gradual reduction of regional differences and uneven development in the various economic sectors, the virtual elimination of an agrarian gentry of which the *Junkers* were a part, a reduced role for the peasantry and pre-industrial handicrafts and concentration of capital in the industrial sphere. Economically, the capitalist class was transformed into a more homogeneous industrial class.

Table 4.1:   Population by employment sector, Deutsches Reich and the Federal Republic, in percentage of employed persons

| | Sector | | |
	primary	secondary	tertiary
1907	35.2	40.1	24.8
1925	30.5	42.1	27.4
1939	25.9	42.2	31.9
1950	22.1	44.7	33.1
1961	13.4	48.1	38.5
1970	8.9	48.6	43.2

Source: Petzina (1977: 179); Abelshauser (1983: 120).

The second change concerns the internal structure of the industrial sector itself. Up to the 1960s, the traditionally important sectors such as coal, steel production and machinery occupied the leading positions. From the 1960s onwards, these sectors were slowly displaced by chemical, electrical and automobile production, and then by the electronic and nuclear industries (Hennig 1974: 211–17; Petzina 1977: 173). While these shifts can be observed in all advanced industrial societies, they are of special significance for West Germany because heavy industry now lost its traditional position of power. Thus, the industrial base of the traditional German pattern of capitalist class formation has been fundamentally transformed.

Third, regarding the concentration and centralization of industrial capital, there was a reversal of trends begun immediately after the war. The Allies had broken up firms such as I. G. Farben that had become highly cartelized and centralized, especially in the Nazi period. Soon, however, especially following the founding of the FRG, German industry was once again on the path of concentration and centralization, as shown in Table 4.2.

Table 4.2: Composition of German industry: size of firms in relation to the total number of firms (A) and to the total number of employees (B), in %.

Size of firm according to number of employees	1933 A	1933 B	1952 A	1952 B	1966 A	1966 B
1–9	88.6	19.6	46.1	2.9	43.7	1.9
10–49	8.1	15.4	34.0	12.4	32.1	9.4
50–99			9.0	9.9	10.2	8.6
100–199	2.4	21.5	5.2	11.5	6.5	11.0
200–499			3.6	17.3	4.7	19.8
500–999	0.8	43.4	1.1	11.7	1.5	12.9
1000+			0.9	34.3	1.2	38.6

Source: Jaeggi (1973).

These processess indicate how economic power has shifted from small to big capital. At the same time they also indicate how the gap between small and large capital has decreased. The capitalist class has been homogenized, and the strata of the old middle class have been stabilized.

Fourth, the rapid expansion of foreign trade and foreign investment concerns especially the role that German industrial capital has played in the development of the European Community and the North Atlantic-dominated world market. It signifies one of the most decisive breaks with the traditional pattern of integration into the world market and the traditional route of modernization. Although there was already a relatively strong internationalizing tendency in the German economy before World War I, it dropped steadily to near autarky during fascism – as can be seen from the fall in the export rate from 17.5 per cent of GNP in 1913 to 6 per cent in 1935–8 (Table 4.3). However, this trend has turned around very markedly. In 1960, the export rate reached the 1913 level, and then rose continuously up to 26.7 per cent in 1980 (Abelshauser 1983). Concurrently with their increasing internationalization, the German commodity markets have also been very substantially redirected away from the traditional markets in East and South-East Europe, and towards Western Europe.[15]

Table 4.3: Dependency on exports, Deutsches Reich and FRG: export rate as relation of exports to GNP, in %

1910–13	17.5
1925–29	14.9
1935–38	6.0
1950	9.3
1960	17.2
1970	23.8
1980	26.7

Source: Abelshauser (1983: 148).

A parallel movement can be observed in German capital markets. Before World War I, Germany clearly lagged behind Great Britain in foreign investment both as capital exporter and importer, and then experienced a marked drop due to the disruption of the world economy during the interwar period. The postwar West German economy, however, has grown to become the world's third greatest capital exporter and importer during the 1970s, behind the United States and the UK (Krägenau 1973: 32; also Spohn 1977; Deubner 1982). Here as well, there has been a shift in orientation from Eastern and South-eastern Europe towards Western Europe and the US, especially for the largest firms.

The basis for these capital movements was the increasing production of German firms in foreign countries and the important role of foreign investment within the FRG. In 1980, for example, 23.6 per cent of the annual total sales were handled by foreign enterprises within the FRG (Olle 1985: 11). Here as well, the multinational companies which have 30 per cent of the sales and 13 per cent of employees in the manufacturing sector (Wohlmuth 1985: 23, 26) have played a decisive role. They, of course, are the core of the increasing internationalization of the West German capitalist class.

Their greater industrial homogeneity and the internationalization of the West German capitalist class represent the most decisive contrast to the past pattern of industrialization. This is in part also true for the role of the big banks and the economic role of the state. Like the cartels, the banks were decentralized after the war but soon regained their previous degree of centralization and concentration. In contrast to their former leading role in the relationship *vis-à-vis* the industrial sector, their role today is more that of a mediator with respect to the financial needs of West German industry (Ronge 1979; Pohl 1982; Gerhards 1982). At the same time, the state has increasingly turned into a mediator between the various industrial interests, in contrast to its previous initiating and controlling functions. This is true even though the state's share in the GNP has risen from 17.7 per cent in 1913 to 30.6 per cent in 1929, 42.9 per cent in 1938 and again from 40.5 per cent in 1950 to 48.4 per cent in 1968 (Petzina 1977). In short, the economic features which were characteristic of the German industrial pattern between 1871 and 1945 have been transformed into an internationalized advanced capitalist economy. In theoretical terms, therefore, it is misleading to conceptualize this development as a transition from 'organized capitalism' to 'state monopoly capitalism' or 'state regulated capitalism'; instead, it represents a dissolution of the peculiar German type of 'organized capitalism' by a western-type liberal-corporatist capitalism (cf. Dahrendorf 1965; Habermas 1973). Let us now examine the consequences of these *economic* transformations for the social aspects of capitalist class formation.

THE SOCIAL RESTRUCTURING OF THE CAPITALIST CLASS IN WEST GERMANY

We have argued that the capitalist class was characterized by a marked social continuity from Nazi Germany to the early years of the FRG. This is true especially of the economic elites in big industry and economic management and administration. The one significant exception was the expropriation and extermination of the Jewish section of the bourgeoisie to the benefit, very largely, of non-Jewish capital. To a lesser degree, lower strata of the capitalist class were decimated in the chaos of the last years of the war and the immediate postwar period. As West German society began to evolve economically and socially, however, the structure of the capitalist class began, gradually but distinctly, to change. This social transformation was determined by the economic changes just sketched, but, on the other hand, it was also carried through by the capitalist class itself.

Concerning the transformation of the overall social structure of which the capitalist class is an integral part, we must keep in mind the fundamental changes in the German class structure during the twentieth century. It is useful in this regard to compare Theodor Geiger's (1932) analysis of the social structure of Weimar Germany with Ralf Dahrendorf's (1965) analysis of West Germany.

Table 4.4:   Social structure of Weimar Germany (1925) and the Federal Republic (1961)

Social structure in Weimer Germany, 1925[a]	%	Social structure of the FRG, 1961[b]	%
Capitalists	1	Elite	1
Old middle class	18	Civil servants (*Beamte*)	12
New Middle Class	18	Middle Strata	20
'Proletariods'	12	Lower Middle Strata	12
Proletariat	51	Labour aristocracy	5
		Workers	45
		Lower strata	5

Sources:
a. Geiger (1932: 36);
b. Dahrendorf (1965: 37).

Both Geiger and Dahrendorf wanted to present not only a picture of the objective social structure in their respective times, but also of the attitudes associated with each class. It is obvious, however, that they apply quite different categorizations and it therefore seems impossible to compare their findings directly. For Geiger, Weimar society should be characterized as a class society because the main strata of the social structure comprise relatively organized and self-conscious groups. The capitalists are an industrial and agrarian economic elite with dominant capitalist-patriarchal attitudes and they are clearly juxtaposed to the wage workers with trade unionist and socialist orientations; between these two groups stand the different strata of the middle classes: the old, the new, and the downwardly mobile 'proletaroids'.

In contrast, we find no class conception in Dahrendorf's portrayal of West German society. Only one group – the higher civil servants (*Beamte*) – are still characterized as a 'class', because of their clear-cut social identity. A middle and working class can still be identified, but, according to Dahrendorf, these correspond more to income levels and only vaguely to class positions. Dahrendorf, then, no longer speaks of classes, but of elite, middle and lower strata combined with some traditional social categories. Geiger, to whom Dahrendorf refers methodologically, had this transformation in mind when he asserted, shortly after World War II, that German class society was being submerged in a melting-pot (Geiger 1949).

This is not the place for a full discussion of these two analyses of German social structure. They do indicate, however, the discontinuities in West German class formation which also affect the social formation of the bourgeoisie. In the Weimar Republic, the different classes had been closed against each other socially and culturally, and politically they confronted each other directly via opposed political organizations and orientations. Now this pattern of class formation, intertwined with traditionally closed estates (Kocka 1979) is no longer present today. Nazism had prepared the ground for this when it destroyed the autonomous working-class and bourgeois parties and created supra-class organizations. During and after World War II, the traditional socio-cultural milieux (Lepsius 1973) were broken up by the streams of refugees from the eastern territories and East Germany. Social, regional and religious differences and boundaries became less distinct.

In the course of the rapid changes in capitalist industrialization, social mobility accelerated within the new working-class and professional strata – groups which correspond more to income levels and only vaguely to economic class positions. Given these shifts, the traditional pattern in social, cultural and political class formation could not be resuscitated. This does not imply that class society as such has been dissolved. Quite the contrary: the further development of industrial capitalism in West Germany brought with it a generalization of the capital–wage labour relation. However, the peculiar class formation pattern, shaped substantially by the older estate structure, has now been superseded by a more mobile and permeable class society (Beck 1986).

The bourgeoisie has not remained unaffected by these changes, of course. Geiger's and Dahrendorf's analyses in themselves do not show how the capitalist class has been transformed, although both have considered this question. One way in which this transformation can be documented, however, is to look at the category of independent producers – capitalists in the widest sense of the world – in German official statistics.

Table 4.5:   Employed persons and their social position in Imperial Germany and the FRG (in per cent)

	1907	1925	1939	1950	1961	1970
Independent producers	20.6	15.6	13.9	14.6	12.2	10.7
Helping family members	15.2	16.9	16.3	13.8	10.0	6.9
Total	35.8	32.5	30.2	28.4	22.4	17.6
Employees, civil servants	7.9	17.1	22.3	21.2	29.0	35.1
Workers	49.9	45.8	46.9	50.5	48.5	47.4
Servants	6.1	4.3	3.9			
Total dependants	64.2	67.5	69.8	71.6	77.5	82.5

Source: Petzina (1977: 180).

In order to show the development of the social composition of the capitalist class, we make the following assumptions. First, the number of independent producers as defined by German statistics and as an indicator for capitalists in the widest sense has clearly decreased in the process of the development of the FRG, from 3.26 million (14.6 per cent) in 1950 to 2.57 million (10.7 per cent) in 1970.

When we now focus on the industrial sectors and compare the distribution of independent producers between the different economic sectors, we find a decrease of the industrial capitalist producers, declining from 0.94 million in 1950 to 0.64 million in 1970 (Petzina 1977: 181).

Table 4.6: *Independent producers and employed persons in total in relation to their social position in Imperial Germany and the FRG (in million)*

	1907	1925	1939	1950	1961	1970
Agriculture	9.88	9.76	8.99	5.11	3.59	1.99
Independent producers	2.5	2.19	1.97	1.25	1.14	0.66
Industry	11.26	13.48	14.6	9.34	12.8	12.96
Independent producers	1.98	1.45	1.38	0.94	0.72	0.64
Third sector	6.31	8.76	11.03	7.62	10.14	11.55
Independent producers	1.57	1.38	1.47	1.07	1.38	1.27
All sectors	27.45	32.0	34.62	22.07	26.53	26.49
All independent producers	6.05	5.02	4.82	3.26	3.24	2.57

Source: Petzina (1977: 181).

Only a fraction of these independent producers, however, are, properly speaking, capitalist producers, as owners of means of production and users of wage labour. On the other hand, the number of managers as the key functionaries of capital has increased. It has been estimated that in 1970, there existed 636,000 capitalists of whom 585,000 were formally functioning owners, 27,000 managers and 24,000 not formally functioning owners (Wienold 1968: 370; Projekt Klassen-analyse 1974: 234ff.).

The change in the social composition of the capitalist class has also brought about a change in its pattern of social mobility, although with important differences with respect to economic elites and non-elites. As far as the economic elite within the capitalist class is concerned, and for the Federal Republic's first two decades, we find that the relatively high level of social closure within that group which is so characteristic of the pre-war period did indeed continue. This continuity, then, which marks the German pattern of conservative modernization, is present despite the fact that parts of the economic elite tainted by Nazism had been replaced. The explanation for that continuity must be sought in the fact that the second rank of this economic elite showed the very same traditional attitudes and forms of behaviour. This replacement in personnel did, however, represent a generational change and as such rejuvenated the economic elites. The new cohort very largely occupied its position until the end of the 1960s, and a new generational turnover in this economic elite then began to occur in the 1970s (Berghahn 1985: 45f.). These two transitions – the first immediately after the war, and the second at the end of the 1960s – can best be seen in the speed of turnover in personnel: its relative rapidity in the early postwar period; its subsequent slowing down, all the way through to the end of the 1960s, and the increase in that speed at the beginning of the 1970s (Zapf 1965: 56; Berghahn 1985: 40).

In contrast to the relative social closure of its economic elite, the capitalist class as a whole did open itself up gradually, due to its greater internal social mobility. This is the case especially for the managerial strata that developed after 1880, but less so for capitalist owners. Thus, while the rate of self-recruitment within the capitalist class had been very high from Imperial Germany to World War II, the rate of self-recruitment decreased distinctly, albeit gradually, in the postwar period. Once again, this rate is greater for managers and leading employees than for the capitalist owners themselves. It is important to see that until the first years of the FRG, the managers and leading employees tended to be recruited from the ranks of higher state officials. Subsequently, the field of recruitment shifted to middle-level officials and the middle classes (Kaelble 1983a: 102–10).

This tendency reflects a loosening of the traditional ties of the capitalist class with the nobility and a strengthening of capital's ties with the middle and even lower classes. The traditional, upwardly-directed pattern of class formation in the capitalist class has been eroded by social mobility from below. The main reason that managerial positions have been opened to the middle strata lies in the increased scale of production and concentration of large enterprises and corporations.

The process of diminishing closure, the gradual opening of the capitalist class, is also suggested by other research findings. First, the rate of academically-trained personnel, already high in Imperial times, has increased even further (Kruk 1972: Appendix table 22; Kaelble 1983a: 105). At the same time, however, while traditionally lawyers predominated in the managerial field, their share has been reduced considerably by the greater share of engineers, natural scientists and economists (Zapf 1965: 178). Secondly, while the regional origin of the capitalist class is still primarily that of the Rhine and Ruhr region (ibid.: 172), we should keep in mind two other shifts: many employers moved from the eastern territories to West Germany, and as the FRG developed, the southern regions of Germany, notably Bavaria and Baden-Württemberg, have become very important bases of recruitment for the capitalist class – an inversion of the ordinary North–South gap. Third, regarding the denominational recruitment pattern, we find some catching up of Catholic employers and managers even though the traditional preponderance of Protestants continues (Zapf 1965: 174).

THE POLITICAL RESTRUCTURING OF THE CAPITALIST CLASS

Even though the continuity of the German capitalist class in terms of its economic and social dimensions prevailed into the early years of the Federal Republic, the massive economic and social changes which were connected with its beginnings influenced the transformation of the FRG. The same is true with respect to the slow political and cultural restructuring of the capitalist class within the radically new political situation in the postwar period. Along with massive economic and social changes, the new political situation had a marked impact on the political-cultural restructuring of the capitalist class. This involved, first of all, the Allies' dissolution of the Nazi elite and the introduction of a western-style liberal-democratic system, as well as the integration by force of West German industry into the western world market (Berghahn 1985: 30f.). It further involved national political changes such as the reorganization of the party system, the re-establishment of an autonomous working-class movement – both influenced by the returning refugees – and finally, the constitution of the FRG as a parliamentary democracy. Developments inside and outside the new country created an entirely different framework for political institutions, and the capitalist class had to reorient itself to these new conditions.

Such a reorientation, however, did not come about without contradictions and tensions. In the beginning, the traditional core of the capitalist class located in the Rhine/Ruhr region attempted to shape the constitution and development of West German society in accordance with their traditional political values (Edinger 1960; Berghahn 1985). These attempts were blocked by the occupation policies of the Western Allies: demilitarization, emphasis on a liberal democratic state and integration into the Western Alliance. The new internal power constellations made a return to the old structures and attitudes impossible as well. The reconstruction of trade unions and working-class parties after the collapse of Nazism; the broadly diffused democratic, anti-capitalist and socialist beliefs and hopes even within Christian Democracy as a common ground for various '*bürgerliche*' strata; and the controlled institutionalization of these forces at first within the occupation administration and then in the new political system of the FRG – all these created opposing forces that, in the long run, could not be ignored by the power centres within the capitalist class. The basic institutional structures of the FRG – especially the *demokratische Rechtsstaat* (democratic state anchored in law) and the *soziale Marktwirtschaft* (social market economy) – represent compromise formulas of a parallelogram of social forces that did not correspond to the traditional political conceptions of the capitalist class.

The traditional political norms of the conservative ruling

class – both the capitalist class and the old nobility combined – were clearly at odds with the political constitution of the new republic. This goes even for the anti-fascist opposition associated with the attempted *coup* of 20 July 1944 which had aimed for a conservative presidential democracy (Rothfels 1969). Nevertheless, these groups had little choice but to accept the political institutions partly imposed by the Western Allies, and partly created by the revitalized democratic parties and working-class organizations. Moreover, within the broader strata of the capitalist class, in the middle classes and the *Bürgertum*, Christian-conservative and liberal-democratic attitudes began to be articulated. These blocked any return to the old authoritarian-conservative pattern of class formation. The Bonn democracy was thus based on a broad consensus even within the capitalist and middle classes, clearly in contrast to its Weimar forerunner. This new consensus also extended to the welfare state where the different political orientations of trade unionism, Social Democracy and political Catholicism met with the social-patriarchal attitudes of the traditional elites (Thränhardt 1986).

This broad consensus notwithstanding, the capitalist reconstruction was nevertheless very controversial even in the early years of the Federal Republic (Berghahn 1985). The industrialists of the Rhine and Ruhr wanted to continue the traditional economic policies of protectionism and cartel-ization, and wanted to make them a condition for Western European integration. In the end, they could not prevail over the liberal-capitalist interests and attitudes of either the Americans or other large segments of West German employers and their articulation in Chancellor Erhard's corporatist liberal economic policy. The basic condition for the defeat of the traditional German capitalists was the unforeseen dynamic of West German economic growth which seemed to prove the correctness of liberal economic policy.

The political integration of the trade unions was controversial as well (Berghahn 1985). In accordance with their principle of *Herr im Hause* (master in their own house) the traditional segments of the capitalist class in heavy industry wanted to prevent any formal institutionalization of working-class and trade union interests. Yet here as well, heavy industry had to succumb to opposing forces: the conception of liberal corporatism put forth by the Americans, the working-class organizations' demands for democratization and socialization of big industries, and, last but not least, the influential social-Catholic conceptions within early postwar Christian Democracy. On this basis, what amounted to some sort of compromise between classes and class fractions, the law of co-determination (*Mitbestimmungsgesetz*), was passed in 1951 – first for heavy industry and later on for all large industrial firms. This legislation, watered down from earlier drafts, nevertheless granted some form of parity for trade union representatives on the boards of these firms (Blumenthal 1956; Thum 1982).

Capital, and particularly the economic elite, opposed the institutionalization of working-class interests not just at the plant level, but at the political-societal level as well. Thus, the industrialists refused to enter into an institutionalized bargaining procedure with the Deutscher Gewerkschaftsbund (DGB), the centralized trade union federation, and they refused direct representation of their interests within the parliamentary system. Instead, members of the economic elite attempted to influence the Adenauer government directly via newly established employers' associations such as the Bundesverband der Deutschen Industrie (BDI), the Bundes-vereinigung deutscher Arbeitgeber (BdA) and the Deutscher Industrie und Handelstag (DIHT) (Braunthal 1965; Simon 1976; Ullmann 1988). Therefore, at least through the early years of the Federal Republic, the relationship between state, capital and labour resembled some form of authoritarian corporatism so characteristic of the history of German industrialization and quite distinct from the western model of liberal corporatism.[16]

In sum, the traditional attitudes of the German capitalist class in relation to democracy, the welfare state and the industrial and political relationship to trade unions, scarcely changed. Nevertheless, as we shall see in the next section, the new economic, social and political setting of the Federal Republic led to a gradual restructuring of the capitalist class, with the least change in its traditional power centre.

As far as their relationship to the Bonn state and its political institutions is concerned, the capitalist class increasingly articulated its interests at the party level via the increasingly conservative Christian Democrats and the liberal-democratic FDP. Below this level of parties, a complex network of institutions, boards and committees penetrated the party and state institutions in order to implement capitalist class interests (Wienold 1986: 368). This political spectre with its authoritarian-democratic, social-conservative and economically liberal currents reflected very adequately the beliefs of the capitalist class and its different factions in the context of the period of dynamic growth of the 1950s and 1960s

When that growth began to slacken, and when the first symptoms of crisis appeared, there emerged some tendencies within the capitalist class that encouraged a Keynesian strategy of crisis management and modernization (Enke 1974; Hoffmann-Lange 1974; Berghahn 1985: chapter 4). That new economic policy was put forward by the SPD which since its adoption of the Godesberg programme in 1959 had ceased to be a dogmatic class party and had transformed itself into a left-wing popular party (Lehnert 1983). This partial political opening of the capitalist class – first towards the 'Grand Coalition' (CDU and SPD), and then towards the 'Social-liberal Coalition' of SPD and FDP – in the transition from the 1960s to the 1970s must be understood in the context of the social opening of the capitalist class; as already noted, it loosened its ties with the old guard of heavy industrialists and gained increasing support from leading employees, managers and the technical intelligentsia, whose members were recruited mainly from middle and lower social strata.

At the level of industrial relations, the social and political opening corresponded to capital's basic acceptance of trade unions as *Sozialpartner* (social partners). The capitalist class now understood the trade unions' integrative function in an economically stable order – all the particular conflicts notwithstanding. At the plant level as well, methods of 'socially responsible management' were introduced; German capital now borrowed from American models and replaced the traditional forms of patriarchal management (Berghahn 1985: 228f.).

This change in attitudes at the economic and political levels led to capital's acceptance and even partial support of 'concerted action' between state, capital and the trade unions, which functioned as some sort of generalized economic bargaining mechanism. *Konzertierte Aktion* was introduced during the Grand Coalition and was particularly effective in the subsequent social-liberal coalition where it was accompanied by a further development of the welfare state (Adam 1972; Berghahn 1985: 301f.). Similarly, the behind-the-scenes support and indeed open engagement for Willy Brandt's *Ostpolitik* on the part of the old heavy industry-based capitalist leadership in the Ruhr must be seen in this context. The political overtures to the Soviet Union and Eastern Europe brought about a large-scale economic expansion into the state socialist countries from which they stood to benefit very substantially.

The establishment of this type of liberal corporatism, however, was accepted by a large segment of the capitalist class only in so far as it involved a necessary process of modernization. It was not accepted in terms of the underlying political implications. As the democratic and welfare reforms of Social Democracy, left liberalism and the trade unions came into being, they were accompanied by the student movement and the growing radicalization of academic youth. In opposition to these developments, neo-conservative forces emerged that were strongly supported by large parts of the capitalist class. In 1972, when Willy Brandt was still Chancellor of the social-liberal coalition, a 'manifesto of employers' was issued that categorically demanded an end to social reforms; otherwise, human civilization would be endangered (Pross 1973). With the oil crisis in 1974, the international and national economic setting changed dramatically. As a consequence, Chancellor Helmut Schmidt's social-liberal coalition was increasingly manoeuvred into a defensive position, and was then superseded by the *Wende* – Chancellor Helmut Kohl's neo-conservative U-turn.[17]

Although this U-turn did not come to fruition immediately, it nevertheless gradually dismantled the central components of social reform that were set up in the preceding period under the SPD's leadership. The new policies had a neo-liberal foot based in the right-wing Free Democrats, and a neo-conservative basis in the CDU. Both these elements corresponded essentially to the interests of the capitalist class in face of stronger world market competition and a marked political radicalization at home. With the *Wende, Konzertierte Aktion* was eventually dissolved, the trade unions were forced to accept a curtailment of the right to strike, and central elements of the welfare state were being attacked (Offe 1986).

Nevertheless, the rise of neo-conservativism and neo-liberalism could not take us back to the traditional political orientation of the capitalist class that was characteristic of the early years of the Federal Republic. The economic, social and political structure of West German society and the pattern of capitalist class formation have evolved too far for that to occur. Instead, the limitations of the *Wende* represent the limitations of capitalist rationality in the face of increasing pressures for democratic rights and social demands that are characteristic of most advanced western industrial societies in the present phase of neo-conservatism.

CONCLUSION

In this survey, we have attempted to sketch the formation of the German capitalist class as an historic, organic and holistic process in order to understand better its present peculiarities. A number of points emerged:

1. In contrast to the formidable discontinuities and ruptures in other social classes, the West German capitalist class was characterized by an astonishing continuity especially in its upper segments until the early postwar period. We strongly suspect a significant intergenerational family continuity in these segments; unfortunately, no studies exist to document this on a case-by-case level.
2. Economically, German capital was characterized by discrepant and uneven development, nationalist, imperialist and monopolistic developmental strategies and a compromise between big agrarian and industrial capital.
3. The transformation and restructuring of German capital took place in the boom period in the early years of the

Federal Republic. The previous developmental pattern was replaced by industrial strategies that produced a more homogeneous and internationally interwoven capitalist class.

4. Socially, despite continuing oligarchic tendencies in the economic elite, the old exclusiveness of the *Junkers* and of industrial capital has been obliterated and a certain opening to other class segments has taken place.

5. Politically, the traditional patriarchalism and the distrust of liberal democracy by the economic elite has been largely abandoned in favour of a political and cultural integration into the parliamentary political system. Nevertheless, in the recent economic and political crises and the popular demands for further democratization, a more traditional authoritarianism has indeed reappeared in the form of neo-conservatism, clearly distinct, however, from the conservatism of the old German capitalist class.

Over the past two decades, the West German capitalist class has been increasingly consolidated. It remains to be seen whether this class will return to its conservative roots in the foundation of the Bismark Empire or whether it has been irrevocably transformed with the foundation of the liberal-democratic West German state.

NOTES

1. For a general survey on the sociology of West German social structure see Bolte and Hradil (1984), Claessens, Klönne and Tschoepe (1978), Dahrendorf (1965), Handl, Mayer and Müller (1977), Kreckel (1983), and Lepsius (1979). On German elite research see Herzog (1985), Wildenmann (1968, 1982), Zapf (1965); particularly on the German business elite see also Pross (1965), Pross and Boettcher (1971), Hartmann (1963), Hartmann, Bock-Rosenthal and Helmer (1973), Kruk (1972), and Stahl (1973).

2. On the social history of German industrialists see Kaelble (1983a), Kocka (1987); on the history of the German *Bürgertum* see Kocka (1987); on West German industrialists Berghahn (1985); on the old middle class Winkler (1983); on the new middle classes Kocka and Prinz (1983); in comparative perspective Kaelble (1983).

3. E.g. Projekt Klassenanalyse (1974) and Institut für marxistische Studien

(1974–75). In contrast to both see Jaeggi (1969, 1973) and Wienold (1986). On the neglected research on the German bourgeoisie see also Rilling (1982).

4. For this class notion see Kocka (1983) and its discussion by Spohn (1985); see also Bodemann and Spohn (1986).

5. Particularly Thompson (1968), its discussion by Donnelly (1976) and Spohn (1985), and its very fruitful application by Katznelson and Zolberg (1986).

6. Although Moore (1969) did not write a separate chapter on Germany it is clear that he refers especially to Carsten (1954), Hamerow (1958) and Rosenberg (1958). In this context his interpretation of the German working class has to be considered (Moore 1978); compare Smith (1983) and Spohn (1988).

7. On the German industrialization pattern in the nineteenth century see Gerschenkron (1943), Barkin (1970) and Spohn (1977).

8. On the relationship between big industry and National Socialism see Turner (1972, 1985), Stegmann (1976), Weisbrod (1978), Abraham (1981) and Eley (1986).

9. This constellation has been characterized as a class symbiosis of *Junker* and bourgeoisie: Machtan and Milles (1980); compare Fischer (1979). On the specifically cultural developments see Plessner (1966).

10. See Wehler (1974), Vondung (1976) and Conze (1980) in respect to the *Bürgertum*, and Rosenberg (1972) in regard to the *Junkertum*.

11. On the political system of Imperial Germany see Wehler (1974), Ritter (1985), and Eley (1986).

12. On the relationship between industry and fascist dictatorship during the Third Reich see Schweitzer (1964), Mason (1978), Neumann (1944) and Sohn-Rethel (1973).

13. On the history of the FRG see Bracher (1981), Narr and Thränhardt (1984), Klessmann (1982), Pirker (1977), and Löwenthal and Schwarz (1974).

14. On the economic history of West Germany see Altvater (1979), Hardach (1976), Abelshauser (1983), and Borchhardt (1985).

15. On the internationalization pattern of the German economy in Imperial Germany see Spohn (1977), for the FRG Deubner, Rehfeldt and Schlupp (1981), and Ziegler (1984).

16. On the corporatism debate see Schmitter and Lehmbruch (1979), Panitch (1986), and Offe (1986).

17. On the ideological trends and sources of German neo-conservatism see Fetscher (1983).

REFERENCES

Abelshauser, Werner (1983) *Wirtschaftsgeschichte der Bundesrepublik Deutschland 1945–1980* (Frankfurt/M.: Suhrkamp).

Abraham, David (1981) *The Collapse of Weimar: Political Economy and Crisis* (Princeton NJ: Princeton University Press).

102   *The Capitalist Class: An International Study*

Adam, Hermann (1972) *Konzertierte Aktion in der Bundesrepublik* (Köln: Bund-Verlag).

Alemann, Ulrich v. (1981) *Neokorporatismus?* (Frankfurt/M.: Campus).

Altvater, Elmar, Hoffmann, Jürgen and Semmler, Willi (1979) *Vom Wirtschaftswunder zur Wirtschaftskrise* (Berlin: Olle/Wolter).

Barkin, Kenneth D. (1970) *The Controversy over German Industrialization 1890–1902* (Chicago: Chicago University Press).

Beck, Ulrich (1986) *Risikogesellschaft, Auf dem Weg in eine andere Moderne* (Frankfurt/M.: Suhrkamp).

Berghahn, Volker (1985) *Unternehmer und Politik in der Bundesrepublik* (Frankfurt/M.: Suhrkamp).

Blackbourn, David and Eley, Geoff (1980) *Mythen deutscher Geschichtsschreibung* (Frankfurt/M., Wien, Berlin: Ullstein).

Blackbourn, David and Eley, Geoff (1984) *The Peculiarities of German History* (Oxford: Oxford University Press).

Blumenthal, W.P. (1956) *Codetermination in the German Steel Industry* (Princeton, NJ: Princeton University Press).

Bodemann, Y. Michal and Spohn, Willfried (1986) 'The organicity of classes and the naked proletarian. Towards a new formulation of the class conception', *Insurgent Sociologist*, vol. XIII (3): 10–19.

Bolte, Karl M. and Hradil, Stefan (1984) *Soziale Ungleichheit in der Bundesrepublik Deutschland* (Opladen: Leske und Budrich).

Borchhardt, Knut (1985) *Grundriss der deutschen Wirtschaftsgeschichte* (Göttingen: Vandenhoek/Rupprecht).

Bottomore, Tom (1979) *Political Sociology* (London: Hutchinson).

Bottomore, Tom (1985) *Theories of Modern Capitalism* (London: Allen & Unwin).

Bracher, Karl D. (1981) *Geschichte der Bundesrepublik Deutschland*, 5 vols (Wiesbaden: Steiner).

Braunthal, Gerard (1965) *The Federation of German Industry in Politics* (Ithaca, NY: Cornell University Press).

Carsten, Francis L. (1954) *The Origins of Prussia* (Oxford: Clarendon Press).

Claessens, Dieter, Klönne, Arno and Tschoepe, Arnim (1978) *Sozialkunde der Bundesrepublik Deutschland* (Reinbek/Hamburg: Rowohlt).

Conze, Werner (1980) 'Konstitutionelle Demokratie – Industrialisierung. Deutsche Führungsschichten um 1900', in *Deutsche Führungsschichten in der Neuzeit*, ed. H.H. Hoffmann and G. Franz, vol. 12 (Boppard a.R.: Boldt), pp. 173–202.

Conze, Werner and Lepsius, Rainer, M. (eds) (1983) *Sozialgeschichte der Bundesrepublik Deutschland* (Stuttgart: Klett-Cotta).

Costas, Ilse (1980) 'Konzentration und Zentralisation in historischer Sicht', in *Monopoltheorie kontrovers. Zur neueren Theorie und Empirie des Monopols*, ed. O. Demele and W. Semmler (Berlin: Olle & Wolter), pp. 39–54.

Dahrendorf, Ralf (1965) *Gesellschaft und Demokratie in Deutschland* (München: Piper).

Deubner, Christian, Rehfeldt, U. and Schlupp, F. (1981) 'Die Internationalisierung der westdeutschen Wirtschaft', in *Deutschland — Frankreich im Systemvergleich*, vol. 2, ed. Robert Bosch Stiftung (Stuttgart: Bleicher), pp. 17-80.

Donnelly, F. K. (1976) 'Ideology and English working-class history, Edward Thompson and his critics', *Social History* (2), 219-38.

Edinger, Lewis (1960) Post-totalitarian leadership in the German Federal Republic', *American Political Science Review*, LIV (1), 58-82.

Eley, Geoff (1986) *From Unification to Nazism* (Boston: Allen & Unwin).

Enke, Edo (1974) *Oberschicht und politisches System der Bundesrepublik Deutschland* (Bern, Frankfurt/M.: Lang).

Fetscher, Iring (1983) *Neokonservative und 'Neue Rechte'* (München: Beck).

Fischer, Fritz (1979) *Bündnis der Eliten. Zur Kontinuität der Machtstrukturen in Deutschland 1871-1945* (Düsseldorf: Droste).

Geiger, Theodor (1932) *Die soziale Schichtung des deutschen Volkes* (Stuttgart: Enke).

Geiger, Theodor (1949) *Die Klassengesellschaft im Schmelztiegel* (Opladen: Kiepenheuer).

Gerhards, M. (1982) *Industriebeziehungen der westdeutschen Banken* (Frankfurt/M.: Sendler).

Gerschenkron, Alexander (1943) *Bread and Democracy in Germany* (Berkeley: University of California Press).

Gerschenkron, Alexander (1963) *Economic Backwardness in Historical Perspective* (Cambridge, Mass.: Harvard University Press).

Giddens, Anthony (1973) *The Class Structure of the Advanced Societies* (London: Hutchinson University Library).

Giddens, Anthony (1974) 'Elites in the British Class Structure', in *Elites and Power in British Society*, ed. Philip Stanworth and Anthony Giddens (Cambridge: Cambridge University Press).

Habermas, Jürgen (1973) *Legitimationsprobleme des Spätkapitalismus* (Frankfurt/M.: Suhrkamp).

Hallgarten, George. W. F. and Radkau, J. (1974) *Deutsche Industrie und Politik von Bismarck bis heute* (Frankfurt/M.: Europäische Verlagsanstalt).

Hamerow, Theodor S. (1958) *Restoration, Revolution, Reaction. Economics and Politics in Germany 1815-1871.* (Princeton, NJ: Princeton University Press).

Handl, J., Mayer, K.-U. and Müller, W. (1977) *Klassenlagen und Sozialstruktur* (Frankfurt/M.: Campus).

Hardach, W. (1976) *Wirtschaftsgeschichte Deutschlands im 20. Jahrhundert* (Göttingen: Vandenhoek & Rupprecht).

Hartman, Heinz (1963) *Der deutsche Unternehmer. Autorität und Organisation* (Frankfurt/M.: Europäische Verlagsanstalt).

Hennig, Friedrich-Wilhelm (1974) *Das industrialisierte Deutschland 1941 bis 1972* (Paderborn: Schöningh).

Herzog, Dieter (1982) *Politische Führungsgruppen* (Darmstadt: Wissenschaftliche Verlagsanstalt).

Hoffman-Lange, Ursula (1976) *Politische Einstellungsmuster in der westdeutschen Führungsschicht* (Mannheim: Dissertation, Universität Mannheim).

Institut für marxistische Studien und Forschungen (ed.) (1974/75) *Klassen – und Sozialstruktur der BRD*, 3 vols (Frankfurt/M.: Verlag Marxistische Blätter).

Jaeggi, Urs (1969) *Macht und Herrschaft in der Bundesrepublik.* (Frankfurt/M.: Fischer).

Jaeggi, Urs (1973) *Kapital und Arbeit in der Bundesrepublik* (Frankfurt/M.: Fischer).

Kaelble, Hartmut (1983a) *Soziale Mobilität und Chancengleichheit im 19. und 20. Jahrhundert* (Göttingen: Vandenhoek & Rupprecht).

Kaelble, Hartmut (1983b) *Industrialisierung und soziale Ungleichheit* (Göttingen: Vandenhoek & Rupprecht).

Katznelson, Ira and Aristide Zolberg (1986) *Working-Class Formation. Nineteenth-Century Patterns in Western Europe and the United States* (Princeton, NJ: Princeton University Press).

Kemp, Tom (1969) *Industrialization in Nineteenth-Century Europe* (London: Longman).

Klessmann, Christoph (1982) *Die doppelte Staatsgründung. Deutsche Geschichte 1945 – 55* (Bonn: Dietz).

Kocka, Jürgen (1973) *Klassengesellschaft im Krieg 1914-1918* (Göttingen: Vandenhoek & Rupprecht).

Kocka, Jürgen (1978) 'Entrepreneurs and managers in German industrialization', in *Cambridge Economic History* (7/I): 492–584.

Kocka, Jürgen (1979) 'Stand-Klasse-Organisation. Strukturen sozialer Ungleichheit in Deutschland vom späten 19. bis frühen 20. Jahrhundert im Aufriss', in *Klassen in der europäischen Sozialgeschichte*, ed. H.-U. Wehler (Göttingen: Vandenhoek & Ruprecht), pp. 137–65.

Kocka, Jürgen (1983) *Lohnarbeit und Klassenbildung* (Bonn: Dietz).

Kocka, Jürgen (ed.) (1986) *Arbeiter und Bürger im 19. Jahrhunndert* (Göttingen: Vandenhoek & Rupprecht).

Kocka, Jürgen (ed.) (1987) *Bürger und Bürgerlichkeit im 19. Jahrhundert* (Göttingen: Vandenhoek & Reprecht).

Kocka, Jürgen and Michael Prinz (1983) 'Vom "neuen Mittelstand" zum angestellten Arbeitnehmer. Kontinuität und Wandel der deutschen Angestellten seit der Weimarer Republik', in *Sozialgeschichte der Bundesrepublik*, ed. W. Conze and R. M. Lepsius (Göttingen: Vandenhoek & Ruprecht), pp. 210–55.

Krägenau, Henry (1976) *Internationale Direktinvestitionen 1950–1973* (Hamburg: Verlag Weltarchiv).

Kreckel, Reinhard (ed.) (1983) *Soziale Ungleichheiten* (Göttingen: Vandenhoek & Ruprecht).

Kruk, Max (1972) *Die grossen Unternehmer* (Frankfurt/M.: Zurich: Deutsch).

Landes, David (1969) *The Unbound Prometheus* (Cambridge: Cambridge University Press).

Lehnert, Detlev (1983) *Sozialdemokratie zwischen Protestbewegung und Regierungspartei 1848–1983* (Frankfurt/M.: Suhrkamp).

Lepsius, Rainer M. (1973) 'Parteiensystem und Sozialstruktur. Zum Problem der Demokratisierung der deutschen Gesellschaft', in *Deutsche*

Parteien vor 1918, ed. G. A. Ritter (Köln: Kiepnheuer & Witsch), pp. 52–80.

Lepsuis, Rainer M. (1979) 'Soziale Ungleichheit und Klassenstrukturen in der Bundesrepublik Deutschland', in *Klassen in der europäischen Sozialgeschichte*, ed. H.-U. Wehler (Göttingen: Vandehoek & Rupprecht), pp. 166–209.

Löwenthal, Richard and H.-P. Schwarz (eds) (1974) *Die zweite Republik. 25 Jahre Bundesrepublik Deutschland* (Stuttgart: Klett & Cotta).

Machtan, Lothar and D. Milles (1980) *Die Klassensymbiose von Junkertum und Bourgeoisie* (Frankfurt/M., Wien, Berlin: Ullstein).

Maier, Charles S. (1971) *Recasting Bourgeois Europe* (Princeton, NJ: Princeton University Press).

Marx, Karl (1969) *Der Achzehnte Brumaire des Louis Bonaparte* (MEW 8. Berlin: Dietz).

Mason, Timothy (1978) *Sozialpolitik im Dritten Reich* (Opladen: Westdeutscher Verlag).

Moore, Barrington (1969) *Social Origins of Dictatorship and Democracy* (Harmondsworth: Penguin Books).

Moore, Barrington (1978) *Injustice. The Social Basis of Obedience and Revolt* (London: Macmillan Press).

Mooser, Josef (1984) *Arbeiterleben in Deutschland 1900-1970* (Frankfurt/M.: Suhrkamp).

Narr, Wolf-Dieter and D. Thränhardt (eds) (1984) *Die Bundesrepublik Deutschland* (Königstein: Athenäum).

Neumann, Franz (1944) *Behemoth* (Toronto: Oxford University Press).

Nipperdey, Thomas (1983) *Deutsche Geschichte 1800-1860. Bürgerwelt und starker Staat* (München: Beck).

Offe, Claus (1972) *Strukturprobleme des kapitalistischen Staates.* (Frankfurt/M.: Suhrkamp).

Offe, Claus and Keane, John (1984) *Contradictions of the Welfare State* (London: Hutchinson).

Offe, Claus (1986) *Disorganized Capitalism. Contemporary Transformations of Work and Politics* (Oxford: Polity Press).

Olle, Werner (1985) 'Der Umfang der Internationalisierung der Konzerne', in *Multinationale Konzerne in der Bundesrepublik Deutschland*, ed. P. H. Mettler (Frankfurt/M.: Haag & Herrchen) pp. 1–18.

Panitch, Leo (1986) *Working Class Politics in Crisis* (Norfolk: Verso).

Petzina, Dietmar (1977) *Die deutsche Wirtschaft in der Zwischenkriegszeit* (Wiesbaden: Steiner).

Pirker, Theo (1977) *Die verordnete Demokratie* (Berlin: Olle & Wolter).

Plessner, Helmuth (1966) *Die verspätete Nation* (Göttingen: Vandenhoek & Rupprecht).

Pohl, Manfred (1982) *Konzentration im deutschen Bankwesen 1848-1980* (Frankfurt/M.: Fritz Knapp Verlag).

Popitz, Hans (1957) *Das Gesellschaftsbild des Arbeiters* (Tübingen: Siebeck & Mohr).

Projekt Klassenanalyse (1974) *Materialien zur Klassenstruktur der BDR* (Berlin: Verlag für das Studium der Arbeiterbewegung).

Pross, Helge (1965) *Manager und Aktionäre* (Frankfurt/M.: Europäische Verlagsanstalt).

Pross, Helge (1973) *Kapitalismus und Demokratie* (Frankfurt/M.: Athenäum).

Pross, Helge and K. W. Boetticher (1971) *Manager des Kapitalismus: Untersuchung über leitende Angestellte im Grossunternehmen* (Frankfurt/M.: Athenäum).

Puhle, Hans-Jürgen (1972) *Von der Agrarkrise zum Präfaschismus* (Wiesbaden: Steiner).

Radkau, Jochen (1983) *Aufstieg und Krise der deutschen Atomindustrie 1945-1975*. (Reinbeck/Hamburg: Rowohlt).

Rilling, Rainer (1982) 'Das vergessene Bürgertum. Über eine Unterlassung der politischen Soziologie', *Das Argument* (131): 34-47.

Ritter, Gerhard A. (1985) *Die deutschen Parteien 1838-1914* (Göttingen: Vandenhoek & Ruprecht).

Ronge, Volker (1979) *Bankpolitik im Spätkapitalismus* (Frankfurt/M.: Suhrkamp).

Rosenberg, Hans (1958) *Bureaucracy, Aristocracy and Autocracy. The Prussian Experience 1660-1815.* (Cambridge, Mass.:   Harvard University Press).

Rosenberg, Hans (1972) *Die Pseudo-demokratisierung der Rittergutsbesitzerklasse* (Frankfurt/M.: Suhrkamp).

Rothfels, Hans (1969) *Die deutsche Opposition gegen Hitler* (München: Deutscher Taschenbuch Verlag).

Schelsky, Helmut (1953) *Wandlungen der deutschen Familie in der Gegenwart* (Stuttgart: Enke).

Schelsky, Helmut (1965) *Auf der Suche nach Wirklichkeit* (Köln, Düsseldorf: Diederichs).

Schmitter, Philippe and Lehmbruch, G. (eds) (1979) *Trends Towards Corporatist Intermediation* (Beverley Hills: Sage).

Schulz, Carola (1984) *Der gezähmte Konflikt* (Opladen: Westdeutscher Verlag).

Schweitzer, Arthur (1964) *Big Business in the Third Reich* (Bloomington: Indiana University Press).

Sheehan, James (1978) *German Liberalism in the Nineteenth Century* (Chicago: University of Chicago Press).

Simon, W. (1976) *Macht und Herrschaft der Unternehmerverbände* (Köln: Pahl-Rugenstein).

Skocpol, Theda (1973) 'A critical review of Barrington Moore's social origins of dictatorship and democracy', *Politics and Society* 4 (1): 1-34.

Smith, Dennis (1983) *Barrington Moore, Violence, Morality and Political Change* (Hong Kong: Macmillan).

Sohn-Rethel, Alfred (1973) *Ökonomie und Klassenstruktur des deutschen Faschismus* (Frankfurt/M.: Suhrkamp).

Spohn, Willfried (1977) *Weltmarktkonkurrenz und Industrialisierung Deutschlands 1870-1914* (Berlin: Olle & Wolter).

Spohn, Willfried (1985) 'Klassentheorie und Sozialgeschichte. Ein kritischer Vergleich der klassengeschichtlichen Interpretationen der Arbeiterbewegung durch E. P. Thompson und J. Kocka', *Probleme des Klassenkampfs* (61): 126–38.

Spohn, Willfried (1988) 'Zum methodologischen Verhältnis von historischer Soziologie, Sozialgeschichte und Geschichtsphilosophie. Am Beispiel einiger jüngerer Interpretationsansätze der Klassenformierung der Arbeiterschaft', *Archiv für Kulturgeschichte* (forthcoming).

Stahl, W. (1973) *Der Elitenkreislauf der Unternehmerschaft* (Frankfurt/M.: Lang).

Stegmann, Dirk (1976) 'Kapitalismus und Faschismus 1929–1934', *Gesellschaft. Beiträge zur Marxschen Theorie* (6): 14–75.

Stent, Angela E. (1982) *From Embargo to Ostpolitik* (Cambridge, Mass.: Harvard University Press).

Stern, Carola and Heinrich A. Winkler (eds) (1979) *Wendepunkte deutscher Geschichte* (Frankfurt/M.: Fischer).

Stedman Jones, Gareth (1974) 'Working-class culture and working-class politics in London 1870 – 1900', *Journal of Social History* (7): 460–508.

Thompson, Edward P. (1968) *The Making of the English Working Class* (Harmondsworth: Penguin Books).

Thränhardt, Dieter (1986) *Geschichte der Bundesrepublik Deutschland* (Frankfurt/M.: Suhrkamp).

Thum, Horst (1982) *Mitbestimmung in der Montanindustrie* (Stuttgart: Deutsche Verlagsanstalt).

Turner, Henry A. (1972) *Faschismus und Kapitalismus in Deutschland.* (Göttingen: Vandehoek & Rupprecht).

Turner, Henry A. (1985) *German Big Business and the Rise of Hitler* (New York: Oxford University Press).

Ullmann, Hans-Peter (1988) *Interessenverbände in Deutschland* (Frankfurt/M.: Suhrkamp).

Vondung, Karl (1976) *Das Wilhelminische Bürgertum* (Göttingen: Vandenhoek & Rupprecht).

Wehler, Hans-Ulrich (1974) *Das Deutsche Kaiserreich* (Göttingen: Vandenhoek & Rupprecht).

Wehler, Hans-Ulrich (1981) '"Deutscher Sonderweg" oder allgemeine Probleme des westlichen Kapitalismus?', *Merkur* (5.5): 478–82.

Weisbrod, Bernd (1978) *Schwerindustrie in der Weimarer Republik: Industrielle Interessenpolitik zwischen Stabilisierung und Krise* (Wuppertal: Hammer).

Wiener, Jonathan M. (1976) 'Review of reviews', *History and Theory* (15.2): 145–75.

Wienold, Hanns (1986) 'Die herrschende Klasse in der Bundesrepublik. Zur Theorie und Empirie der Bourgeoisie', in *Herrschaft, Krise, Überleben*, ed. Hans-Günter Thien and H. Wienold (Münster: Westfälisches Dampfboot), pp. 335–73.

Wildenmann, Rudolf (1968) *Eliten in der Bundesrepublik Deutschland* (Mannheim: Universität Mannheim).

Wildenmann, Rudolf (1982) *Führungsschichten in der Bundesrepublik Deutschland (Tabellenband)* (Mannheim: Universität Mannheim).

Winkler, Heinrich A. (ed.) (1972) *Organisierter Kapitalismus.* (Göttingen:

Vandenhoek & Rupprecht).

Winkler, Heinrich A. (1979) *Liberalismus und Antiliberalismus* (Göttingen: Vandenhoek & Rupprecht).

Winkler, Heinrich A. (1983) 'Stabilisierung und Schrumpfung: Der gewerbliche Mittelstand in der Bundesrepublik Deutschland', in *Sozialgeschichte der Bundesrepublik Deutschland*, ed. W. Conze and R. M. Lepsius (Stuttgart: Klett & Cotta), pp. 187–209.

Wohlmuth, Karl (1983) 'Multinationale Konzerne und Wirtschaftspolitik in der Bundesrepublik Deutschland', in *Multinationale Konzerne in der Bundesrepublik Deutschland*, ed. P. H. Mettler (Frankfurt/M.: Haag & Herchen), pp. 19–50.

Zapf, Wolfgang (1965) *Wandlungen der deutschen Elite* (München: Piper).

Ziegler, Rolf (1984) 'Das Netz der Personen- und Kapitalverflechtungen deutscher und österreichischer Wirtschaftsunternehmen', *Kölner Zeitschrift für Soziologie und Sozialpsychologie* (36): 585–614.

5 Italy

Alberto Martinelli and Antonio M. Chiesi[1]

FOREWORD

The recent history of the Italian capitalist class provides an interesting case of re-acquisition of business power and influence. In the last twenty years the Italian capitalist class has moved from a position of weak political power and low legitimation to a position of strong political influence and widespread legitimation. Analogous shifts have occurred in other countries as well, but what is peculiar to the Italian case is that the change was dramatic and extensive. In order to understand this 'success story' we must recall the timing and sequence of the processes of development and modernization in Italy and the role of the bourgeoisie.

Italy was a 'latecomer' in the process of capitalist development of the western countries (Gerschenkron 1962; Fuà 1980). The formation of a modern industrial society was accomplished after the end of the Second World War in less than two decades, between the early 1950s and the late 1960s. This deep and rapid transformation, the 'Italian miracle' as it was called at the time, took place after a century of much slower and difficult economic growth, mostly confined to the North-west – the Milan/Turin/Genoa triangle. In the long period of preparation, since the take-off at the end of the nineteenth century to the 1950s, the Italian bourgeoisie grew in a market already dominated by the other industrial powers. It relied heavily on an alliance with strong pre-industrial estates and sought the protection of the state. Traditional patterns of family and community life slowed down the modernization process and were only partially adapted to capitalist social relations.

The *Risorgimento*, the political process of Italian nation-building, was only partially a social revolution against pre-modern aristocracies. It created a rather fragmented nation. This made it difficult for a unified market to emerge and for bourgeois hegemony to be established. This situation forced the Italian capitalist class to grant considerable political power to other social classes[2] and to leave ideological and cultural initiatives to intellectual movements very critical of the capitalist economy, such as Catholic doctrine and Marxism.

This interpretation of Italian capitalist development, which can be labelled the 'thesis of the weakness of the Italian bourgeoisie', needs to be qualified and put into historical perspective in order to take into account the timing and sequence of the development process. As argued elsewhere (Martinelli 1980), in fact, the support given by the capitalist class to both reactionary and conservative parties[3] was no historical 'accident'; it was a political choice functional to the process of intense capital accumulation and to the formation of oligopolies in symbiosis with the state. The process of capital concentration that usually accompanies economic development did not take place so much through the growing power of major firms in the market as through the granting of special privileges by the state; and the competition among business groups was, first of all, a competition to obtain favours from the government.

The traditional model of business giving political and financial support to authoritarian governments in exchange for repression of workers' demands and protection for external competition was, however, no longer workable at the moment of transition to a more industrial society. In the booming years of the late 1950s and early 1960s, economic integration in the international market proceeded very rapidly and the diversified growth of the economy fostered the contradictions which usually stem from accelerated growth. Trade unions became stronger[4] and sought full citizenship and basic reforms, while dominant social groups defended the status quo and their privileges. A different and more sophisticated relationship between the capitalist class and the state was needed, one capable of ensuring an effective and smooth transition to a mature industrial economy. This implied both a change in the strategy of organized business and an increase in the political and social costs of the government parties' mediation.

The boom years were really a turning-point: they fostered serious contradictions and the need for a political management of the transition. At the same time, the bourgeoisie was provided with the opportunity to exercise a hegemonic role in the process of modernization. This opportunity was not seized for a complex of reasons, among the most prominent of which were the staunch opposition of the Communist Party and of the related trade unions (CGIL), the lack of a strategic vision by most of the government coalition parties, and the fears and cultural backwardness of large sectors of the business class and their associations (Martinelli 1980).

The open opposition to the centre-left government from certain sectors of the bourgeoisie, and the successful politics of 'watering down' most relevent reforms pursued by other sectors, seemed at the time a success for business; but it was a meagre success which put short-term interests ahead of the long-term and was paid for by increased party control of key management decisions in the state-owned firms and banks. The rather myopic defence of vested interests by separate sectors of business had the net effect of weakening the general position of the bourgeoisie and of helping the transformation of the Italian polity into a political regime dominated by the Christian Democrats. Moreover, the minor reforms of the 1960s helped sharpen social contradictions and foster protest movements at the end of the decade.

The labour struggles of the 'hot autumn' of 1969 and the following years, and the related protest of students and women,, were deeply anti-capitalist and anti-business and brought the Italian capitalist class to its historically lowest level of political influence and cultural legitimation. This was a time when union leaders argued that wages are an 'independent variable of the economic equation' and political leaders and scholars alike discussed the forms of the necessary transition from capitalism to a different economic and political regime. Union power at the plant level was strong, and governments did not implement a new policy without the prior consent of unions. Strikes and protest demonstrations occurred daily.

Why only ten years later was the picture substantially different? In order to provide an answer we shall look, on the one hand, at the changing structure of Italian capitalism and at the social profile, the geographical scope and sphere of influence of the capitalist class; and on the other, we shall examine the major strategies of this class as a political actor *vis-à-vis* union strategies and government policies, and at specific features of business culture. This analysis will be developed in the following sections, but some key features can be anticipated here.

First, the present social and political centrality of this class is a consequence of the consolidation and expansion of the country's industry. In response to general increases in the prices of factors of production, because of the oil crisis and the labour struggles of the early 1970s, international competition and technological innovation have greatly increased. These processes fostered strategies of productive rationalization in large firms[5] and designed a new map of business power in Italy with shifting alliances and new equilibria among major groups. At the same time Italy witnessed a high degree of entrepreneurial vitality, with thousands of new firms being formed every year and an extension of industrialization to the whole country. A widespread view argues that the diffusion of small firms in the 1970s was a result of their ability to avoid legal and union constraints through their position in the 'black economy'. Another view stresses the ability of small firms to find competitive niches. Whatever the reason, it is true that this component of Italian business was successful and competitive abroad in industries like metalwork, textiles, clothing, furniture, etc. The only sector which in the 1970s did not seem able to meet the new challenges was that of state-controlled firms, which were losing productivity and also their intellectual prestige.

Entrepreneurial growth and rationalization strategies contributed to enlarge the social and geographical scope of the capitalist class, providing its leaders and political associations with a mass base. At the same time, the working class was shrinking because of capital-intensive technologies. The increasing internationalization generalized the rules of the game of the market and provided legitimation of business strategies which weakened union power, according to what we may call 'the political use of the market'.

The poor performance of state-controlled firms *vis-à-vis* private ones strengthened popular confidence in the value of private enterprise and in the related values of business productivity, competitiveness, individual responsibility, professional competence and organizational flexibility. It also fostered attempts to 'export' those values to hostile domains such as the state bureaucracy. As far as the strategies of business, labour and government are concerned, we argue that business could take advantage of the changes in the international economy better than unions or government, although it was exposed to the negative effects of economic stagflation in a very delicate phase of its development.

The processes of social mobilization and of collective identity building, which took place in the late 1960s and early 1970s, gave to Italian organized labour a high degree of bargaining and political power. But in a capitalist economy, which is deeply integrated in the world market, union power cannot pass a critical level, above which it blocks the mechanisms of accumulation and investment, i.e. the very premise of its demand for wage increases. When this level is reached, either unions become part of a political coalition that changes the economic and political regime, or they have to reduce their veto power and transform it into some policy of co-determination at the firm level and into greater influence in government policy-making.

In Italy there was not the social consensus – either inside or outside the labour movement – necessary for a revolutionary change. On the other hand, unions were also not willing or prepared to play a role similar to that of German trade unions, which take part in the decision-making process at the firm level (*Mitbestimmung*). What they tried to do was to influence government policies in areas such as welfare, industrial policy, employment, etc. The strategy of political exchange pursued by Italian unions brought consistent gains to labour in the second half of the 1970s and early 1980s, but the government was never transformed into an organic neo-corporatist regime. In the meantime, increasing internationalization generalized the rules of the competitive game at the world level, setting constraints on union strategies, and strengthened Italian business through connections with the capitalist class in other countries. Technological and organizational innovation and rationalization weakened the union base in the large firms through labour-saving investments, productive decentralization, increased flexibility and some deregulation. Profit margins increased and the influence of business values and management critieria expanded to larger sectors of Italian society.

We intend to explain these processes by focusing on the social origins and characteristics of the Italian business élite, its cleavages and coalitions, the political representation of business interests and the increasing importance of business culture in Italian society.

THE ORIGINS AND MAIN SOCIAL FEATURES OF THE ITALIAN BUSINESS ELITE

The fact that Italian capitalism developed late had two important consequences for the formation of its capitalist class. First, Italian industry has been consistently dependent on the cycle of international demand (Graziani 1970). Second, the state has actively intervened to promote economic development, serving as a 'substitution factor' in the mechanism of primitive accumulation (Gerschenkron 1962). These two factors lie at the origin of an important dualism of the economy: on the one hand are companies, many of them small, which are subject to international competition, which adopt flexible strategies and which frequently restructure; on the other are those companies, often large and state-owned, that enjoy a domestic monopoly. The dualism of the economic structure produces cleavages and different strategies in the capitalist class. Some big financial groups, still mainly family-controlled, can escape this dualism. They maintain the advantage of a monopolistic or quasi-monopolistic position in the international market conditions (e.g. Fiat, Pirelli, Olivetti and, to a lesser extent Montedison). The social characteristics of the Italian capitalist class cannot be understood without analysing the historical origins of state intervention in the economy and the creation of state capitalism through the public shareholding formula. Herein originated the large group of managers, whose political interests have sometimes been interpreted as opposed to those of private capitalists and their dynasties.

It is widely agreed that an essential prerequisite of economic development is a period of capital accumulation. The countries of the second wave of industrialization developed more quickly than those in the first wave due to the adoption of what Gerschenkron (1962) calls 'substitution factors'. In Germany, for instance, the role played by banks and their interplay with industry gave rise to a capitalist class strongly oriented towards finance. In Italy the function of international finance has been assumed by state intervention since the end of the century. This intervention contributed not only indirectly to the development of industry, through the adoption of protectionist policies; it also promoted important investment projects, such as the railway network, and implemented the development of heavy industry, financing investments in this sector and guaranteeing a market for its products.

During the fascist period, due to the dramatic consequences of the Great Depression, the main banks and some of the largest industries in the country became state-owned. The rationale of this strategy was to buy in order to promote recovery and afterwards to sell again to private capitalists, in order to maintain the principles of a market economy and private property.

After the Second World War this policy was abandoned, but the Italian economy still witnessed increased direct state intervention. The Christian Democratic party, which became the major government party after the war, aimed at tightly controlling the main power centres of civil society through party-connected managers. Thus, the state shareholding formula was no longer a provisional structure devoted to the temporary rescue of important private companies; it became a policy tool for the direct control of the economy. This control was not only a way to obtain resources for the party, but was part of a more general strategy of consensus formation through economic development and social reform. This political strategy was actually based on the formation of a managerial status group, functionally connected with the politicians, which was called the 'state bourgeoisie'.

In the history of the Italian business elite we can identify a number of entrepreneurial types, whose characteristics vary according to the phase of economic development and the nature of the political regimes in which they emerged. In economic terms, the major divide is the period of rapid economic growth in the 1950s and 1960s. In political terms the major divide is the formation of the democratic regime after the Second World War. If we make use of available empirical data, based on entrepreneurial biographies (Chiesi 1977), we can distinguish four entrepreneurial types.

During the second half of the nineteenth century, the main capitalist type was the 'traditional entrepreneur', whose cultural and economic roots lie in the pre-capitalist economy. The textile industry, and afterwards also the manufacture of metal goods and the food industries, that were developing since the formation of the unified kingdom, are located mainly in the countryside at the foot of the Alps. These industrial activities, which sometimes involve large plants, originate in crafts that were formerly dependent on nearby cottage industry. Therefore, most of these capitalists represent the second generation of wealthy artisans, middle landowners and provincial merchants, and in some cases sons of professionals. The landed gentry does not seem to have contributed to the ranks of these entrepreneurs and did not take part in industrial initiatives. The contribution of the proletariat to the formation of entrepreneurship was also very marginal. The exceptions involve a number of establishments whose founders of low and middle social origin were usually self-taught.

The traditional entrepreneur's training took place mainly in the workplace alongside his own father, through a period of apprenticeship and management training. Apprenticeship was usually completed abroad in establishments of the same sector, where the new technologies were learned, and also in German, Swiss or English banks. Property was family-controlled, following a model that survives to this day among the small and middle entrepreneurs of eastern and central Italy. Decisions related to the firm were considered family decisions, taken by its leader in its name. The family was usually large, following the peasant tradition; and high fertility rates had important consequences for the social closure of the class. In this way the family was easily able to ensure its reproduction, but in the meanwhile it increased capital fragmentation. The firms were divided among heirs using pre-capitalistic criteria, according to which larger sums of capital are given to the elder son, who has been designated as successor since childhood, and has been socialized to the entrepreneurial role better than his brothers.

Limited political participation at the central government level is evidence of the backwardness of this component of Italian capitalism and signifies the lack of a long-term industrial strategy, although the traditional entrepreneur did not lack a number of political spokesmen, who defended his interests and sought to secure state protectionism. The traditional entrepreneur was politically active only at the local level, where his firm exerted considerable economic influence. On the contrary he did not enjoy important relations with the central political power, and hence he remained outside the state apparatus, which was partly occupied by the subsidized entrepreneurs. Only the latter pursued a rational plan of long-run economic development through the industrialization process.

The political role of the traditional entrepreneur was therefore passive, while in his ideology the defence of the free market is often at odds with protectionist demands. Unlike the other types, the traditional entrepreneur was not the bearer of the emerging values of the spirit of capitalism, but was rather inclined to uphold the rural values of deference and tradition which allowed him to exploit the structural flexibility of the labour market and the ebb and flow of rural manpower, which followed the international economic cycle. Rural ties, which still conditioned the proletariat, were considered functional to the social order and an antidote against social distress.[6]

The second type in our typology is that of the subsidized entrepreneur. They did not form a large group[7] but they played a decisive role in the origin and development of heavy industry. They were also responsible for some specific features of Italian capitalism. This type of entrepreneur developed because of direct state intervention that supplied credit, gave endowment funds, sustained internal demand and offered protection from foreign competition. The subsidized entrepreneurs enjoyed total freedom to invest profits in other sectors or in financial speculations and in any kind of personal initiative, in order to constitute their own family capital.[8] In other words there was an osmosis of capital from the huge investments backed by the state to private initiatives which took advantage of current business opportunities. These capital movements between the two spheres were fostered by merchant banks, which are typical of another kind of capitalist, the financier.

The origin of the subsidized entrepreneur was at first closely linked to the nation-building process and later the early phase of Italian imperialism and the nationalistic movements of the early twentieth century. The economic performance of heavy industry was in fact dependent on the evolution of the international crisis and on the colonial aims of the ruling class. The subsidized entrepreneur was part of this, and his business flourished if relations with government and the ministries were tight and organic. The importance of these relationships can be appreciated if one bears in mind the frequent participation of subsidized entrepreneurs in the *Risorgimento*. A full third of such entrepreneurs held parliamentary positions. Moreover, biographical information reveals frequent alliances and common purposes with outstanding government members. These personal links can substantially account for the origin and development of this entrepreneurial type.

The third important figure at the origin of Italian capitalism was the financier. His main social characteristic was the frequent control of share capital without family relations. This control was less personalistic, more mediated and diffused through financial devices. Usually the entrepreneur's control was exerted through minority blocks of shares in one or more holdings that in turn controlled banks, industries, estates, trading companies, etc. Sometimes these companies operated abroad in Italian spheres of influence, such as the Balkans and, later, Latin America. In other words, we are speaking of what, in his historical works on mid-nineteenth-century France, Marx called the 'financial aristocracy'. Although in the Italian case the economic power of this social group was more limited than in France, there were significant similarities: in both cases this group had pre-capitalistic origins, it enjoyed international links, and it was heavily engaged in underwriting the public debt. At the turn of the century, the Italian financial elite transformed its capital by forming the first joint-stock companies with the intervention of a few private banks. The combining of financial and industrial capital took place only during the fascist period, mainly in the energy, chemical and concrete sectors. Especially during the fascist period the financier was an insider in the political sphere. He occupied not only parliamentary, but also government posts, and he owned the newspapers. He attributed to political activity an importance similar to that of the subsidized entrepreneur.

The fourth historical type of entrepreneur, born during the fascist period, is the manager of state-owned firms. This kind of entrepreneur developed under the protection of the Christian Democratic Party during the 1950s, and also of the Socialist Party since the first centre-left coalition governments. The geographical origin of this entrepreneurial type was different from the previous ones because it was not concentrated in the traditional regions of industrial develop-ment but widespread all over the country.[9] For the most part, there are two career patterns of the public manager. The first one is technical and bureaucratic, involving people from higher positions in the civil service, endowed with an outstanding technical background, sometimes acquired in a previous academic career. The second pattern, which is political, involves those who had been previously engaged in the professions – mainly lawyers and journalists – and backed the regime. Among the technical careers some significant cases of mobility from private firms are present, demonstrating consistent managerial mobility between the two sectors.

Since the 1960s, the capitalist class has changed tremen-dously, and today the four historical types are hardly distinguishable. In order to provide an outline of the present situation we shall now present some results of a number of surveys on Italian business leaders.

SOCIAL CHARACTERISTICS OF THE BUSINESS ELITE

Empirical research on social mobility contributes to the study of business élites. Table 5.1 summarizes the result of a number of Italian surveys that can be compared[10] with data on the USA and Japan. Father's occupation is interpreted as a proxy of social origin. A first general result comes out clearly in all the periods and in all the analysed countries: self-made men are very few. Italy does not seem to confirm Schumpeter's hypothesis that entrepreneurs can spring from any social background with equal probability. Rather the results seem to confirm the existence of a hereditary business elite, i.e. business dynasties with abundant economic and other privileges. This happens despite the gradual decline of family control in big corporations and the consequent development of managerial capitalism.

Table 5.1 also shows a specificity of the postwar Italian case, compared with the two other countries: lower mobility from the ranks of blue-collar workers than in the USA, and a higher

Table 5.1: Father's occupation as social origin indicator of entrepreneurs (percentage values)

Father's occupation	Italy		USA	Japan
	1860–1940	1977	1952	1960
Big entrepreneur		25.3	23	11.5
Small entrepreneur	59.8	5.3	18	21.6
Artisan	6.3	2.3		
Manager	0.0	14.0	8	10.5
Profession	8.9	14.6	14	9.7
Teacher	0.0	1.7		
Clerk	3.6	16.9	8	7.5
Salesman	13.4	6.6		2.5
Goverment official	1.8	6.6	2	11.5
Farmer	0.0	1.7	9	6.7
Landowner	5.4	1.7		17.3
Skilled worker	0.0	.7		
Unskilled worker	.9	2.0	15	1.3
Other	0.0	.7	3	.9

Source: Italy 1860–1940 (Chiesi 1977); Italy 1977 (Martinelli et al. 1981a); USA (Warner and Abegglen 1955); Japan (Mannari 1974).

one from the ranks of clerks and middle management;[11] moreover, both in the USA and Japan small business and landowners play a more important role in the formation of the business élite.

Turning our attention to small business, a number of studies show a high degree of upward mobility as typical of the formation of local systems of firms, especially in the central and southern regions[12], but also in the northern ones.[13] On the other hand, the small chance that the son of a small entrepreneur will become a big business leader is important evidence of the sharp break between the worlds of small and big business in Italy.

Another issue that has been thoroughly studied in Italy is the consequences of the concentrated geographical origin of entrepreneurs, which is related to the promotion of development in the southern regions. The concentration of development in the north-western regions since the first take-off has been associated with the mainly northern origin of the business class, or, more precisely, a Lombard and to a lesser extent a Piedmontese origin. During the fascist period, and especially in the 1950s, greater direct state intervention in the economy and the increasing role played by public managers resulted in increasing recruitment of managers from the central and southern regions (Dalla Chiesa 1979).

Because of the impermeability of the Italian business élite, the entrepreneur's education does not work as a mobility channel, but rather as a certification mechanism and a means of role socialization. As in France (Bourdieu and de Saint Martin 1978) and other countries, the length of education and especially the elitist content of education is correlated with membership in entrepreneurial dynasties and higher social origin. In Italy, the entrepreneurs coming from the petty bourgeoisie manifest a higher proportion of lower quality educational backgrounds than their colleagues of higher social origin (Martinelli et al. 1981a). Nevertheless, the lower level of internal stratification of the Italian academic system does not give rise to situations like that in France, where the mechanism of élite socialization in the Grandes Ecoles and the *ésprit de corps* among schoolmates, play for the furture managers the role that parenthood, relatives and marriage alliances play for the heirs of entrepreneurial dynasties.[14]

Yet we can state that in Italy a small number of universities have been, and still are, centres for students who are interested in getting certified for managerial roles. Since the end of the last century Milan and Turin polytechnics have traditionally trained entrepreneurs and managers with technical backgrounds. Since the end of the Second World War the Catholic University of Milan has contributed to the education of a large number of public managers and has helped forge their ideology. Bocconi University provides mainly economic and financial training and, perhaps more than the previously mentioned universities, serves as an upward mobility channel for students coming from the petty bourgeoisie, fostering their acquaintance with the heirs of big capitalist families and entry into their firms. The ties among Bocconi alumni strengthen relations among firms, banks, other financial institutions and the professions.

As Italian (Martinelli et al. 1981a) and French (Monjardet 1971; Birnbaum 1978) surveys show, career patterns seem to be deeply influenced by social background, measured through father's occupation, and the ownership structure[15]. Proprietors of high social origin enjoy a quicker career in terms of years to reach the top, related to the same company (the heir). Those who are not proprietors and who do not have high social origin follow a longer career, often changing appointments before reaching the top. In this case the career takes the typical features of bureaucratic promotion. The career pattern of those who do not own shares but come from bourgeois families is quite different. They often enter the business after a previous professional or political occupation. Co-option to the boards is in this case a sign of a successful career for a professional or a politician. A high inter-sectoral mobility is also a feature of this career.

Other important characteristics of the Italian business class are related to the influence that the traditional family structure has exerted on the nature of entrepreneurship. Given the importance of family relations for the means of control over big business, and for the successful development of small business areas[16], it is interesting to discuss the possible factors causing the persistence of family capitalism in Italy, in spite of the significant presence of state managers. It is not easy to explain this persistence during the managerial revolution. The best-known works stress that the family is an insufficient basis for accumulation (Hilferding 1910), the consequences of the separation between property ownership and control (Berle and Means 1933), the development of technostructures and the consequent bureaucratization and prevailing meritocratic criteria, which are in principle incompatible with the dynastic elements of entrepreneurial functions (Chandler 1966). Schumpeter, too, concentrating on the unique personal qualities of entrepreneurs, implicitly points out the problematic nature of transferring competence and motivation over entrepreneurial generations.

Nevertheless the history of big capitalist families in Italy is characterized by mechanisms able to counteract effectively the above-mentioned tendencies. Insufficient accumulation on the basis of the family and the dangers of progressive taxation systems and inheritance taxes have been avoided through financial strategies,[17] minority control,[18] holdings and sub-holdings[19] and the constitution of foreign holdings.[20] The increasing organizational complexity of the firm has confronted the entrepreneur with the need to transfer decision-making power to managers. But this need has often involved transferring mostly non-strategic decisions or fostering managerial skills in the most talented family members. On the other hand, the maintenance of veto power, often carried out in tandem with co-option onto the boards, may be considered the last rampart of the entrepreneurial family before the rising managers and the prelude to their total expulsion from control.

All things considered, we can state that the recent decline of a number of entrepreneurial families has not brought a decline of dynastic capitalism, but rather a higher concentration of control, together with the emergence of new family-controlled groups (Chiesi 1986).[21]

CLEAVAGES AND COALITIONS IN THE BUSINESS CLASS

As shown in previous paragraphs, the Italian business class has never been homogeneous and scholars in different periods have tried to identify the most important interest groups and coalitions. In this chapter we shall try to explain the long-term cleavages, as distinguished from the temporary formation of pressure groups and implicit interest coalitions that usually fade away together with the immediate historical conjuncture that has helped shape them. Therefore we do not examine important controversies such as the one which took place after the war between the financial oligopolies and the export-oriented firms with regard to the role of state intervention trading policies, etc. Rather, we concentrate our attention on the two main permanent cleavages between private capitalists and state managers (*Borghesia di stato*) and between small firms and large oligopolies.

We think that the contrast between private and state-owned companies has been over-stressed, especially by scholars who tend to draw unwarranted generalizations from a single case. Expanding state control over the economy reached its highest point of development at the beginning of the 1970s, coincident with the first oil shock and the subsequent economic crisis. It has been interpreted as evidence of the emergence of a new power coalition (Galli and Nannei 1976; Scalfari and Turani 1974) between the unproductive middle classes of the public sector and the politicians of the government parties.[22] This interpretation highlights, perhaps in a Manichaean way, a deep contrast between the private business class, whose power can be tempered by the automatic mechanisms of market competition and the need for efficiency and productivity, and the state bourgeoisie, which absorbs the country's economic resources, replacing market mechanisms with those of political exchange.

Empirical research has not convincingly demonstrated the state manager's specificity, in terms of social characteristics, career patterns (Martinelli et al. 1981a) or structural positions in interlocking directorates (Chiesi 1982). Apart from the wider geographical distribution of state managers' origins, the data indicate considerable mobility of top managers between the private and public spheres. Moreover since the early 1980s the values of efficiency and competitiveness on the free market have been openly declared and pursued by the state managers. In the name of these values some profitable firms have been sold to private capitalists as a painful but necessary move to aid the rest of state holdings; and a few but important cases of joint ventures between private and state-owned capital have been worked out, as recent projects in the communications sector demonstrate.

It is true that a recent study comparing the structure of the network of interlocking directorates of ten industrialized countries (Stokman et al. 1985) demonstrates a partition of the Italian network into distinct private and public centres, while the other countries show a unique centre usually formed by financial institutions. Nevertheless, a network study of the structural characteristics of the Italian financial élite (Chiesi 1982) gives evidence of the presence of a core of 200 directors, sitting on the boards, regardless of whether the companies are public or private.

The second structural cleavage in the Italian capitalist class is between small firms and big oligopolies, which is more clear-cut than in other western economies, because of the small number of middle-size firms. The development of small business took place mainly in the northern regions during the 1950s and 1960s and in the central and south-eastern regions during the 1970s, coincident with a temporary crisis of most oligopolies.

The small firms have always been dependent on the oligopolies because of industrial decentralization and supply relations. Since the 1950s political parties have fostered the development of small business and encouraged a specific ideology based on the traditional values of hard work, efficiency and job creation, often in opposition to the idea of bureaucratic rigidity and monopoly rent attached to oligopolies. Moreover, the substantially convergent views of the Christian Democrats and the Communists on this subject have produced a number of policies in favour of small firms.[23]

The small firm has been able to confront successfully international competition and to create high living standards in once marginal areas of the country thanks to a variety of factors: a higher degree of flexibility compared with large firms, which have to deal with institutionalized union power at the plant level; a remarkable capacity for vertical integration in production systems at the local level (Trigilia 1986); and the advantage of lower welfare contributions and tax charges.[24]

During the 1970s this set of advantages, together with economic difficulties and industrial relations problems in large firms, has reduced the historical imbalance between the two sectors. Some rich local banks that are an outcome of this diffused economic development came to rescue the major private bank, Banco Ambrosiano, when it went bankrupt. Some local firms have been able to reduce the historical gap between small and large firms. During the 1980s this development has been officially recognized, and outstanding figures in the local economy have been nominated to head Confindustria, the confederation of private industrialists.

The recent growth of a shared culture favourable as never before to the capitalist values of market, efficiency and meritocracy has been accompanied by a structural development of Italian capitalism that has progressively reduced the latent contradictions between the two cleavages in the Italian business class. But in spite of this development, Italian capitalism still retains certain structural contradictions which could endanger the recent legitimation and new cohesion of the capitalist class.

The increasingly central role of the stock exchange has fostered the diffusion of shares among the middle classes and the diffusion on popular grounds of the concept of personal risk. Moreover, as a cheap channel of financing for the firms, it has allowed a considerable increase in the assets of large firms. Therefore the stock exchange has been useful for the traditional oligopolies rather than for the emerging firms at the local level.

The consolidation of assets, besides offering fiscal reliefs, which did not meet with any real opposition in Parliament, has helped along a remarkable process of rationalization and financial development of the large capital groups, through mergers and alliances. Foreign capital has been involved as never before in this movement, through joint ventures[25] and direct acquisitions by foreign firms. Nevertheless, the original small number of big firms has not changed and investments have been oriented substantially more to the financial sector than to the industrial one.

Increasing international integration has brought foreign investments to Italy. But this remarkable investment wave has not yielded proportional growth in production or change in the commodity composition of the import–export balance. The productive power of Italian capitalism has not yet been able to modify its relative position in the international division of labour, towards more advanced segments with a higher proportion of research and development, technology and value added.

THE POLITICAL REPRESENTATION OF BUSINESS INTERESTS

In a capitalist economy the bourgeoisie holds power by virtue of the fact that it controls the means of production and has the power to invest. Sheer economic power is a necessary but not a sufficient condition for a ruling class to rule, even in a capitalist society. The degree to which and the manner in which the capitalist class rules is related to three major sets of variables:

1. the degree of effectiveness of the organized action both of single firms and of business associations, i.e. the extent to which the capitalist class is able to act as a homogeneous and independent class and influence relevant government policies;
2. the degree of legitimation of business values, the extent of ideological differences in the capitalist class and the ability of this class to exercise cultural hegemony in society;
3. the structure of the party system and of government institutions and the nature of the policy-making process.

Given the object of this chapter, we shall focus on the first two sets of variables, but we shall take into account also the third in so far as it contributes to clarifying the specific nature of the relationship between business and politics in Italy.

Business action always has important political consequences, in so far as it decides imperatively the allocation of
basic resources,[26] but in order to act politically the capitalist
class requires certain conditions: (a) the awareness that the
power to invest is no longer sufficient to control the political
process and to realize its interests; (b) a certain degree of
independence, for wherever local businessmen depend heavily,
as in some underdeveloped countries, on resources controlled
by foreign capital, they cannot play a significant role and tend
to act as a comprador bourgeoisie; (c) the capitalists are able to
perceive their common interests *vis-à-vis* other classes and
enjoy a minimal degree of internal cohesion, a sense of
solidarity and a legitimate leadership strong enough to impose
discipline and individual sacrifice; (d) the capitalist class is able
to formulate its goals in terms of commonly accepted values[27]
and to make its position appear as a status embodying certain
legitimate rights and entitlements; (e) parties, government
institutions and the whole policy network must be articulated
in such a way as to make the political representation of
business interests legitimate and effective.

Compared with workers, capitalists are less willing to
engage in collective action and less easily mobilized for the
pursuit of collective goals. While workers are individually
weak in the labour market and are quick to realize that their
interests are dependent on the formation of a collective
political will, capital owners prefer to respond individually to
market constraints and opportunities (Offe and Wiesenthal
1979). Besides, competition rather than cooperation is the
dominant form of social relations in the market and
entrepreneurs tend to pursue a number-reducing strategy
rather than the number-increasing strategy of political
mobilization (Martinelli et al. 1981b). Moreover, in the
political domain capitalists meet other social groups on terms
which, unlike those in the marketplace, do not grant them an *a
priori* advantage (Schmitter and Streeck 1981). For all these
reasons, political action for business can be assumed to
represent a 'second-best solution' with regard to economic
action in the pursuit of interests; and, within the realm of
political action, associative behaviour in trade and employers'
associations is often, mostly for large firms, a less preferred

strategy than individual lobbying for favourable government policies.

In the Italian context, the conditions for the political mobilization of the capitalist class and the exercise of political influence in the policy process have long been present. The discretionary power to invest has certainly not been sufficient to control the political process in the framework of parliamentary democracy. On the one hand, union power, which has been more or less strong but generally significant, has made the institutionalization of class conflict, the setting of shared rules of the game in labour disputes, and the guarantee of a stable labour supply, primary concerns for capital owners. On the other hand, the systematic intervention of the state in the economy has impinged on the discretionary power of business and has forced the capitalist class – or significant segements of it – to develop forms of collective action in order to realize their interests.

The Italian capitalist class has complex patterns of recruitment and is diversified in a number of major industrial-financial groups and a multitude of often dynamic and competitive small firms. The cleavages and conflicts that take place within the class and the changing coalitions among major fractions have, however, never prevented business associations from playing a continuous political role with varying strategies and organizational structures in the different phases of Italian economic development. This associative role has, however, always been accompanied by the individual strategies of major firms, each with its own channel of access to the policy arena and with different degrees of effectiveness.

The whole system of business interest representation in Italy is deeply politicized. Political factors account for some of the most important changes that have taken place in the structure of the system, above all the creation of Intersind and Asap, the two associations of state-controlled firms. On several occasions their behaviour as collective actors has been strongly influenced by political parties, which play a prominent role in the Italian society and polity. The election of the presidents of business associations, both public and private, is often influenced by party allegiances. And, as we shall argue, the uneasy relationship between Confindustria, the major business interest association, and the Christian Democratic Party, the largest political party, is a key question in the political creation of the capitalist class in Italy.

A second major feature of the Italian system of business associations is the type and degree of internal differentiation.[28] There are three important criteria of differentiation. These are based on the previously discussed structural cleavages of Italian capitalism:

1. territorial vs. sectoral. Unlike the situation in most countries, territorial associations play a more important role than sectoral ones;[29]
2. type of property, i.e. private vs. state-owned capital;
3. size, specifically within private capital, where small firms have a relatively larger representation in a specific federation, Confapi, in competition with Confindustria.

The lack of functional specialization between trade and employers' associations has produced some acute problems of coordination and management; while differentiation between economic sectors, type of property and size has fostered conflicts of boundary definition, such as the conflict over the representation of the so-called 'advanced tertiary sector' between Confindustria and Confcommercio, and has prevented organized business from working out a unified strategy *vis-à-vis* government and labour.

CULTURAL HEGEMONY AND BUSINESS SUBCULTURES

Let us now consider how capitalist class rule is related to the degree to which bourgeois values are not only legitimated but also hegemonic[30] in the society. The role played by the bourgeoisie in the process of capitalist development creates the conditions for the construction of a successful ideology of growth and modernization. Bourgeois intellectuals elaborate concepts and theories which legitimate capitalist control. A typical example is provided by the concept of technical rationality. It is presented as an expression of innovation, progress and well-being for all, but can also be used to control the labour force (Baglioni 1974).

The degree to which the capitalist class of a given country can be hegemonic may, however, vary widely (Bendix 1956). It depends on the timing and sequence of the industrialization process, which in turn is influenced both by international and domestic factors, such as the country's position in the international division of labour and its historical 'genetic code'. The pattern and degree of dependence on foreign economic interests, foreign political power and foreign ideologies are relevant, in so far as they influence both the degree of change directed by outside forces and the opportunity for a national bourgeoisie to emerge. The impact of the historical past is felt mostly in the ways in which traditional cultural patterns and social relations are maintained, transformed and mixed with modern values and attitudes, and in the ways in which alternative ideologies of economic growth and political modernization, such as Marxism and nationalism, can develop.

As we have argued earlier, in Italy the process of formation of a modern, industrial society was highly accelerated after the Second World War and took place in a rather short period of time. In the previous decades the Italian bourgeoisie grew up in a context not favourable to its consolidation as a hegemonic class. From the wars of independence to the First World War, both liberalism and positivism provided men and ideas for the development of a secular, scientific and cosmopolitan culture, which could be used to legitimize the hegemonic role of the bourgeoisie; but they could institutionalize themselves into parliamentary or research institutions only to a limited extent and, with the exception of a few great figures like Cattaneo, Pareto and Pantaleoni, they remained on the margin of European intellectual debate. Moreover, Croce's critique of positivistic science, although correct in many aspects contributed to weaken attitudes favourable to modern science in general; while Mosca's and Pareto's critique of parliamentary institutions, although in many respects legitimate, helped to undermine confidence in liberal values. Finally, with the rise of fascism, the democratic versions of secular, modern culture were repressed.

The absence of a thorough bourgeois revolution, to use the expression of Gobetti (1924), and the weak and divided nature of modern liberal culture, created the ground for the growth of two other major subcultures. The *Catholic* subculture was intrinsically unopposed to basic capitalist institutions, such as private property, wage labour and markets, but traditionally opposed to the basic principles of modern culture,[31] such as rational science and technology versus the superiority of faith over science, modern individual liberties versus hierarchy and obedience, and 'democracy by the people' versus 'democracy for the people' (Bobbio 1986). The *Marxist* subculture was, on the contrary, an intellectual current born in the industrial bourgeois revolution. It was modern in the sense of providing a scientific analysis of social change, and predicting continuous, rapid and widespread technological change and a thorough transformation of social relations; but it strongly opposed the capitalist mode of production, parliamentary democracy and the bourgeois state. These two subcultures, deeply entrenched in the peasant and working classes, and capable of developing strong organizations around church institutions and the Socialist and Communist Parties respectively, were able to survive the fascist period and present themselves as the ideological bases for the mass movements of the young Italian republic.

In the decades of rapid economic growth and thorough social transformation after the Second World War, both major subcultures underwent profound adaptations to the capitalist economy and parliamentary democracy. The Catholic subculture developed a social doctrine of Christian solidarism and the Marxist subculture an economic ideology of planning and union power. But their very vitality made difficult the growth of other subcultures, secular and cosmopolitan, liberal and social democratic, demanding the international integration of Italy abroad and reform policies at home. In the other advanced industrial countries subcultures of the third type define most of the political culture – in their conservative and progressive versions – and they confine religious creeds and radical ideologies to the margin of political culture. In this situation it is easier for the bourgeoisie to find values and categories to legitimize modern industrial society and its key economic institutions.

In Italy the two dominant subcultures, originally anti-modern or anti-business, have gradually transformed themselves in order to provide both political and intellectual leadership for the management of a complex industrial society, where the capitalist role is no longer challenged. It is unclear in the present Italian situation who is hegemonic with respect to whom; in other words, whether and how far Catholics and Communists have silently put aside some key elements of their cultures, such as traditional authority or class struggle, in order to continue to be accepted in a capitalist, democratic society; or capitalists have transformed themselves into 'good Christians' and 'social reformers' to be able to live in a country with a strong Catholic heritage where most people show leftist beliefs.

The present situation has however witnessed the success of bourgeois values, which sporadic clashes with Catholic doctrine and Marxist ideology do not seem to threaten. Examples of this kind of ideological debate are, on the Catholic side, the recent plea of the cardinal of Milan, urging the moral responsibility of entrepreneurs and, on the Marxist side, the recurrent and vague pleas of the Italian Communist Party for a 'new model of development', mostly concerned with collective services and post-material needs. These critics do not, however, call into question the legitimate role of business. They seem to be defensive responses to an aggressive entrepreneurial culture. Efficiency, freedom of enterprise, individual responsibility, professional competence and material reward are values gaining momentum and acceptance. They have oriented the restructuring of the economy, the recovery of most of the state-controlled firms and of portions of the welfare system and have timidly appeared even in the inefficient state bureaucracy. Business leaders are active speakers on the national scene and they try to influence behaviour and attitudes. Employers' organizations are paying more attention to the question of education and research, and to the system of mass communications.

All these are interesting symptoms, but they are far from establishing a thorough and consolidated cultural hegemony of the bourgeoisie. Major political parties have cultural traditions and present strategies which are only partially compatible. In different ways, Catholic traditionalism and Christian solidarism, on the one hand, and the social reformism of the Communist and Socialist Parties, on the other, try to strike compromises with bourgeois values and at the same time compete with them and with each other for cultural hegemony.

Besides, the cleavages in the Italian business elite are associated with important cultural differences. Alongside a core of basic, shared values, relevant differences exist in the culture of the capitalist class, according to social and geographic origins, age, level and type of education, type of industry and firm, etc. With some simplifications, and limiting ourselves to the entrepreneurial and managerial culture, we can identify a few major types: the 'free market type', the 'secular humanist' and the 'Christian socialist' (Gallino 1987).

The first type is characterized by his concern with managerial efficiency, strategic planning, organizational control and performance, and by a market-centred notion of development.[32] The second type is concerned mainly with the motivation of personnel, the informal life of business organizations, and the priority given to social sciences in technical and managerial disciplines.[33] The third type, more frequently present in the state-controlled sector of the economy and more politically oriented than the other types, is characterized by the attempt to reconcile corporate and national policy goals, such as the development of strategic sectors and the industrialization of the *Mezzogiorno*; and by a close relationship with political power.[34]

It is worth emphasizing that the secular humanist has almost disappeared while the free enterpriser and the Christian Socialist have assumed some of the secular humanist's features. Meanwhile a fourth type, perhaps representing an evolution of the free enterpriser is now emerging as the dominant figure. This is the multinational technocrat, who is very confident in the modern techniques of management – mostly strategic finance, strategic marketing and organizational design; whose reference group is the international business community and whose institutionalized guidelines are the rules of the game of the world market. This is a manifestation of the increasing integration of the Italian business class into the international economy.

CONCLUSION

In the preceding sections we have tried to demonstrate two main hypotheses by analysing the historical origins and main social features of the Italian business elite, the identification of the most important interest groups and coalitions, the problems related to the political representation of business interests and the formation of business subcultures. The first hypothesis is that the recent development of the Italian capitalist class provides an example of increasing political and, to some extent, cultural influence. This is related to a process of modernization of production machinery, a widespread use of new technologies, and a recent phenomenon of entre-preneurship in once peripheral areas of the country. The second hypothesis concerns the consequent reduction of the specificities of the Italian business elite compared with other developed capitalist countries, even though industrial maturity has been attained only recently; the state as entrepreneur plays a more central role than in other countries, and the business elite still finds difficulty in exerting a cultural hegemony.

NOTES

1. This chapter is a cooperative effort. Sections 1, 5 and 6 were written by Alberto Martinelli and sections 2, 3 and 4 by Antonio M. Chiesi.
2. At first especially the landowners and then the petty bourgeoisie.
3. Such as the fascist party in the period between the two world wars and Christian Democracy in the 1950s, in spite of their basic differences.
4. Especially since the end of the fifties the trend towards full employment in core industrial sectors strengthened the position of the workers in the labour market.
5. I.e. capital-intensive investments in automation, decentralization of phases of the productive process, concentration, internationalization, etc.
6. This widespread ideology was well expressed by the most outstanding textile industrialist of the past century, Alessandro Rossi (Baglioni 1974).

7. In our research on the biographies of 190 big business leaders before the Second World War, this kind is only one-third as numerous as the traditional entrepreneurs.

8. The dynastic character that also affects this kind of entrepreneur is evidenced by the fact that more than half the entrepreneurs in our sample belonged to only four families.

9. During the fascist period, 40 per cent of the analysed cases were born in central and southern Italy, while only 22 per cent came from Lombardy. These figures do not change substantially after the war. By contrast Lombardy accounts for 66 per cent of the origins of the traditional entrepreneurs and 42 per cent of the financiers.

10. These surveys were conducted over different periods. If we assume that the rate of mobility can differ according to the stage of economic development (Warner and Abegglen 1955), the comparisons in Table 5.1 are in some ways affected by this bias. Moreover it is not always possible to check if the category labels match in the different surveys. Finally, country universes are sometimes defined by different numbers of top positions for each firm. For all these reasons the comparisons can be only suggestive and must be limited to the more evident differences.

11. The available data on Italy (column 1 and 2 of Table 5.1) seem to show an increasing contribution of non-bourgeois strata to the formation of entrepreneurship and a more important role played by the typical bureaucratic figures of the large corporations, such as the middle management and white-collar workers.

12. See, among others, the contribution by Bonazzi et al. (1972) and Catanzaro (1979).

13. See, for example, Frigeni and Tousijn (1976) and Bratina and Martinelli (1978).

14. The importance of schools like the Ecole Polytechnique and ENA is well known in France.

15. I.e. the degree of separation between property ownership and control according to the literature inspired by the well-known Berle and Means study (1933).

16. Paci (1982) has found an indirect but strong relationship, often affecting several generations, between the origin of small firms in central Italy and the rural family structure. Frigeni and Tousijn (1976) draw attention to the decentralized family firm that represents an innovative response to the need for organizational change. In this context the diversification of production and the organizational integration of small business are particularly appropriate to the traditional large family structure that plays a productive function for the market.

17. By the end of the 1970s it was still possible to resort to cross-participation, like that which allowed the Pesenti family to control a diversified group with low financial resources.

18. In 1984 Fiat tripled its share capital, raising about $1.4 billion from shareholders. The members of the Agnelli family took part with a tiny proportion of a few percentage points of the total capital increase, thanks to the indirect minority control through their family holding and

the increasing proportion of shares without voting rights.

19. The rapid expansion of the financial group controlled by the De Benedetti family is certainly helped by the intensive use of a sequence of controlling holdings.

20. Several important firms, historically related to well-known entrepreneurial families, are formally controlled by foreign holdings. The family members usually hold the top management positions and officially own only a very small number of shares.

21. This is also due to other factors such as the modernization and development of the stock exchange and the loss of motivation and competence among heirs.

22. Stressing the parasitic behaviour of the *borghesia di stato*, this hypothesis forgets the unquestionable contribution of the public sector to industrial development in the 1950s.

23. The legislation defines the characteristics of the artisan sector and allows for tax relief and favourable credit conditions for the artisans. Strong craftsmen's associations, functionally linked to the main political parties, supply counselling and lobbying.

24. Sometimes this is a result of tax evasion and moonlighting.

25. Especially in computers, telematics, chemicals and agri-business sectors.

26. The role of the capitalist class as a political actor has been analysed mostly with regard to trade and employers' associations (Schmitter and Streeck 1981; Windmuller and Gladstone 1984) or to industrial policies and industry–government relations (Zysman 1983; Useem 1984; Grant 1987) or sectors (Wilks 1984) or single companies (Pettigrew 1985; Cohen and Bauer 1985). But on the whole, this field has produced a much smaller body of research than the study of unions, although the gap is now narrowing.

27. Here the question of political representation is limited to the question of cultural hegemony.

28. Unlike many other countries, such as West Germany, Austria and Sweden, in Italy there are no separate associational structures performing trade and employer functions. These functions coexist within the same overall organization and the territorial associations. This does not imply a unified system like that of the *Conseil national du patronat* in France, since function does not constitute the crucial divide. Besides, industrial firms are organized in associations separate from commerical firms, banks, insurance companies, service firms, etc.

29. This can be explained historically as a response to geographically organized trade unions and is related to the importance of labour struggles in the Italian context.

30. Hegemony, as distinguished from sheer dominance, means a capacity to pursue class interests in the form of some notions of the general interest and to work out a *Weltanschauung* for the intellectual appraisal and the political steering of the process of change. Gramsci's concept of hegemony defines a situation where power based on the control of the factors of production is rationalized through an ideology which aims at gaining consensus between dominant and subordinate groups.

31. As the encyclicals of the popes show; not only the conservative ones by Pius IX, but also the progressive ones by Leo XIII.
32. Several top managers of Italian business have been of this type, such as Valletta, who headed Fiat in the interregnum between Giovanni Agnelli the founder and Giovanni Agnelli the grandson.
33. Adriano Olivetti is the best-known representative.
34. Mattei, the founder of Eni group, is the best-known figure of this kind.

REFERENCES

Baglioni, G. (1974) *L'ideologia della borghesia industriale nell'Italia liberale* (Torino: Einaudi).

Bendix, R. (1956) *Work and Authority in Industry* (London: John Wiley).

Berle, A.A. and Means, G.C. (1933) *The Modern Corporation and Private Property* (New York: Macmillan).

Birnbaum, P. (1978) *La classe dirigeante française* (Paris: Presses Universitaires de France).

Bobbio, N. (1986) *Profilo ideologico del '900 italiano* (Torino: Einaudi).

Bonazzi, G., Bagnasco, A. and Casillo, S. (1972): *Industria e potere* (Torino: CERIS, L'impresa edizioni).

Bourdieu, P. and Saint Martin M. De (1978) 'Le patronat', in *Actes de la recherche en sciences sociales*, 20–1.

Bratina, D. and Martinelli, A. (1979) *Gli imprenditori e la crisi* (Bologna; il Mulino).

Catanzaro, R. (1979) (a cura di): *L'imprenditore assistito* (Bologna: il Mulino).

Chandler, A. D. (1966) *Strategy and Structure* (New York: Doubleday).

Chiesi, A. M. (1977) 'Una ricerca sulle biografie imprenditoriali nell'Italia liberale e fascista', in *Quaderni di Sociologia*, 3.

Chiesi, A. M. (1982): 'L'elite finanziaria Italiana', in *Rassegna Italiana di Sociologia*, 3.

Chiesi, A. M. (1986) 'Fattori di persistenza del capitalismo familiare in Italia', in *Stato e Mercato*, 18.

Cohen, E. and Bauer, M. (1985) *Les grandes manoeuvres industrielles* (Paris: Belfond).

Dalla Chiesa, N. (1979) 'L'imprenditore centro-meridionale', in *Sviluppo e Organizzazione* (Milano: Scuola di Direzione Aziendale, Università Bocconi).

Frigeni, R. and Tousijn, W. (1976) *L'industria delle calzature in Italia* (Bologna: il Mulino).

Fuà, G. (1980) *Problemi dello sviluppo tardivo in Europa* (Bologna: il Mulino).

Galli, G. and Nannei, A. (1976) *Il capitalismo assistenziale* (Milano: Sugarco).

Gallino, L. (1987) *Dell'ingovernabilità* (Milano: Comunità).

Gerschenkron, A. (1962) *Economic Backwardness in Historical Perspective* (Cambridge, Mass.: Harvard University Press).

Gobetti, F. (1924) *La rivoluzione liberale* (Bologna: Cappelli).

Grant, W. and Sargent J. (1987) *Business and Politics in Britain* (London: Macmillan).

Graziani, A. (ed.) (1970) *L'economia italiana dal '45 ad oggi* (Bologna: il Mulino).

Hilferding, R. (1910) *Finanzkapital* (Frankfurt: Europäische Verlag).

Mannari, H. (1974) *Japanese Business Leaders* (Tokyo: University of Tokyo Press).

Martinelli, A. (1977) 'Borghesia industriale e potere politico', in A. Martinelli and G. Pasquino (eds) *La politica nell'Italia che cambia* (Milano: Feltrinelli).

Martinelli, A. (1980) 'Organized business and Italian politics', in P. Lange and S. Tarrow (eds) *Italy in Transition* (London: Frank Cass).

Martinelli, A., Chiesi A. M. and Dalla Chiesa, N. (1981a) *I grandi imprenditori italiani. Profilo sociale della classe dirigente economica* (Milano: Feltrinelli).

Martinelli, A., Schmitter, P. and Streeck, W. (1981b) 'L'organizzazione degli interessi imprenditoriali', in *Stato e Mercato*, 3.

Monjardet, D. (1971) 'Career patterns of company presidents and control of the firm in France', in J. J. Boddewin (ed.) *European Industrial Managers: West and East* (White Plains: IASP).

Offe, K. and Wiesenthal, H. (1979) 'Two logics of collective action', in *Political Power and Social Theory*, vol. 1.

Pettigrew, A. (1985) *The Awakening Giant* (Oxford: Basil Blackwell).

Scalfari, E. and Turani, G. (1974) *Razza padrona*, (Milano: Feltrinelli).

Schmitter, P. and Streeck, W. (1981) *The Organization of Business Interests. A Research Design* (Berlin: Wissenschaftszentrum).

Stokman, F. N., Ziegler, R. and Scott, J. (1985) (eds) *Networks of Corporate Power* (Cambridge: Polity Press).

Trigilia, C. (1986) *Piccole imprese e grandi partiti* (Bologna: il Mulino).

Useem, M. (1984) *The Inner Circle: Large Corporations and the Rise of Business Political Activity in the U.S. and the U.K.* (New York: Oxford University Press).

Warner, W. L. and Abegglen, J. C. (1955) *Big Business Leaders in America* (New York: Harper).

Wilks, S. (1984) *Industrial Policy and Motor Industry* (Manchester: Manchester University Press).

Windmuller, J. P. and Gladstone, A. (1984) (eds) *Employers Associations and Industrial Relations* (Oxford: Oxford University Press).

Zysman, J. (1983) *Government, Markets and Growth* (Ithaca, New York: Cornell University Press).

6 Japan[1]

Koji Morioka

INTRODUCTION

In Japan there are few studies which focus on the capitalist class. But if we examine these studies in depth, we can recognize three main streams of thought. First are the statistical analyses of the capitalist and working classes developed by Ryūken Ōhashi (1971) and other social statisticians (Itō 1978; Iwai 1978; see also Doi 1986), who have conducted some excellent surveys of changes in class composition after the Second World War. Their studies show that postwar capitalist development in Japan has been so rapid that class structure has changed radically. Nevertheless, they do not concentrate on the capitalist class, but rather on the working class, and furthermore their concept of the working class is too broad, since they lack a middle-class category.

Second are the studies of present-day capitalism, controlled by a small number of giant monopolistic corporations, which have been done by Hiroshi Okumura (1978; 1984), Yoshikazu Miyazaki (1982; 1985), Isamu Kitahara (1980; 1985) and others. In spite of certain variations, they all emphasize that in such corporations there is no ruling individual capitalist who has overall controlling power. Instead there is 'management control' resulting from the increasing dispersion of stock ownership. These arguments are based on the fact that private ownership by shareholders means private ownership not of real capital or means of production but only shares as 'fictitious capital', and the top management is the representative of corporate capital itself. But these studies do not examine in any detail facts about the capitalist class, especially individual entrepreneurs or small capitalists who are subordinate to the large corporations. They are principally concerned with theoretical problems connected with the controversies about 'management control' and 'finance capital'.

Third are studies of Japanese elites. These have been conducted mainly in the field of non-Marxist sociology (Mannari 1960; 1974; Asō 1967; 1983). They argue that elite formation in Japan is profoundly connected with the Japanese educational system and academic cliques. Simply put, many managers, bureaucrats and politicians have graduated from a few famous national and private universities. But these analyses do not make apparent the socioeconomic reasons why capitalist reproduction in Japan is so closely connected with the educational system. On the contrary, many of them deny the very existence of a capitalist class.

In this chapter I integrate these three main streams of thought and survey some general features of the capitalist class and other classes in Japan.[2] I then consider the major features of the industrial policies enacted by the Japanese state. The state has very effectively aided the growth of the dominant segment of the capitalist class, and this explains why Japanese capitalism has been so much more successful than North American and Western Euopean capitalism since the Second World War.

JAPAN'S CAPITALIST DEVELOPMENT AND CHANGES IN CLASS COMPOSITION AFTER THE SECOND WORLD WAR

The era of capitalist development in Japan started with the Meiji Restoration in 1868. But before the First World War Japan was a capitalist society with semi-feudal parasitic landownership based on landlord–tenant relations in rural areas. The ruling classes comprised the capitalist class and the landowning class. Many of the latter were parasitic on the tenant peasants, and they extorted high rents in kind which usually amounted to more than half the total harvest. The largest landowner was the Emperor, who in 1918 owned about 2.06 million hectares of land.

In the early 1920s, Japanese capitalism had already become established and had then immediately transformed itself into imperialism at the monopolistic stage of capitalism. Economic and political hegemony was in the hands of the *zaibatsu*, an organization of finance capital peculiar to prewar Japan, but from the standpoint of class composition agriculture was still superior to industry. The peasantry, including landowning farmers, were more numerous than the working class even in 1935 when capitalism had reached its most developed prewar stage. The peasantry accounted for almost half (47 per cent), and the working class almost a quarter (23 per cent) of the labour force (Ōhashi 1971: 23). The second World War radically altered this composition as a result of the rapid increase of workers in war industries. The agrarian reform carried out during the American occupation of Japan transferred to peasants all the land they were then cultivating as tenants, abolished the foundations of the semi-feudal landlord system, and prepared the ground for the development of a domestic market; but the peasantry was still more numerous than the working class in 1950.

A dramatic change occurred after 1955 when economic recovery was achieved and 'high economic growth' began. During the period from 1955 to 1970 Japan's gross national product in real terms increased about nine-fold, and from 1970 to 1985 about two-fold. This was the very process of capitalist development, since it divorced the means of production from labour, transformed labour into wage-labour and caused the rapid increase of workers. According to the statistics presented by Ōhashi and his followers, shown in Table 6.1, the peasantry decreased from 37.7 per cent of the labour force population in 1955 to 8.3 per cent in 1985, while the working class increased from 43.6 per cent to 69.4 per cent during the same period. The figure for the working class had doubled in two decades, from 17.4 million in 1955 to 34.2 million in 1975. These workers were mainly absorbed by the construction and heavy chemical industries which were supported by public investment and industrial policy. The result was the concentration of production and population in metropolitan areas. The percentage of workers in the labour force population in metropolitan areas is much higher than in rural areas (see Iwai 1978). According to Hiroshi Iwai and Mitsuo Fujioka (1985), in 1980, in the metropolitan areas of Tōkyō, Kanagawa, Aichi, Kyōto, Ōsaka, Hyōgo, and Fukuoka, 68.9 per cent were working class and 2.8 per cent peasantry. In these areas the conservative party (Liberal Democratic Party), the centrist parties (Kōmei Party and Democratic Socialist Party), and the progressive parties (Socialist Party of Japan and Japanese Communist Party) receive almost equal support. In recent general elections, in Tōkyō and Ōsaka the conservative received fewer votes than the progressives, and the SPJ got fewer votes than the JCP.

Let us now turn to Table 6.1. This table, constructed according to Ōhashi's method, highlights changes in the internal composition of the working class. For example, it shows that the proportion of white-collar workers and unproductive workers have continuously increased, but the proportion of productive workers began to stagnate or decrease around the mid-1970s. However, a few adjustments need to be made to these figures, since Ōhashi and his followers define the working class too broadly. If we adopt the definition used by Rob Steven (1983), who conducted a comprehensive study of classes in Japan, we arrive at the figures in Table 6.2. While Table 6.1 shows that the capitalist class numbered 3.6 million (6.4 per cent) and the working class 37.1 million (64.9 per cent) in 1980, Table 6.2 shows that the capitalist class numbered 7.8 million (14.3 per cent) and the working class 28.4 million (51.2 per cent) in 1979. This indicates some very serious discrepancies in the analysis of the capitalist class in present-day Japan. Before discussing these, let us first consider the economic structure of Japanese capitalism, which conditions the class structure and the political superstructure.

GIANT CORPORATIONS AND MONOPOLISTIC CAPITALIST ASSOCIATIONS

Postwar Japanese economic development has resulted in the

Table 6.1: *Class composition according to the Ōhashi method*

	Number (thousand persons)						Per cent					
	1955	1965	1970	1975	1980	1985	1955	1965	1970	1975	1980	1985
Population 15 years and over	59,282	73,136	78,721	84,608	89,482	94,893	100.0	100.0	100.0	100.0	100.0	100.0
Labour force (inc. totally unemployed)	39,908	48,294	52,826	54,265	57,231	60,271	100.0	100.0	100.0	100.0	100.0	100.0
Employed (inc. not at work)	39,154	47,629	52,109	53,016	55,811	58,218	98.1	98.6	98.6	97.7	97.5	96.6
Capitalist class = (1) + (2) + (3)	807	1,756	2,633	3,159	3,642	3,546	2.0	3.6	5.0	5.8	6.4	5.9
(1) Individual entrepreneurs	73	15	48	100	78	75	0.2	0.03	0.09	0.2	0.1	0.1
(2) Directors and managers	630	1,629	2,475	2,933	3,422	3,362	1.6	3.5	4.7	5.4	6.0	5.6
(3) Government officials	104	112	110	126	142	109	0.3	0.1	0.2	0.2	0.2	0.2
Military, police and guards	431	575	646	735	772	791	1.1	1.2	1.2	1.4	1.3	1.3
Self-employed workers' stratum = (5) + (6)	21,251	18,501	18,384	16,085	15,639	14,077	53.2	38.3	34.8	29.6	27.3	23.4
(5) Self-employed and family workers	20,894	17,907	17,535	14,903	14,273	12,461	52.4	37.1	33.2	27.5	24.9	20.7
(a) Farmers, lumbermen, fishermen	15,046	11,097	9,570	6,880	5,657	4,977	37.7	23.0	18.1	12.7	9.9	8.3
(b) Workers in mining, manufacturing, construction, transport and communication	2,463	3,017	3,873	3,755	3,865	3,433	6.2	6.2	7.3	6.9	6.8	5.7
(c) Sales workers	2,776	2,859	2,892	2,905	3,246	2,657	7.0	5.9	5.5	5.4	5.7	4.4
(d) Service workers	608	936	1,200	1,363	1,505	1,394	1.5	1.9	2.3	2.5	2.6	2.3

(6) Professional and technical workers	357	592	849	1,182	1,366	1,616	0.9	1.2	1.6	2.2	2.4	2.7
(7) Family workers within the groups cited above	11,975	9,222	8,438	6,852	6,352	5,344	30.0	19.1	16.0	12.6	11.1	8.9
Working class [from (8) to (14)]	17,419	27,463	31,163	34,286	37,127	41,855	43.6	56.9	59.0	63.2	64.9	69.4
So-called white collar = (8) + (9)	4,977	8,225	9,668	11,386	12,500	14,767	12.5	17.0	18.3	21.0	21.8	24.5
(8) Professional and technical workers	1,634	2,240	2,825	3,299	4,003	5,071	4.1	4.6	5.4	6.1	7.0	8.4
(9) Clerical and related workers	3,343	5,985	6,843	8,087	8,496	9,697	8.4	12.4	13.0	14.9	14.8	16.1
Productive workers = (10) + (11)	8,956	14,089	15,455	15,423	16,343	17,184	22.4	29.2	29.3	28.4	28.6	28.5
(10) Farmers, lumbermen, and fishermen	798	576	434	405	412	386	2.0	1.2	0.8	0.8	0.7	0.6
(11) Workers in mining, manufacturing, construction, transport and communication	8,158	13,513	15,021	15,018	15,931	16,798	20.4	28.0	28.4	27.7	27.8	27.8
Unproductive workers = (12) + (13)	2,733	4,484	5,323	6,228	6,864	7,851	6.8	9.3	10.0	11.5	12.0	13.0
(12) Sales workers	1,409	2,558	3,161	3,840	4,411	5,069	3.5	5.3	6.0	7.1	7.7	8.4
(13) Service workers	1,324	1,926	2,162	2,388	2,452	2,782	3.3	4.0	4.1	4.4	4.3	4.6
(14) Totally unemployed	754	665	717	1,249	1,420	2,053	1.9	1.4	1.4	2.3	2.5	3.4
Not in labour force	19,373	24,841	25,895	30,343	32,099	34,442	48.5	51.4	49.0	55.9	56.1	57.1
Population 14 years old and under	29,992	25,140	24,823	27,332	27,578	26,093	75.2	52.1	47.0	50.4	48.2	43.3
Total population	89,273	98,275	103,720	111,940	117,060	121,026	223.7	203.5	196.5	206.3	204.5	200.4

Source: Population Censuses. Cited from Tanaka (ed.) 1987.

Table 6.2: Total population over the age of 15, by economically active class, non-active class, and sex, 1979 (1000 persons)

	Males		Females		Total	
	No.	%	No.	%	%No.	%
Total population over 15 years	42,825	–	45,472	–	88,297	–
Economically active (adjusted)	34,017	100	20,720	100	54,736	100
Bourgeoisie	7,389	21.7	423	2.1	7,812	14.3
Petty bourgeoisie	4,827	14.7	4,629	22.5	9,456	17.3
Peasantry	2,552	7.5	2,661	12.9	5,213	9.5
Middle class	2,527	7.4	1,262	6.1	3,789	6.9
Working class	16,834	49.3	11,601	56.4	28,435	51.2
Total	34,129	100	20,576	100	54,705	100
Adjustment	–112		+144		+32	
Not economically active	8,808	100	24,751	100	33,559	100
Bourgeoisie (owners)	1,133	12.9	60	0.2	1,193	3.6
Middle class (students)	3,994	45.3	3,325	13.4	7,319	21.8
Peasantry (on farms)	(940)		(1,938)		(2,878)	
Working class (latent and stagnant)	1,829	20.8	8,524	34.4	10,353	30.9
Keeping house	119	1.4	9,478	38.3	9,597	28.6
Other	1,733	19.7	3,364	13.6	5,097	15.2

Note: The notes to this table have been omitted because they contain cross references to the source book.
Source: Steven (1983).

rapid growth of a small number of large corporations. First, let us see the levels of overall concentration to substantiate the fact that these large corporations exercise enormous controlling power. According to the latest report of the National Tax Administration Agency, in 1984 there were 1.62 million companies (incorporated businesses): 869,000 joint-stock companies, 704,000 limited companies and others. Considering these companies according to size (Table 6.3), 1.31 million small companies with capitalization of less than 10 million yen accounted for 80.6 per cent of the total number of companies, but they accounted for only 10.2 per cent of total capital, and 11.9 per cent of total profits. On the other hand, 2726 large corporations with capitalization of over 1000 million yen made up only 0.2 per cent of the total number of companies, but they accounted for 59.9 per cent of total capital

Table 6.3: Level of general concentration, 1984 (million yen)

Classes by capitalization	Number of corporations	Capitalization	Profit
less than 10 million	1,309,941 (80.6%)	13,532,716 (10.2%)	3,244,984 (11.9%)
10 million and over	295,302 (18.2%)	6,362,926 (18.4%)	5,821,102 (21.4%)
100 million and over	16,292 (1.0%)	3,959,807 (11.5%)	3,932,643 (14.4%)
1000 million and over	2,726 (0.2%)	20,724,487 (59.9%)	14,248,153 (52.3%)
Total	1,624,261 (100%)	34,579,941 (100%)	27,246,882 (100%)

Source: Zeimu tōkei kara mita hōjin kigyō no jittai [The Real Situation of Corporations from the Viewpoint of Taxation Statistics] (1986).

and 52.3 per cent of total profits. In the manufacturing sectors, the relative shares of the large corporations are still higher (see Senoo 1983).

There are 383 giant monopolistic corporations with capitalization of over 10,000 million yen, and their position indicates an enormous level of capital concentration. In 1984, they accounted for 40.4. per cent of total capital and 34.5 per cent of total profits. Each of them is approximately equal in the size of its capital to 13 large corporations with capitalization of over 1000 million yen, excluding the 383 giant monopolistic corporations (Kokuzeichō 1986a).

These giant corporations have affiliated with other giant corporations through borrowing from the large banks, exchanging stocks, cross-appointing directors, and establishing trading and banking connections. Some powerful enterprise groups have thus emerged: Mitsui, Mitsubishi, Sumitomo, Fuyō (Fuji Bank), Sanwa, and Dai-Ichi Kangyō Bank. These big bank-centred enterprise groups are different from prewar capital groups, such as the '*zaibatsu*' (*zai* means finance or business, *batsu* means interest or family group) in which the affiliated corporations were controlled by the head (stockholding) company. Immediately after the Second World War the family connections of *zaibatsu* were eliminated. From the period of reconstruction to the period of high economic growth large corporations did not have enough capital of their own, and the stockmarkets were to small to allow them to procure necessary capital by issuing shares, so the large coporations had to obtain their capital as loans from the large banks which were supported financially by the Bank of Japan.

The result is the big bank-centred enterprise groups with a system of *keiretu-yūshi* (affiliated financing): each group's core bank gives loans to the affiliated corporations in each group. In addition, the financial institutions, such as life insurance companies, and main general trading companies also play an important role as intermediaries in each group. Such intragroup financing and trading has been supplemented by the mutual holding of stocks and interlocking directorates in each group (Miyazaki 1976). Table 6.4 shows the controlling power of six of the largest enterprise groups in the Japanese economy.

Table 6.4: Major six enterprise groups' shares in the Japanese economy

	Employees	Total assets	Gross sales	Ordinary profit
1980	4.91%	15.34%	15.59%	12.08%
1982	4.77	15.18	15.96	13.86
1984	4.63	15.37	16.43	16.92

Note: Excluding finance institutions and insurance companies.
Source: Kigyō keiretsu sōran [A General View of Linked Companies] (1986).

The business operations of the large corporations are concentrated in a relatively small number of branches of industry, such as electricity, gas, electrical machinery and appliances, iron and steel, non-ferrous metals, automobiles, petrochemicals, etc. In these branches, the giant corporations form monopolies with other corporations, that is, they form monopolistic trade associations to eliminate competiton and to regulate conflict among fellow corporations.

In addition to economic functions, such associations also have political functions. They collect political funds, especially campaign money for the Liberal Democratic Party and some of the opposition parties, with the exception of the Japanese Communist Party. They make contact with politicians and bureaucrats to introduce, alter or abolish laws which concern them, and to promote public spending in their interests. Approximately 70 per cent of the political funds of the LDP comes from these monopolistic capitalist associations. We can see here a veritable hotbed of political corruption and plutocracy.

There is another type of monopolistic capitalist association, namely *zaikai* (*zai* means finance or business, *kai* means world or circles), such as Keidanren (Federation of Economic Organizations), Nikkeiren (Japan Federation of Employers' Association), Nihon Shōkō Kaigisho (Japan Chamber of Commerce & Industry), Keizai Dōyūkai (Japan Committee for Economic Development). Keidanren is something like a board of directors of 'the Corporation of Japan'. As I shall discuss later, its top leaders are composed of the representatives of giant monopolistic corporations and enterprise groups. Nikkeiren is something like a labour section of 'the

Corporation of Japan', providing guidelines for wage agreements and conducting a campaign to restrain wage increases. The *zaikai*, which is the head of a financial oligopoly, helps resolve frictions in individual monopolistic corporations, individual branches of industry and various segments of the capitalist class, and decides industrial strategies, especially industrial policies. Its leaders also undertake adjustments of economic and political conflicts between Japan and foreign countries. In the relation between Japan and the United States of America, the results usually favour the US since Japan is dependent on the US in both the military and diplomatic fields.

The leaders of monopolistic capitalist associations take part in councils organized by the government. In 1986, in 20 main councils related to economic and industrial policies, almost half the total seats (199 out of 404) are occupied by the leading financiers, who connive with bureaucrats and conservative politicians to reach advantageous decisions for themselves in these councils. Other members, such as trade union representatives and so-called men of learning and experience are always in the minority, and they are often supporters of the business world (Zenei Rinjizōkan 1986). Under present political circumstances, the LDP government can pass the Bills proposed by these councils in the Diet (Parliament) without any important amendment. The connection between government and business is embodied in the personnel exchanges between them: frequently, senior public officials are employed by the large private enterprises, and the top leaders of monopolistic corporations take posts in public corporations. Industrial policies are also formulated and pursued under such a government–business relationship.

INDUSTRIAL POLICY AND THE CAPITALIST CLASS

Capitalist development in postwar Japan has been strongly promoted by industrial policy: fiscal, financial, legislative and administrative measures for the purpose of building up or scrapping particular industries.

The most important governmental institution of industrial

policy in Japan is the Ministry of International Trade and Industry (MITI). In MITI, there are three main bureaux for particular industries (the Basic Industries Bureau, the Machinery and Information Industries Bureau, and the Consumer Goods Industries Bureau), two agencies (the Agency of Natural Resources and Energy, including the Petroleum Department and Coal Mining Department, and the Small and Medium Enterprise Agency), and four bureaux for policy adjustment (the International Trade Policy Bureau, the International Trade Administration Bureau, the Industrial Policy Bureau, and the Industrial Location and Environmental Protection Bureau). Each industrial bureau includes various divisions for various industries. For example, the Machinery and Information Industries Bureau has an Industrial Machinery Division, Electronics and Electrical Machinery Division, Automobile Division, Aircraft and Ordnance Division, Vehicle Division, etc.

Industrial policy appears to be drafted and executed largely by MITI, but it is also influenced by other economic bureaux such as the Ministry of Finance (budget, tax, customs and tariff, finance, securities, banking, insurance and international finance), the Ministry of Transport (shipping, shipbuilding, ports and harbours, railway, road transport and civil aviation), the Ministry of Construction (road, construction equipment and construction contracting business), the Economic Planning Agency, the Science and Technology Agency, and the National Land Agency.

These governmental institutions of industrial policy have their counterparts in the form of trade associations (industrial organizations) in the business world. Although there are also trade associations which comprise small and medium enterprises, the main trade associations are monopolistic capitalist associations of particular industries, such as Japan Iron & Steel Federation, Federation of Electric Power Companies, Petroleum Association of Japan, Japan Chemical Industry Association, Japan Automobile Manufacturers' Associations Inc., Electronic Industries Association of Japan, and others.

These associations share with the governmental institutions the function of making and executing industrial policy, and many economists and technocrats are transferred from giant monopolistic corporations to governmental institutions to work on industrial policy. As a result, a personnel link has been established between governmental institutions and the trade associations. Moreover, these monopolistic capitalist associations constitute their own 'government' which has administrative institutions for industrial and economic policies, namely Keidanren. Successive presidents of Keidanren, Ichirō Ishikawa (Nissan, chemicals), Taizō Ishizaka (Tōshiba, electronics and electrical machinery), Kōgorō Uemura (the Wartime Control Association, coal), Toshio Dokō (Tōshiba), Yoshihiro Inayama (Nippon Steel, iron and steel), and Eishirō Saitō (Nippon Steel), were representatives not only of an individual enterprise or a particular industry but also of the dominant segment of the Japanese capitalist class. Ishizaka, Uemura, Inayama all graduated from Tōkyō University and worked as senior officials of the government for some years after graduation. Generally in Japan the most prominent capitalists are not owner-capitalists or big shareholders but people who have worked as skilled executives of industrial policies favouring the interests of the '*zaikai*', as government officials or as directors of private companies (Kakuma 1981).

Industrial policy has included a series of protective measures, such as discriminatory tariffs, preferential commodity taxes on national products, import restrictions, low-interest loans and special amortization benefits. But one of the most important measures of industrial policy is 'gyōsei shidō' (administrative guidance) based on the government's licensing and approval authority, which originated in state control of wartime industries (Johnson 1982; Miyajima 1987). The guiding priciples of this administration have often stressed the elimination of 'excessive competition'[3] (*katō kyōsō*) and the promotion of 'industrial rationalization', which must encourage not 'effective competition' but rather concerted action, and accelerate the tendency towards monopolization and cartelization.

Although these measures are related to specific industrial organizations, there are broader measures providing physical infrastructure – industrial parks, telecommunications, roads, ports, railways, electricity and water supply for industrial use – through public investment. Public investment in motorway construction has had essential importance for the growth of the automobile industry. Road construction and improvement accounted for 40 per cent of the public works expenses from 1960 to 1970, during which time the automobile industry was expanding rapidly.

The increase in public works expenditure has caused an increase in the number of civil or construction contractors. As a result, civil contractors have gained influential political positions as new capitalists in rural areas. Ex-Prime Minister Kakuei Tanaka was a typical example of this kind of politician in postwar Japan. He was successful, a self-made civil contractor, and successively held the position of Minister of Posts and Telecommunications, Minister of Finance, MITI Minister, and Prime Minister after being elected a member of the Diet at the age of 29. The so-called 'Plan to Remodel the Japanese Archipelago' presented by Tanaka in 1972 (which suffered a setback because of hyperinflation), was intended to provide an extraordinarily high rate of public works expenditure on road, rail (*sinkansen*) and other transportation facilities.

Industrial policy has also been shaped by various special laws. With regard to the electronic industries, especially the computer industry, its full-scale research and development started with the Electronics Industry Promotions Special Measures Law in 1957. This law created various measures such as government subsidies for research and development, special loans and special tax relief, according to each stage of test research, commencement of production, mass production and rationalization of production. Although the law has been altered several times, the largest projects in the field of computer research and development since the enactment of the law have been wholly achieved with the aid of government subsidies (Sinjyō 1984). It would have been impossible for the Japanese computer industry to grow rapidly and to catch up with that of the US without these protective measures.

Taking into consideration not only these institutions and measures of industrial policy but also their political and social background, one must add the following three points. First, in postwar Japan, the LDP, which was found in 1955 by the merger of the Liberal Party and the Japan Democratic Party, has been able to continue single-party rule for a long time. Consequently the close and stable connection or coalescence among conservative politicians, bureaucrats and financial magnates is well established, and industrial policies can continue without any serious interruption.

Second, the course of capitalist development in postwar Japan has been powerfully influenced by the Japan–US Security Treaty, which was imposed by the US in 1951 and revised in 1960 as a more aggressive military alliance despite a strong opposition movement. Under this treaty, the US has established more that 100 military bases and facilities in Japan, and compelled Japan to rearm and expand armaments. These circumstances suggest why the US allowed Japan to delay the liberalization of capital transactions, especially direct investment by American enterprises, until the late 1960s (Allen 1978). In my opinion the US did so partly through its need to cultivate and strengthen Japanese capitalism as an anti-communist stronghold in Asia, and partly in compensation for its military burden on Japan, especially its continuing occupation of Okinawa (which continued until 1971). If Japan had taken capital liberalizing measures in the 1950s in line with the Western European nations, industrial development in postwar Japan would have been radically different.

Finally, the Japanese Constitution prohibits Japan from maintaining military forces and public opinion strongly supports this peace constitution. This has restricted the ratio of armaments expenditure to GNP, which is small in comparison with other advanced capitalist countries, although the peace provision of the Constitution has been violated since 1950. In other words, this provision has made it possible to appropriate an inordinately large amount of public funds for expenditure on industrial policy. Without the peace constitution, Japan's industrial productivity after the Second World War would not have been increased faster than that of other nations.

JOINT-STOCK COMPANIES AND THE CAPITALIST CLASS

As we have seen, the Japanese economy and Japanese politics are controlled by a small number of giant monopolistic corporations. But it is not commonly thought that the management ranks in large corporations are active segments of the capitalist class and that Japanese society is ruled by the capitalist class. Economists and sociologists often deny the existence of capitalists in large corporations because of the wide dispersion of share ownership. To discuss this we have to examine the 'corporate capitalism' controversy which has dealt with 'management control' in joint-stock companies (Scott 1985; 1986).

In Japan, theories of corporate capitalism dealing with the problems of ownership and control in large corporations have been advanced mainly by Hiroshi Okumura, Yoshikazu Miyazaki and Isamu Kitahara. They argue that capitalist control based on private ownership of capital or means of production has disappeared, and that the corporation itself has become the subject of ownership and control, so far as large joint-stock companies are concerned. But their arguments differ in a number of ways. Okumura (1984; 1985) discusses executives in large corporations without any concept of a capitalist class. He claims that 'corporate capitalism' is peculiar to 'the Japanese-style joint-stock company' and calls it 'the corporation-centred system'. According to him, the nature of labour–management relations in Japan also derives from this system.

Miyazaki (1982; 1985) argues that there are three types of control: (1) individual (family), (2) corporate, and (3) management. According to his analysis of the 300 largest corporations in 1975, 18 corporations (6 per cent of the total number) are individually (family) controlled, 147 corporations (49 per cent) are corporate controlled, 112 corporations (37.3 per cent) are management controlled, and six corporations (2 per cent) are controlled by the government or local public organizations. In his opinion, control based on ownership has reappeared in the form of corporate control. Kitahara (1985: 268–72) criticizes Miyazaki by saying that the control of affiliated corporations or subsidiaries is not based on ownership of their shares but on ownership of the real capital of the parent corporation itself. In other words, a parent corporation controls the affiliated corporations or subsidiaries not as a shareholder but as a capitalist.

Marxist economic theories of the joint-stock company are based on Marx's *Capital* and Hilferding's *Finance Capital*. But these theories specify no definition of an active capitalist in a joint-stock company. According to Marx (1959 [1894]: 436), the formation of a joint-stock company causes 'the transformation of the actually functioning capitalist into a mere manager, administrator of other people's capital'. Hilferding (1981 [1910]) states that the transformation of an individual enterprise into a joint-stock company means the conversion of an industrial capitalist into a money capitalist. Where then is a functioning or industrial capitalist in a joint-stock company?[4] If we investigate the reason why they lose sight of the active capitalist, we realize that Marx and Hilferding assume that dividends absorb the whole profit of a joint-stock company and do not recognize the transformation of profit into capital within a joint-stock company. In Hilferding's case, this is related to his theory of promoter's profit.[5]

In a joint-stock company as a collective capitalist or associated capital, profits are divided into two portions, excluding interest on borrowed money capital, corporation income tax and other taxes: corporate profit and dividends to shareholders. The former is further divided into three portions: directors' fees and managers' wages, administrative costs (including entertainment expenses), and funds for accumulation within the corporation. In this case, capitalists are divided into two groups: directors and managers who control the business operations, and shareholders who acquire dividends. The latter are regarded as capitalists only when their dividends and capital gains are large enough for them to live without other incomes.

Returning now to the Japanese case, let us re-examine Table 6.1. Ōhashi divides the capitalist class into three groups: (1) individual entrepreneurs, (2) directors and managers of corporations, and (3) government officials. According to this classification, the capitalist class totalled 3.64 million in 1980 and 3.55 million in 1985.

The results of the 1985 National Census tell us that the total number of directors for that year was 2.68 million. But according to the Statistics of the National Tax Administration Agency (Kokuzeichō 1986b), directors numbered 4.04 million (2.43 million in joint-stock companies). The difference stems mainly from duplication in the case of interlocking directorates. Regarding joint-stock companies, 57 per cent of the total number of directors belonged to small and medium enterprises with capitalization of less than 10 million yen. The number of directors with capitalization of over 1000 million yen was only 70,000, i.e. 3 per cent of the total. Average annual earned income per director was 4.54 million yen in the former group, and 11.69 million yen in the latter. The directors who earned over 20 million yen numbered about 30,000.

From these figures we gain the impression that directors' earned incomes are low, contrary to general belief. Generally speaking it is probably true that their personal incomes in Japan are lower than in other advanced capitalist countries, and that the income gap between the capitalist class and the working class in Japan is smaller than in other capitalist countries. But to discuss directors' incomes as a whole we have to consider other sources of income such as interest, dividends and capital gains. In a small number of giant corporations, the total annual incomes of presidents or chairmen range from 100 million yen to 400 million yen. What is more, directors can spend their corporation's entertainment allowances on themselves, and in 1984 these amounted to 3.6 billion yen, whereas dividends totalled 2.9 trillion yen (Kokuzeichō 1986b), and the sums paid to them on retirement often amount to hundreds of millions.

Steven estimates that the bourgeoisie numbered 7.8 million in 1979, as Table 6.2 shows. He includes as capitalists not only members of boards of directors (*torishimariyaku*), department managers (*buchō*) and factory managers (*kōjōchō*), but also section managers (*kachō*) and division managers (*kakarichō*). There is no doubt that division managers, along with other senior managers, share capital's function of controlling the labour process, but they differ from other senior managers in

Table 6.5:   Average monthly earnings by position (1985)

Position	Ratio of persons engaged	Average age	Average monthly earnings		
			Contract earnings	Contract earnings: Overtime allowance	Contract earnings: Responsible position allowance
Branch manager	0.2	49.7	602,086	1,648	92,452
Administration department manager	1.0	50.2	552,559	813	57,833
Administration department assistant manager	0.6	48.5	516,191	1,387	52,526
Administration section manager	4.3	45.0	441,869	3,743	39,866
Administration section acting manager	1.5	41.1	416,571	28,297	19,607
Chief clerk (Division manager)	6.1	40.2	359,528	34,268	5,335
Clerk in charge	7.7	37.2	316,985	35,348	1,545
Clerk	78.6	29.3	212,658	22,789	0
Factory manager	0.3	50.4	514,689	157	41,522
Technical department manager	1.4	49.3	510,986	1,281	42,976
Technical department assistant manager	0.8	48.0	482,763	1,567	38,017
Technical section manager	6.1	44.5	417,953	2,416	34,171
Technical section acting manager	1.3	41.8	375,217	18,282	23,045
Chief technician (Division manager)	8.1	40.3	369,907	53,332	3,406
Technician in charge	10.9	37.7	335,708	55,351	1,672
Technician	71.1	31.2	260,335	48,572	0

Note: Data are based on the survey of private establishments with 50 or more regular workers which belong to enterprises employing 100 or more regular workers.
Source: Shokushubetsu minkan kyūyo jittai chōsa [Survey of Compensation in Private Industry by Occupation] (1986).

that they have scarcely any say in using entertainment allowances and hardly participate in making decisions on capital accumulation. Moreover, the position allowance of a division manager is much lower than that of other senior managers (see Table 6.5) and the average wage of a division manager is not much higher than that of a worker who graduated from university (see Table 6.5 and 6.8). Although division managers do not belong to the working class, they are close to the upper strata or privileged sections of the working class in terms of their consciousness. What I have said about division managers is also true of foremen in factories. I think therefore that division managers as well as foremen should be placed in the middle class.

On the other hand, to establish the boundaries of the capitalist class we have to take into account other types of capitalist such as shareholders and money capitalists. With respect to the accumulation of money capital through the banks, security corporations and other financial institutions, it is important to understand that the more joint-stock companies develop and the greater the significance of government bonds and debentures becomes, the more the accumulation of money capital will mean the accumulation of fictitious capital, i.e. claims to future production or proprietary claims to labour. Therefore, the large proprietors who own these fictitious capitals, as well as shareholders, must also be included as capitalists.

In Japan, however, there are no accurate statistics about the distribution of shareholders and securityholders, and hence we can only use some simple data. Let us look at Table 6.6 which

Table 6.6:   Distribution of listed shares, 1806 companies (1984)
(1000 persons, 1000 stocks)

Classes by number of shares	Number of shareholders	Number of shares
0–1,000	4937 (24.0%)	1,284,575 (0.5%)
1,000–5,000	12040 (58.6%)	22,557,135 (8.7%)
5,000–50,000	3322 (16.2%)	33,906,262 (13.1%)
50,000–5000,000	199 (1.0%)	27,335,365 (36.6%)
500,000–5,000,000	47 (0.2%)	67,184,071 (26.0%)
5,000,000 and over	7 (0.0%)	105,896,444 (41.0%)
Total	20552 (100.0%)	258,163,852 (100.0%)

Note: Including duplication in the case that a shareholder has shares in two or more companies.
Source: Ōkurashō shōkenkyoku nenpō [Annual Statistical Report of the Securities Bureau. The Ministry of Finance] (1986).

examines 1806 listed (on Tōkyō, Ōsaka and Nogoya stock exchange) corporations. The large shareholders with over 50,000 shares account for 1.2 per cent of the total number of shareholders, but they own 77.6 per cent of the total number of shares. Most of them are institutional investors, such as banks and life insurance companies, and corporate shareholders. (Financial institutions, incorporated businesses and security corporations hold about 75 per cent of the total number of shares.) Shareholders with over 5,000 shares but less than 50,000 shares number 3.32 million. Many of them are individual shareholders we may consider capitalists. But no one can properly estimate how many individual shareholders are capitalists, since it is difficult to ascertain from any data the economic characteristics of individual shareholders, and whether they are classified as directors, workers or housewives in other statistics.[6]

In addition, there are no statistics which show exactly the concentration of wealth, because in Japan there is no taxation of capital gains. This makes Japan a capitalist's paradise (see Ishizaki 1983; also Hayashi Y. 1985 [1958]). Capital gains result from rises in the price of land, shares, debentures and

Table 6.7: The distribution ratio by decile groups of income, financial assets, and real assets per household (1972-74)

	Incomes Households including farms'	Financial assets Households excluding farms'	Real assets Households excluding farms'
1st	0.8	0.5	0.5
2nd	3.6	1.6	1.4
3rd	5.4	2.5	2.1
4th	6.6	3.5	2.9
5th	7.9	4.6	3.8
6th	9.2	6.0	5.0
7th	10.8	7.9	6.7
8th	12.7	10.6	9.7
9th	15.5	15.9	16.0
10th	27.4	46.9	51.9
Total	100.0	100.0	100.0

Note: Decile groupings were made according to each separate item.
Source: Ishizaki (1983) and Ogawa (1985).

other securities, and are realized when ownership titles are sold. It is necessary to emphasize that share prices have risen remarkably, and that land prices in the metropolitan areas have also risen steeply compared with the fluctuation of the general price index for the last decade. From 1978 to 1985, the share price index rose from 87.6 to 210.2, and the land price index in urban areas from 89.8 to 131.0, whereas the general price index rose from 89.4 to 111.4.

To show the level of concentration of wealth in the hands of a small number of people, we can use only very rough estimates such as those in Table 6.7. It demonstrates that the more income households earn, the more financial and real assets they have, and that the greater part of financial and real assets are owned by a small number of large proprietors. As a result of the extraordinary rise in the price of shares and land, this tendency has been strengthened in recent years.

SMALL AND MEDIUM ENTERPRISES, INDEPENDENT BUSINESSMEN AND THE PEASANTRY

According to the Fundamental Law on Small and Medium Enterprises, business establishments with capitalization of less than 10 million yen and with fewer than 50 employees in commerce and services (fewer than 100 in the retail wholesale trade), and establishments with capitalization of less that 50 million yen and with fewer than 300 employees in other industries are classified as small and medium enterprises, respectively. According to this definition, and using the Establishment Census, small and medium enterprises in 1981 comprised 99.8 per cent of a total of 6.3 million establishments (excluding the public sector), and they employed 85 per cent of a total of 46 million employees (including the self-employed). Each firm employs on average seven persons, but over half the total number of small and medium enterprises are very small ones with four or fewer employees. One-third of the small and medium enterprises carry on wholesale and retail trade, and the overwhelming majority of them are actually self-employed petty retail merchants. A quarter of the small and medium enterprises engage in manufacturing. Over half the small and medium enterprises in manufacturing (65.5 per cent, 569,000 in 1981) are subcontractors who deliver parts and semi-finished goods to parent companies.

Let us just remember the level of overall concentration shown in Table 6.3. Again and again, hundreds of giant monopolistic corporations subjugate hundreds of thousands of small and medium enterprises. This is the peculiar 'dual structure of the Japanese economy'. Perhaps it would be even more appropriate to call it 'the shock absorber' or 'profit absorber' mechanism of Japanese capitalism, because whenever an economic crisis or shock occurs, the giant monopolistic corporations can pass the difficulties on to the large number of small and medium enterprises, especially subsidiaries and subcontractors, by forcing them to reduce costs and personnel. As a result, the financial position of, and working conditions in, small and medium enterprises become worse each time there is a crisis or shock.

It is sometimes said that the high growth rate of the Japanese postwar economy was induced by the energetic investment of private enterprises, especially large corporations (Noda 1975). This is true if we add that such energetic investment was made possible by the incessant profit-squeezing and repeated bankruptcy of small and medium enterprises. In the public consciousness, a large corporation is immortal, and a small and medium enterprise mortal. The 1986 White Paper on Small and Medium Enterprises says that the rapid changing or quitting of the trade of small and medium enterprises has contributed to the restructuring of Japanese industry.

Entrepreneurs in small and medium enterprises are divided into two categories: individual or small capitalists and independent business people (self-employed persons). In Japan, the former number at least 1.5 million (see Table 6.10), and are the largest active rearguard of the capitalist class. Here we should consider a few points about individual capitalists from the viewpoint of class analysis.

First, they are so deeply subordinate to the large corporations and so divided among themselves by strong competition and a low profit rate, that they can hardly cooperate with each other, and for this reason they have great difficulty in forming a political alliance with the working class despite having common interests in the face of the monopolistic corporations.

Second, in the small and medium enterprises, workers face and enter directly into conflict with individual capitalists, partly because the capitalist who manages each small and medium enterprise is a visible individual, partly because the big capitalists who stand behind the individual or small capitalists, and actually control and exploit small and medium enterprises, are invisible to workers. What is more, in 1986 there were 31.4 million unorganized workers (72 per cent of a total of 43.7 million), and the majority of them worked for small and medium enterprises. They have great difficulty, therefore, in struggling against the individual capitalists who employ them and the giant monopolistic corporations who stand behind them.

Independent business people are unevenly distributed in the field of retail business. There were 2.04 million establishments in wholesale and retail trade in 1985. Ninety per cent of these are shops with fewer that ten employees, and over half (1.03 million) are shops with one or two employees (of which 90 per cent are small shopkeepers). Their earnings including family employees' wages, are not necessarily higher than the average wages of a worker, and their businesses always face threats that result from the development and penetration of large shops such as department stores and supermarkets. In fact, small shopkeepers have decreased in recent years. These conditions also apply to a large number of small factory owners and most of them are petty manufacturers who are situated at the lowest level of the pyramidal subcontract system. For these and other reasons independent business people have organized themselves fairly well to defend their business and living against large corporations and the government. For example, The National Federation of Traders' and Producers' Organizations (*minshō*), which is one of the mass organizations of small and medium shopkeepers and factory owners, had 386,000 members in March 1986 (JCP 1987).

As already mentioned, the peasantry shrank rapidly after

the Second World War, in contrast with the rapid growth of the working class. From 1955 to 1985, the number of employees in agriculture declined from 15 million to 5 million, and the number of full-time farmers' households declined from 2.1 million to 0.6 million. But the total number of farmers' households decreased only from 6 million to 4.4 million. Nowadays many farmers work only part-time on the land, and part-time in local factories or public organizations.

The Japanese peasantry has been rapidly proletarianized since the postwar agrarian reform and the high growth of the post-1955 economy, but a truly capitalist agriculture in which capitalist-tenants or farmers employ wage-labourers has never been developed. Even many full-time farmers own less than two hectares of land, excluding Hokkaido. They produce commodities for sale on the market but depend on hardly any wage-labour. However, peasants have been oppressed by the large corporations through the purchase of chemical fertilizers, feeds and agricultural machines, and have suffered from the government's agricultural policy which has promoted the import of agricultural products from USA. On the other hand, because land prices in urban areas have risen rapidly, a small number of farmers in suburban areas have made money by selling their land and have changed into a sort of money capitalists.

In Japan, the peasantry shares many common interests with the working class, but their class consciousness is closer to that of the petty bourgeoisie and their political attitude is considerably more conservative because they cling to the land as their only means of production and depend on the weak agricultural protective policy of the ruling party. Workers who live in rural areas display similar tendencies and many of them are not unionized. Many workers in rural prefectures, as well as most of the peasantry, support the LDP. In the last general election, the LDP obtained 80 per cent of its seats in the House of Representatives in the rural electoral districts, constituting only 60 per cent of the total population, because of unfairly distributed number of seats; namely, the difference in the weight of individual votes between rural and metropolitan areas. But it will be difficult for the LDP and its government to sustain the present political and electoral situations because the current trade friction between Japan and USA compels Japan to import more and more agricultural products, including rice, and to restructure the agraraian economy. If the government continues to adopt a restructuring policy which eliminates small farms, the agricultural areas will not be able to remain conservative strongholds.

HIGHER EDUCATION AND THE REPRODUCTION OF CLASSES

The Japanese educational system has been basically composed of four parts since the Second World War: six years primary school, three years middle school, three years high school, four years university with another five years for postgraduate degrees (El-Agraa and Ichi 1985). In 1986 the higher educational system comprised 465 universities, some of which offered postgraduate courses, 548 junior colleges and 62 technical colleges (only 4th and 5th grade students). The total number of registered students was about 2.24 million (66 per cent male, 34 per cent female). The proportion of school students going on to universities and colleges increased from 10 per cent in 1960 to 38.4 per cent in 1975, and it has remained at that level since then (Ministry of Education 1986).

The high participation rate in the higher education system is one of the most characteristic features of contemporary Japan. From the socio-economic viewpoint there seem to be two main reasons why individuals decide to go on to higher education. The first is the wage and promotion discrimination based on educational background, the second, the resultant pension discrimination based on an individual's professional career. Table 6.8 shows that university graduates earn more than high school graduates, and employees in large enterprises earn more than in small and medium enterprises. Generally, in Japan, the higher the education people have, the larger the enterprises they are employed in, and this tendency enlarges the wage differences between university graduates and high school graduates. For example, in 1985 the monthly salary of male workers aged 40–44 who graduated from university and worked in enterprises with over 1000 employees was 425,000

Table 6.8:   *Wages by firm size, education, age, and sex, 1985 (1000 yen)*

Firm size (persons)	High school graduates			University graduates		
	1000 and over	100–999	10–99	1000 and over	100–999	10–99
Males						
Age						
18–19	128.2	122.3	119.2			
20–24	148.8	140.9	145.0	159.0	154.7	152.9
25–29	191.1	174.0	178.8	196.9	184.7	186.3
30–34	235.3	213.3	210.8	270.2	237.8	235.2
35–39	274.8	249.2	240.1	338.9	302.6	288.3
40–44	328.3	287.0	262.9	424.7	362.2	333.8
45–49	352.1	303.7	270.7	494.1	416.7	376.2
50–54	371.9	301.8	264.5	544.2	449.1	379.2
55–59	326.3	262.0	243.0	520.6	457.8	390.2
60–64	238.6	217.2	214.2	350.0	426.7	352.5
65–	211.9	191.3	194.5	353.7	426.5	324.0
Females						
Age						
18–19	118.8	114.5	104.8			
20–24	135.8	125.2	116.1	152.3	147.3	136.8
25–29	164.3	138.4	125.8	181.7	170.8	156.9
30–34	187.0	149.8	131.2	232.2	209.7	187.6
35–39	195.7	151.8	134.7	260.1	268.9	213.0
40–44	218.0	151.5	139.5	301.7	306.2	262.9
45–49	241.2	153.8	143.2	333.3	326.0	255.4
50–54	255.8	163.2	150.2	422.8	360.0	289.1
55–59	275.1	176.4	153.3	362.6	435.7	378.7
60–64	259.1	170.9	156.8	356.5	418.9	267.2
65–	226.9	159.6	157.2	194.2	237.3	352.0

Note: Monthly contract earnings of regular workers excluding overtime allowance.
Source: Chigin kōzō kihon tōkei chōsa [Basic Survey of Wage Structure] (1985).

yen, whereas the salary of male workers aged 40–44 who were employed after graduating from high school and worked in enterprises with 10–99 employees was 263,000 yen. If we take bonuses into account the wage differences between these two groups increase from 100:66 to 100:54. This differential is even more marked in the case of female workers. Those employed in small enterprises after graduating from high school receive only 46 per cent of the monthly salary of university graduates employed in large enterprises.

Table 6.9: *Professional and technical workers*

(Employees 15 years old and over)

(Occupational classification)	
Scientific researchers	68,400
Engineers and technicians	1,292,300
Public health and medical workers	1,330,300
Law and justice workers	14,600
Registered accountants and licenced tax accountants	6,500
Professors and teachers	1,384,700
Religious workers	39,000
Authors, reporters and editors	90,100
Fine artists, photographers and designers	113,500
Musicians and stage artists	79,000
Other professional and technical workers	652,400
Total	5,070,800

Source: The 1985 Population Census

The spread of higher education influences class compositon. If we look at Table 6.9 we can see that large numbers of people are employed in professional and technical occupations: science, technology, health service, education, law and justice, accountancy, journalism and art, etc. Excluding directors, self-employed workers and family employees, they numbered 5.07 million in 1985. From 1955 to 1985 their numbers tripled while their proportion in the population doubled, although it is still lower than in the European countries. In my opinion these people should be mostly classified as middle-class.

Ohashi and his followers have no middle-class category. They recognize only three classes (excluding military and police personnel): (1) the capitalist class, (2) self-employed persons (including peasantry and independent business people), (3) working class. Table 6.1 (using Ohashi's categories) classifies professional and technical workers such as university lecturers and school teachers, employees in the medical and health services, and technical workers as belonging to the working class, but Steven categorizes them along with supervisors and the military and police in the middle class. He estimates that they total some 3.79 million.

According to orthodox Marxist views in Japan, the middle

class means the 'petty bourgeoisie' such as small producers or self-employed persons. But in my opinion, although I do not accept C. Wright Mills' theory (1951) which considers all white-collar workers to be middle-class, the category of middle class is also useful to designate professional and technical workers (Table 6.9), and managerial personnel of intermediate rank. I have already explained the class characteristics of the latter. So far as the former are concerned, they are usually engaged in specific sustained mental labour, and can perform their own job relatively free from control by employers. Usually they have gone on to higher education and earn relatively higher wages than other workers. I would add, by way of a caution, that the middle-strata consciousness which most people have in present-day Japan, has nothing to do with the middle-class category, which is a phenomenon within the working class.

With respect to the reproduction of the capitalist class, many new recruits are the offspring of parents already employed as managerial officials in large corporations, individual entrepreneurs, professional and technical workers, and personnel in public administration (Asō 1983). Higher education in prewar Japan has had a profound effect on today's executives in large corporations. One-third of the 32,000 directors in the listed corporations graduated from two national universities (Tōkyō University and Kyōto University) and two private universities (Keiō University and Waseda University) (Shūkan Daiyamondo Bessatsu 1987), and this tendency is unlikely to change in the near future. Not only in the administrative bureaucracy but also in the industrial bureaucracy, there are rigid academic cliques. The link between business and government is also dominated by them. As a result, it is widely believed that the elite of Japanese society is recruited not from the workings of Japanese capitalism, but rather via the educational ladder. But in fact, as I have already mentioned, the elite has been formed through the mechanism of capitalism; and higher education has developed so broadly, and Japanese society is so highly competitive, that it is easy for the capitalist class, as the ruling class, to recruit capable people as directors, managers, bureaucrats and politicians, whose chief functions are to maintain the capitalist system and to promote capital accumulation.

CONCLUSION

On the basis of the foregoing it is possible to contruct Table 6.10 which shows the estimated class composition of Japan in 1985. I have already explained the definition of each class. Comparing Table 6.10 with Tables 6.1 and 6.2 reveals some large differences. But we must consider the limits of statistical analyses of class composition. They do not show clearly the class structure under contemporary monopoly capitalism, nor do they show conflict or cooperation either within the same class or between different classes. They do not explain how the capitalist class rules, and how the working class is exploited. In conclusion I shall discuss briefly the characteristic features of relations between capital and labour in contemporary Japan.

It is often said that the postwar Japanese economy has achieved a miraculous success because of Japanese-style management, which has been accompanied by workers' industriousness, submission to the group, on-the-job training and company-based trade unionism. It cannot be denied that these are important features of the worker's life in Japan. but they do not explain the reasons for the Japanese economic 'miracle'.

One of the most important reasons why Japan succeeded can be seen from the experiences of British capitalism in the first half of the nineteenth century, which developed rapidly because of long working hours, the use of advanced machinery, and a sharp increase in the number of workers. To see through the 'miracle' theory of the Japanese economy, we have only to look at current long working hours, microcomputers and the quality circles movement with self-training at home or outside the workplace. Since the economic crisis in the mid-1970s, which broke out after the first oil shock, many Japanese enterprises have rapidly introduced computer systems including industrial robots, and have promoted quality circles for reducing waste, intensifying labour and increasing productivity (George and Levine 1984).

Table 6.10:   Estimated class composition, 1985

(1000 persons)

	Numbers	Per cent
Population 15 years and over	94,893	157.4
Labour force	60,271	100.0
Employed (inc. not at work)	58,218	96.6
Capitalist class	3,597	6.0
Directors and senior managers[1]	2,031	3.4
Individual capitalists[2]	1,457	2.4
Capitalistic rentiers[3]	na	–
Government officials	109	0.2
Military and police	453	0.8
Middle class	20,611	34.2
Peasantry (inc. family workers)	4,977	8.3
Independent businessmen (inc. family workers)	9.070	15.0
Employees	6,564	10.9
(Middle managers)[4]	(1,493)	(2.5)
(Professional and technical workers	(5,071)	(8.4)
Working class	35,630	59.1
Clerical and related workers	9,284	15.4
Productive workers	16,453	27.3
Sales and Service workers[5]	7,840	13.0
Totally unemployed	2,053	3.4
Not in labour force	34,442	57.1
Population 14 years and under	26,093	43.0
Total population	121,026	200.0

Notes: 1. I have subtracted 1,310,000 owners of small companies with capitalization of less than 10 million yen and 21,000 managers (station masters, chief operation officers, and managers of post, telegram and telephone offices) from the figure (3,362,000) in Table 6.1. Senior managers refer to managers of corporations, such as factory managers, department managers and section managers.
2. Individual capitalists here indicate 147,000 individual entrepeneurs in unincorporated enterprises with 10 or more workers and 1,310,000 small companies' owners mentioned above. To estimate these numbers I used sources 2 and 3, and Table 6.3.
3. There are no statistics which show distinctively the number of capitalistic rentiers in Japan.
4. I multiplied 22,297,000 workers in all enterprises with 30 or more workers by 6.6 per cent (the proportion of division managers, namely, chief clerks and chief technicians) and added 21,000 station masters, chief operation officers, and managers

of post, telegram and telephone offices. These numbers came from Table 6.5, the notes 1 and 4.
5. I added 338,000 security guards included in Table 6.1, military, police and guards.
As regards other items some adjustment was also needed to the figures in Table 6.1 as a result of the adjustments above.
Sources: The 1985 Population Census; Kojin kigyō keizai chōsa nenpō (Unincorporated Enterprise Survey) (1986); Jigyōsho tōkei chōsa nenpō (Establishment Census) (1986); Zeimu tōkei kara mita hōjin kigyō no jittai (Real Situation of Corporations from the Viewpoint of Taxation) (1986).

But at the same time, working hours, especially overtime working, which had been declining during the high-growth period in the 1960s, have increased. According to the White Paper on Labour (Ministry of Labour) of 1986, Japanese workers laboured on average 2152 hours in 1983. That is 539 hours more than workers in West Germany, 495 more than in France, 254 more than in the USA and 214 more than in Britian.

What we see here is classic capitalist exploitation. In Japan there is no effective legal limit to the absorption of surplus labour. The Labour Standard Law limits a working day to eight hours, but it allows almost unlimited overtime work. Although overtime pay now forms a large part of workers' income, the premium wage for overtime work (the additional rate is 25 per cent, which is legally the minimum, but actually normal) is actually much lower than the usual wage, because the indirect wages and bonuses amounting to 40–50 per cent of the total wages per annum are not included in the premium. Capitalists can make extra profit by forcing workers into overtime work, and workers are often made to do extra unpaid work both in the workplace and at home (Hayashi K. 1986). It is currently said that overtime work including 'service overtime work' amounts to 40–50 hours per month. An essential lack of limit to working hours means a lack of fundamental human rights in factories and offices (Kiso keizai kagaku kenkyūsho 1987). Besides, although working conditions have deteriorated, workers have great difficulty in striking because of 'harmonious' labour relations inspired by trade union leaders. The number of trade disputes has decreased from 10,462 in 1974 to 2,002 in 1986 (The Labour Disputes Statistics by the Ministry of Labour 1986; see also Fujimoto 1984).

The condition of the working class in Southeast Asia

generally is much worse. Working hours in Korea, Taiwan, Singapore and other newly industrialized countries (NICs) are far greater than in Japan. In recent years, an increasing number of Japanese enterprises, including small and medium businesses, have relocated in these countries. At the same time, many high-technology products have been imported from Asian NICs and many foreign workers come to Japan from these countries, ostensibly as tourists, musicians, stage dancers or students, but really in order to work illegally. Trade friction between Japan and the United States and the resultant high exchange rate of the yen have accelerated this movement. Under these circumstances, just as American and European workers face competition with Japanese workers, Japanese workers face severe competition with other Asian workers.

Precisely for these reasons the Japanese capitalist class has been obstinately opposed to reducing working hours. Officially, the government recognizes that reducing working hours is necessary to promote the health and welfare of workers and to spur domestic demand, and encourages the implementation of a five-day working week (Economic Planning Agency 1986). But the Labour Standard Law, renewed in 1987, changed the regulations on working hours from a daily to a weekly basis, and overrode the eight-hour daily work system in exchange for a slight shortening of the legal weekly limit on working hours. And it introduced the 'flexible working hours system', legalizing longer normal working hours and 'service overtime work'.

With all these privileges, Japan's industrial productivity and international competitiveness will continue to increase faster than that of other capitalist countries, and Japan will become more and more the originator of a world-wide restructuring of capitalism.

NOTES

1. I am most grateful to Mr Bob Bright and Professor Hiroshi Iwai for assisting me with some useful advice. It goes without saying, however, that the responsibility for any errors and inadequacies rests solely with me.
2. In contemporary Japan neo-Marxist theories of the state and classes such

as those of Nicos Poulantzas (1973 [1968]) and Ralph Miliband (1969) have been introduced, mainly in the field of politics, but empirical studies on classes in Japan have not been greatly influenced by these theories. In Japan, state theories seem to be separate from class analyses.
3. 'Excessive competition' is not quite accurate as a translation of *'katō kyōsō'*. The former is the concept to express objective conditions of particular industries, whereas the latter implies something subjective which means to be unreasonable from the viewpoint of a value judgement (Komiya, Okuno and Suzumura 1984: 12–13).
4. For a detailed discussion of Hilferding's notion of promoter's profit, see Kōji Morioka (1985; 1987a [1979]). Hilferding confuses promoter's profit, the source of which is the money capital invested by shareholders, with industrial profit gained by banks from industrial joint-stock companies. His emphasis on the dominance of bank capital over industrial capital, neglecting the capital accumulation (internal reserve) within joint-stock companies, is also a result of the fact that he has reduced promoter's profit to industrial profit.
5. To analyse the features of developed joint-stock companies, it is important to recognize first that a subject of capital accumulation is a corporation itself. In the world of competition between capitals, individual corporations appear as individual capitalists, therefore individual corporations themselves appear as active capitalists.
6. In Japan, the proportion of individual shareholders had decreased since the Second World War. However, their number has now increased again and stood at 20.47 million in March 1986. This growth reflects recent low interest rates and the jump in share prices. Although an overwhelming majority of shareholders are not considered as capitalists, the increased number of individual shareholders with the development of employee share-ownership schemes has a serious impact on middle-strata consciousness.

REFERENCES

Allen, G. C. (1978) *How Japan Competes: An assessment of international trading practices with special reference to 'dumping'* (London: The Institute of Economic Affairs).
Asō Makoto (1967) *Erīto to kyōiku* [Elites and Education] (Tōkyō: Fukumura Shuppan).
Asō Makoto (1983) 'Gendai Nihon ni okeru erīto keisei' [The Making of Elites in Contemporary Japan], in Naoi Atsushi, Hara Junsuke and Kobayashi Hajime (eds) (1986) *Rīdingusu Nihon No Shakaigaku* [*Readings; Japanese Sociology*] *8, Shakai kaisō shakai Idō* [*Social Strata and Social Mobility*] (Tōkyō: Tōkyō daigaku shuppankai) 229–42.
Chūshō kigyōchō [Small and Medium Enterprise Agency] (1986) *Chūshō Kigyō Hakusho* [*White Paper on Small and Medium Enterprises*] (Tōkyō: Okurashō insatsukyoku).

174   *The Capitalist Class: An International Study*

Doi Eiji (1986) 'Kenkyū dōkō; kaikyū' kōsei'[Survey of the Studies on Class
Composition] *Shakai kagaku to shiteno tōkeigaku* [*Statistics as Social
Science*] 2 (Tōkyō: Sangyō tōkei kenkyūsha) 242–56.
Economic Planning Agency, Japanese Government (1986) *Economic Survey
of Japan* 1985/1986 (Tōkyō: Ministry of Finance).
El-Agraa, Ali M. and Ichii Akira (1985) 'The Japanese Education System
with Special Emphasis on Higher Education', *Higher Education* 14
(Amsterdam) 1–16.
Fujimoto Takeshi (1984) *Kokusai hikaku Nihon no rōdō jyōken* [*Working
Conditions in Japan: A Comparative Study*] (Tōkyō: Shin nihon
shuppansha).
George, Mike and Levine, Hugo (1984) *Japanese Competition and the
British Workplace* (London: Centre for Alternative Industrial and
Technological Systems).
Hayashi Kentarō (1986) 'Issues on the Conditions of Workers in Japan'.
Retsumeikan University, *Sangyō shakai ronshū* [*Review of Industrial
Society*] vol. 21, no. 4 (March) 33–45.
Hayashi Yoshio (1985 [1958]) *Sengo Nihon no sozei kikō* [*The Tax Structure
in Postwar Japan*] (Tōkyō: Yūhikaku).
Hilferding, Rudolf (1981 [1910]) *Finance Capital*, edited with an
Introduction by Tom Bottomore (London: Routledge & Kegan Paul).
Ishizaki, Tadao (1983) *Nihon no shotoku to tomi no bunpai* [*Distribution of
Income and Wealth in Japan*] (Tōkyō: Tōyō keizai sinpōsha).
Itō Yōichi (1978) 'Gendai Nihon no kaikyū kōsei to sinhonka' [Class
Composition and Capitalists in Contemporary Japan], in Keizai riron
gakkai [Japan Society of Political Economy] ed. *Gendai shihonshugi to
kaikyū* [Contemporary Capitalism and Classes] (Tōkyō: Aoki shoten)
3–34.
Iwai Hiroshi (1978) *Gendai Nihon no chiiki kaikyū kōsei* [*The Local Class
Composition in Modern Japan*], *Chōsa to shiryō* [*Researches and
Materials*], 26 (Osaka: Kansai University).
Iwai Hiroshi and Fujioka Mitsuo (1985) 'Daitoshi kaikyū kōsei no henka to
kōreika' [Changes of Class Composition in Metropolitan Areas and
Ageing], *Keizai*, no. 254 (June) 49–75, no. 255 (July) 177–87.
Japan Communist Party (1987 [1985]) *Japanese Politics and Communist
Party* (Tōkyō: Japan Press Service).
Johnson, Chalmers (1982) *MITI and the Japanese Miracle: The Growth of
Industrial Policy, 1925–1975* (Stanford: Stanford University Press).
Kiso keizai kagaku kenkyūsho [The Institute of Fundamental Political
Economy] (ed.) (1987) *Rōdō jikan no keizaigaku* [*Economics of Working
Hours*] (Tōkyō: Aoki shoten).
Kitahara Isamu (1980) 'Ownership and Control in the Large Corporation',
Keiō Economic Studies, vol. 8, no. 2, 19–34.
Kitahara Isamu (1985) *Gendai shihonshugi ni okeru shoyū to kettei*
[*Ownership and Decision in Contemporary Capitalism*] (Tōkyō: Iwanami
shoten).
Kokuzeichō [National Tax Administration Agency] (1986a) *Zeimu tōkei*

kara mita hōjin kigyō no jittai [*Real Situation of Corporations from the Viewpoint of Taxation Statistics*] (Tōkyō: Okurashō insatsukyoku).

Kokuzeichō (1986b) *Zeimu tōkei kara mita minkan kyūyo no jittai* [*Real Situation of Private Incomes from the Viewpoint of Taxation Statistics*] (Tōkyō: Okurasho insatsukyoku).

Komiya Ryūtarō, Okuno Masahiro and Suzumura Kōtarō (eds) (1984) *Nihon no sangyō seisaku* [*The Industrial Policy of Japan*] (Tōkyō: Tōkyō daigaku shuppankai).

Mannari Hiroshi (1960) *Bijinesu elíto* [*Business Elites*] (Tōkyō: Chyuō kōronsya).

Mannari Hiroshi (1974) *The Japanese Business Leaders* (Tōkyō: University of Tōkyō Press).

Marx, Karl (1959 [1894]) *Capital*, vol. 3 (London: Lawrence & Wishart).

Miliband, Ralph (1969) *The State in Capitalist Society* (London: Weidenfeld & Nicolson).

Mills, C. Wright (1951) *White Collar: The American Middle Class* (London: Oxford University Press).

Miyajima Hideaki (1987) 'Senji tōsei keizai eno ikō to sangyō no soshikika' [Controlled Cartelization in the Early Stage of Wartime Economy] *Kindai Nihon kenkyū* [*Journal of Modern Japanese Studies*] 9 (Tōkyō: Yamakawa shuppansha). 103–27.

Miyazaki Yoshikazu (1976) *Sengo Nihon no kigyō shūdan* [*The Enterprise Groups in Postwar Japan*] (Tōkyō: Nihon keizai shinbunsha).

Miyazaki Yoshikazu (1982) *Gendai shihonshugi to takokuseki kigyō* [*Contemporary Capitalism and Multinational Corporation*] (Tōkyō: Iwanami Shoten).

Miyazaki Yoshikazu (1985) *Gendai kigyō ron niyūmon* [*An Introduction to the Theory of Modern Corporation*] (Tōkyō: Yuhikaku).

Morioka Kōji (1985) 'Hilferding's Finance Capital and Promoter's Profit', in *Kansai University Review of Economics and Business*, vol. 13. nos 1–2, 87–110.

Morioka Kōji (1987a [1979]) *Dokusen shihonshugi no kaimei, zōho shinpan* [*An Elucidation of Theories on Monopoly Capitalism, the enlarged and revised edition*] (Tōkyō: Shinhyōron).

Morioka Kōji (1987b) 'Gendai Nihon no shihonka kaikyū' [The Capitalist Class in Contemporary Japan] *Kiso keizai kagaku kenkyūsho* (ed.) (1987) Kōza. Kōzō Tenkan [Series: The Structural Change], vol. 4, Ningen hattatsu no minshushugi, [*Democracy for Human Development*] Tōkyō: Aoki shoten).

Noda Kazuo (1979 [1975]) 'Big business organization', in E. F. Vogel (ed.) *Modern Japanese Organization and Decision-making* (Tōkyō: Tuttle) 115–45.

Ogawa Masako (1985) *Shin 'kaisō' shōhi no jidai* [*The Age of New 'Strata' Consumption*] (Tōkyō: Nihon keizai shinbunsha).

Ohashi Ryūken (ed.) (1971) *Nihon no kaikyū kōsei* [*Japan's Class Composition*] (Tōkyō: Iwanami shoten).

Okumura Hiroshi (1976) *Nihon no rokudai kigyō shūdan* [*The Six Major*

Enterprise Groups in Japan] (Tōkyō: Daiyamondosha).

Okumura Hiroshi (1978) *Kigyō shūdan jidai no keieisha* [*The Executives in the Age of Enterprise Groups*] (Tōkyō: Nihon keizai shinbunsya).

Okumura Hiroshi (1984) *Hōjin sihonshugi* [*Corporate Capitalism*] (Tōkyō: Ochanomizu shobō).

Ōkurashō [Ministry of Finance] (1986) Ōkurashō Shōkenkyoku Nenpō [*Annual Statistical Report of the Securities Bureau*] (Tōkyō: Ōkurashō insatsukyoku).

Poulantzas, Nicos (1973 [1968]) *Political Power and Social Classes* (London: New Left).

Rōdōshō [Ministry of Labour] (1985a) *Chingin kōzō kihon tōkei chōsa* [*Basic Survey on Wage Structure*].

Rōdōshō [Ministry of Labour] (1985b) *Shokushu betsu minkan kyūyo jittai chōsa* [*Survey of Compensation in Private Industry by Occupation*].

Rōdōshō [Ministry of Labour] (1986 and 1987) *Rōdō hakusho* [*White Paper on Labour*] (Tōkyō: Nihon rōdō kyōkai).

Scott John (1985 [1979]) *Corporations, Class and Capitalism*, second, completely revised, edition (London: Hutchinson).

Scott, John (1986) *Capitalist Property and Financial Power: A Comparative Study of Britain, the United States and Japan* (Sussex: Wheatsheaf Books).

Senoo Akira (ed.) (1983) *Gendai Nihon no sangyō shūchū* [*Industrial Concentration in Contemporary Japan*] (Tōkyō: Nihon kezai shinbunsha).

Sinjyō Kōji (1984) 'Konpyūta sangyō' [Computer industry], in Komiya, Okuno and Suzumura (1984): 297–323.

Steven, Rob (1983) *Classes in Contemporary Japan* (London: Cambridge University Press).

Syūkan daiyamondo bessatsu [*Weekly Diamond, Special Issue*]. *'87 nen ban kigyō rankingu* [*Enterprises Ranking in 1987*].

Tanaka Naomi (ed.) (1987) *Tōkei shiryōshū* [*Statistical Sources*] (Tōkyō: sangyō kenkūsha).

Zenei rinji zōkan [*Special Issue*]. *1986 Seiji keizai sōran* [*Survey of Japanese Economy and Politics*] (Tōkyō: Nihon kyōsantō).

7 Canada*

Robert J. Brym

THE CANADIAN QUANDARY

Students of comparative economic development have traditionally found Canada a difficult country to classify. In so far as its
Gross National Product per capita and manufacturing
productivity are high, Canada resembles the world's most
highly industrialized countries. As in the semi-industrialized
countries, however, the value of manufactured goods
produced in Canada is low compared to the value of raw
material exports, and foreign ownership is widespread in some
important branches of the economy.

The closely related study of Canada's capitalist class evinces
the same sort of confusion. Thus, some Canadian capitalists
have been characterized as members of a weak 'comprador'
elite on the Latin American model, growing wealthy by
helping US-based multinationals exploit the country's independent economic development. In contrast, other researchers have
analysed Canadian capitalists and found a mature and powerful class that has come to play an increasingly important role in
international economic affairs – a promising junior partner in
the global capitalist system. This stature was recognized in
Tokyo in May 1986 when Canada, along with the other six
countries represented in this book, formed the Group of
Seven. The mandate of G-7: to oversee the world economy,
with the specific task of coordinating international economic
policy (Walkom 1986).

Before the early 1970s there was little research on the
Canadian capitalist class. Since then, however, research in this

area has become a growth industry.[1] And throughout this period research has been animated chiefly by the antinomy just noted: Is the Canadian capitalist class weak or strong, dependent or imperialistic? In the 1970s, dependency theory, popularized by André Gunder Frank (1969) and others, was enthusiastically adopted by a whole generation of Canadian researchers. In the 1980s this approach to understanding the Canadian capitalist class and the country's complex pattern of economic development and underdevelopment was roundly criticized by more orthodox 'internationalist' Marxists (cf. Portes and Walton 1981). One aim of this chapter is to assess the validity of these competing views by critically examining research on the social organization and economic boundaries of the Canadian capitalist class.

A second important issue that has enlivened debate on the Canadian capitalist class centres on the question of class rule: In what sense (if any) do Canadian capitalists control the state? In the early to mid–1970s answers to this question were overwhelmingly influenced by the 'instrumentalist' views of Ralph Miliband (1973 [1969]). The thrust of his argument was that capitalist states are controlled through direct and indirect ties between individual capitalists and state institutions. By the late 1970s the popularity of this viewpoint had waned and the 'structuralist' theory of Nicos Poulantzas (1975 [1968]) was taken up by many researchers. Increasingly it was argued that the state serves capitalist interests not because of the strength of personal ties, but because it functions within a capitalist economic system that systematically constrains policy to benefit the long-term interests of the capitalist class as a whole. The Canadian evidence bearing on this debate will also be reviewed below.

DEPENDENCY THEORY AND THE CAPITALIST CLASS

In Canada in the 1970s 'dependency' signified an unequal relationship between Canada and the USA, a relationship in which the USA used its superior power to secure a wide range of economic advantages over Canada. According to Canadian proponents of dependency theory (see especially Levitt 1970; Britton and Gilmour 1978), one of the chief features of the Canada/USA relationship is the control of substantial portions of the Canadian economy by US-based multi-nationals. This facilitates the outflow of a great deal of capital from the country in the form of profits, dividends, interest payments, royalties and management fees. In the absence of foreign control, that capital would presumably be available for domestic investment and job creation.

The magnitude of the problem is indicated by the large and growing deficits on the non-merchandise account of Canada's international balance of payments since the Second World War. In 1977, for example, the deficit amounted to $7 billion. About 75 per cent of the deficit resulted from capital transfers such as those just listed.

Not only does US direct investment cause a net capital drain, but (the adherents of dependency theory continue) the foreign capital that remains invested in Canada creates fewer jobs than would an equal amount of domestic investment. That is because foreign capital is invested in Canada for two main purposes: to provide a secure source of raw materials for manufacturing in the USA, and to produce manufactured goods for the Canadian market (Williams 1983). Plants established to produce only for the Canadian market are by definition prevented from trying to compete for international sales, from engaging in research and development, and in many cases from doing any more than assembling parts made outside the country. Thus, foreign direct investment constrains growth in the manufacturing sector – which is one important reason why Canada imports substantially more manufactured goods than it exports (in 1977, $11 billion more). Moreover, massive US direct investment in the resource sector is an inefficient creator of jobs: generally speaking, a unit of investment in resource extraction creates fewer employment opportunities than a unit of investment in manufacturing since resource extraction is generally more capital-intensive.

As a corollary it was further argued that 'Canada's dependency is a function not of geography and technology but of the nature of the country's capitalist class' (Laxer 1973: 28). This idea was first elaborated in a highly influential article by

Tom Naylor (1972; see also Naylor 1975). According to Naylor, the whole sweep of Canadian economic history is characterized by Canada's role as a supplier of raw materials to, and a purchaser of manufactured goods from, a progression of imperial centres: first France, then Great Britain, and finally the USA. Naylor allowed that out of this trade there emerged a Canadian capitalist class specializing in the construction and operation of transportation facilities, as well as insurance, banking and short-term credit services. But he further insisted that this class historically has had a vested interest in blocking the development of a vigorous and independent manufacturing sector in Canada. After all, he reasoned, using raw materials in Canada rather than shipping them abroad, and producing manufactured goods in Canada rather than bringing them in from elsewhere, would undermine the trading and related activities on which the Canadian capitalist class's prosperity was founded. The high import tariffs on manufactured goods instituted by the 1879 National Policy, and eagerly backed by members of Canada's mercantile bourgeoisie, serve Naylor as an outstanding example of how Canada's capitalist class stunted independent industrial growth. The tariff wall encouraged the hothouse growth of foreign (mainly US) branch plants in Canada – plants designed to service only the local market and engage mainly in assembly and warehousing.

This argument, which came to be known as the 'merchants against industry thesis', was widely accepted until the mid-1970s. Consider, for instance, the important studies undertaken by Wallace Clement (1975; 1977). One of the tasks Clement set himself was to analyse the density and pattern of ties among dominant corporations in Canada – ties formed by individuals sitting simultaneously on more than one corporate board of directors. The senior executives and members of the boards of directors of the country's dominant corporations, or members of the corporate elite, actually comprise two main groups according to Clement. First, the indigenous elite consists of people, for the most part Canadian-born, who head corporations engaged mainly in commercial and transportation-related activities. Their business is conducted chiefly inside, but also to a degree outside, Canada. (Exemplary are the large Canadian banks that have set up branches throughout the Caribbean.) Second, the comprador elite consists of people, some Canadian-born, others not, who merely manage the Canadian branch plants of multinational corporations. The economic activities of these branch plants are also largely restricted to Canada itself, although in some cases they serve as intermediaries for US direct investment in third countries. (For example, the Ford Motor Co. of Canada, which in turn holds 100 per cent of stock in the Ford Motor Co. of Australia, New Zealand, South Africa and Singapore.) Most of the multinationals with branch plants in Canada have head offices in the USA, and most of them are engaged in manufacturing and resource extraction.

Clement does not suggest that the cleavage between indigenous and comprador fractions of the Canadian corporate elite implies conflict or rivalry between the two groups. Quite the contrary. The two groups play complementary roles in Canadian economic life, one basically financial, the other basically industrial and resource-related. Moreover, their boards of directors are highly interlocked, important financiers frequently serving on the boards of foreign-controlled companies engaged in manufacturing and resource extraction, and vice versa. And they share a continentalist outlook on the nature of Canada/US relations, as is evidenced by their opposition to the growth of an indigenous Canadian manufacturing sector that could disrupt the existing pattern of economic relations between the two countries.

CAPITALIST CLASS CLEAVAGES

The 'merchants against industry thesis' was the first aspect of dependency theory to come under critical scrutiny. The thesis stands or falls partly on the degree to which indigenous manufacturers in Canada formed a relatively small, poor and uninfluential segment of the capitalist class, constrained in its development during the latter part of the nineteenth and first part of the twentieth centuries by more numerous, wealthy and powerful commercial entrepreneurs. If, however, it can be shown that native industrialists were not so insignificant as the dependency theorists maintain, then a central element of the merchants against industry thesis is called into question.

Several historians of Canadian industrial growth have made precisely this point, and they have done so with a wealth of material attesting to the industrialization that began in the British North American colonies as early as the 1850s. There is no denying the predominance of 'staple' production (especially lumber and wheat) in the pre-Confederation years. But Stanley Ryerson oberves that in Upper Canada in the 1850s there was 'a consolidation of the new elite of railroad and factory owners; the shaping of that ruling class of industrial capitalists who were to be the real (not merely the titular) "fathers" of Confederation' (Ryerson 1973 [1968]: 269; see also Ryerson 1976; Kealey 1980).

Certainly, by the 1880s and the 1890s industrialization was well under way and by the early decades of the twentieth century Canadian manufacturing industry was well developed, even by international standards. Thus, Gordon Laxer (1983; 1985) presents data showing that in 1913 Canada was the world's seventh largest manufacturing nation, outranked only by the USA, Germany, UK, France, Russia and Italy. The great bulk of the products manufactured in Canada were not semi-processed, but fully finished goods such as farm implements, footware, furniture, and so forth. With only 0.4 per cent of the world's population, Canada produced 2.3 per cent of all manufactured goods in the world in 1913 (compared to Japan's 1.2 per cent and Sweden's 1.0 per cent).

Nor was Canada's commercial sector particularly over-developed in the first decades of this century, at least in comparison with that of the USA. Jack Richardson (1982: 291) computed the ratios, for Canada and the USA, of national income generated by commercial businesses to national income generated by industrial activity. He discovered that between 1920 and 1926 the Canadian ratio was the same or lower than the US ratio, depending on the precise definitions of 'commercial' and 'industrial' activity used. This is just the opposite of what one would expect to find if the merchants against industry thesis were valid.

In this light it seems unjustified to speak of a tiny and uninfluential manufacturing elite in late nineteenth and early twentieth-century Canada. The current weakness of Canada's manufacturing sector is undeniable, but one may reasonably conclude that the twentieth century was well advanced before its frailty became obvious.

Why Naylor and Clement none the less held otherwise is partly a result of a definitional quirk. They alluded to Marx's distinction between industrial or productive capitalists who engage in 'the sphere of production' (i.e. manufacturing) and mercantile or non-productive capitalists who engage in the 'sphere of capital circulation' (i.e. banking, insurance and the like). According to Marx, only productive capital directly adds value to raw materials. Moreover, industrial capital is characterized by a comparatively high ratio of fixed to circulating capital – which is to say that manufacturers tend to invest relatively more in plant and equipment than do mercantile capitalists, who prefer short-term liquid investments. That is why, in Marx's view, sustained and substantial economic development depends on the robustness of industry: only manufacturers organize the actual addition of value to raw materials by promoting the accumulation of long-term fixed investments.

The view that industry is generally the chief engine of economic development is, I think, unobjectionable. What is problematic is that Naylor and Clement classified entrepreneurs active in the railroad industry – one of the most important branches of the economy in late nineteenth-century Canada – not as industrialists but as financial or commercial capitalists engaged in trade. Yet, according to L. R. Macdonald (1975: 267, 268), 'railways had much the highest proportion of fixed to circulating capital of any nineteenth-century enterprise' in Canada; and Marx himself 'went out of his way in *Capital* to insist that the transportation industry was productive because it added value to commodities; for him, a railway was an industry, not a trade.' In other words, if Naylor and Clement had characterized the railroad barons as productive rather than financial capitalists, they might not so readily have jumped to the conclusion that productive capitalists were a minor force in Canadian economic life.

In addition, little evidence supports the view that there was a conflict of interest between financial and industrial capitalists.

Financial capitalists in late nineteenth-century Canada had nothing against the formation of domestic manufacturing concerns. As Macdonald (1975) demonstrates, many financial capitalists promoted the growth of manufacturing and even became manufacturers themselves. Richardson (1982: 287-8) shows that this early tendency for merchants actually to become industrialists was clearly visible in the Brantford, Ontario economic elite of the 1890s and in the Toronto economic elite of the 1920s. In Brantford, 55 per cent of the 22 members of the economic elite were active in mercantile and industrial firms at the same time. In Toronto, 53 per cent of the 164 most powerful men in the economic elite simultaneously held directorships in both types of corporations. If the economic interests of financial and industrial capitalists were opposed one would not find such clear evidence of an identity of interest and, indeed, of personnel, between these two groups.

Some analysts of the late twentieth-century Canadian capitalist class have taken this last point a step further. They question whether it makes any sense at all to talk about two main groups in the Canadian capitalist class and hold that it may be altogether more accurate to posit a merger of commercial and industrial interests, at least in contemporary times. The most important researches that develop this theme are by William Carroll, John Fox and Michael Ornstein (1982) and by William Carroll alone (1982; 1984; 1986).

Carroll, Fox and Ornstein examined interlocking director-ates among 100 of the largest financial, merchandising, and industrial firms in Canada in 1973. They discovered, first, that these firms are remarkably highly integrated by top corporate officials and managers serving simultaneously on more than one board of directors. Ninety-seven of the 100 firms were connected by single-director interlocks and 70 of the 100 by multiple-directorship ties. They also discovered no evidence to support the view that the largest Canadian firms are clustered in disconnected subgroups or cliques based on nationality of ownership or on sphere of economic activity. Such cliques would presumably have been discovered if the cleavages within the capitalist class posited by the dependency theorists did in fact exist. Finally, Carroll, Fox and Ornstein found that non-financial corporations controlled by Canadians had few links to their foreign-controlled counterparts; but both domestic and foreign-controlled corporations were linked to large Canadian financial institutions. In other words, banks lie at the centre of the network of interlocking directorates, serving as the principal points of articulation and integration for the corporate elite.[2]

Some of these interpretations are confirmed and elaborated in Carroll's work. Carroll (1982; 1986) examined the boards of directors of the 100 largest Canadian industrial, financial and merchandising firms at five-year intervals between 1946 and 1976. He discovered the existence of dense ties between Canadian-controlled financial firms and Canadian-controlled industrial firms; and markedly less dense ties between Canadian-controlled financials and US-controlled industrials operating in Canada. Moreover, the directorship ties among indigenous Canadian financial and non-financial firms become more dense over time, while the ties between Canadian financials and US-controlled industrials have become less dense. Carroll (1984) separately analysed the 'inner group' of 298 key Canadian corporate interlockers. He found that dominant indigenous interests predominate in this group, and they represent all major sectors of large-scale capital. These findings all contradict the predictions of dependency theory.[3]

CAPITALIST CLASS BOUNDARIES

On the basis of available evidence I conclude that the cleavages in the Canadian capitalist class which the dependency theorists purported to detect were greatly overdrawn. Does dependency theory fare any better with regard to the question of the capitalist class's boundaries? Carroll (1982; 1986) for one thinks that the Canadian capitalist class is now autochthonous and independent, not continental and dependent. Steve Moore and Debi Wells (1975) come to much the same conclusion, while Jorge Niosi (1981 [1980]; 1982; 1983; 1985) offers a more qualified assessment. Let us consider the evidence on which they base their conclusions.

Carroll (1982: 98) underscores the fact that the assets of top Canadian firms were overwhelmingly Canadian-controlled at the end of the Second World War and they exhibit the same characteristic today: in 1946 and in 1976 about 86 per cent of such assets were Canadian-controlled (about 56 per cent Canadian-controlled in the manufacturing sector alone) while roughly 11 per cent were US-controlled (approximately 33 per cent in the manufacturing sector). There was a period in the 1950s and 1960s when overall US control of assets in the largest Canadian firms nearly doubled, but that era began to fade into history after 1970. Similarly, Niosi (1981 [1980]: 32; 1983: 132) cites government statistics showing that, among all non-financial companies in Canada, the value of assets under foreign control as a percentage of all assets has steadily decreased from 36 per cent in 1970 to 26 per cent in 1981. In manufacturing alone the decline was from 58 per cent in 1970 to 41 per cent in 1983 (Urquhart 1984). Minimally, these figures support the view that Canadian capitalism has become more indigenous and less controlled by non-Canadians over the past two decades.

It is also worth noting that this independence has been reflected in the propensity of Canadian companies to increase their foreign investments: the boundaries of the capitalist class's activities are, in other words, less and less circumscribed by the country's political borders. The ratio of US direct investment in Canada to Canadian direct investment in the US declined from 6.7 in 1970 to 2.8 in 1985. The ratio of total foreign direct investment in Canada to total Canadian direct investment abroad fell from 4.6 in 1970 to 2.7 in 1979. Government forecasters expect the latter ratio to fall to 1.0 by 1992. Significantly, in 1969 less than 62 per cent of Canadian direct investment abroad was investment by Canadian-controlled companies; that figure increased to 83 per cent by 1978. In absolute terms, Canada was the seventh largest overseas investor in the world by 1976 (after the USA, the UK, West Germany, Japan, Switzerland and France). In relative terms, too, Canada's overseas investment record was impressive: in 1978 Canadian indirect investment abroad amount to $700 per capita – not much less than the US figure of $750; and by 1980 the annual rate of growth of Canadian investment abroad was 13.7 per cent, compared to 9.0 per cent for the USA ('Border exchanges', 1987; Moore and Wells 1975:

72; Niosi 1982: 24, 25; 1983: 132-3; 1985; US Department of Commerce 1986: 780, 782).[4]

On the basis of these figures some analysts are inclined to urge outright rejection of the view that the Canadian capitalist class is basically dependent and continentalist and largely constrained in its business dealings to Canadian soil. Carroll, Moore, Wells and others think of Canadian capitalists as having come of age, engaging in their own economic ventures overseas and no longer subordinate to US interests. However, this is probably going rather further than facts warrant. For, as Niosi (1982; 1983: 133-4; 1985) points out, Candian-controlled multinationals are still technologically dependent on research and development in the USA and other countries, and they are restricted to supplying only a narrow range of products and services abroad (non-ferrous metals, banking, real estate, paper, farm machinery, distilling, synthetic rubber, footwear, telecommunications equipment). Furthermore, the decline in foreign control of the Canadian economy witnessed over the past twenty years has largely been confined to extractive and mineral processing industries (especially oil and gas, potash, coal, asbestos, and metals). The Canadian manufacturing sector is, as the dependency theorists stressed, still very weak. Much of it is still foreign-controlled, and because of the strict limits this places on its growth it still employs a smaller proportion of the labour force than is the case in highly industrialized countries (Black and Myles 1986). It does not even come close to supplying Canadians with all the manufactured goods they need. And much of the manufacturing that takes place in Canada involves the mere assembly of parts made elsewhere (Williams 1983). For these reasons, Niosi concludes – quite sensibly I think – that the Canadian capitalist class cannot at present be characterized either as purely continentalist and dependent or as purely independent of foreign interests; either as tightly constrained to engage in business almost exclusively in Canada or as freely able to engage in wide-ranging business ventures abroad. The Canadian capitalist class manifests aspects of all these features because of the domestic and international economic and political conditions within which it has evolved. I shall mention some of these conditions in the next section.

DOMESTIC POLITICAL ECONOMY, INTERNATIONAL CONTEXT AND ECONOMIC DEVELOPMENT

In the 1970s the characterization of the Canadian capitalist class as dependent represented an advance in social scientific thinking in so far as it drew attention to important structures and processes previously neglected in the study of the country's economic development. In particular, dependency theory highlighted the broader international context of economic development. It challenged the widespread assumption that the trajectory of a given country's growth or stagnation should be analysed exclusively in terms of that country's internal conditions. At the same time, however, dependency theorists thought of the international context only in bilateral terms (Friedmann and Wayne 1977). In the Canadian case, for example, the nature of Canada/US ties were held to be responsible for both the character of Canada's development and the structure of its capitalist class in recent times.

As we have seen, the internationalists of the 1980s challenged the validity of some key empirical implications of this theory. In the process, they sketched a more accurate picture of the structure of the Canadian capitalist class. We now know that banks lie at the centre of the network of interlocking directorates, that foreign control of the Canadian economy is waning, that Canadian multinationals have become important players in several economic spheres, and so forth.

Notwithstanding these important contributions, the internationalists, like the dependency theorists, have minimized the significance of internal economic and political processes in shaping Canadian capitalism. This point has been made especially effectively by Gordon Laxer (1983; 1985a; 1985b). Laxer has recently explored the ramifications of the following paradox. The late-industrializing countries that were able to overcome severe domestic capital shortages and generate robust independent manufacturing sectors were those with strong agrarian classes. In such countries as Japan and Sweden the agricultural sector traditionally encouraged expanionist military endeavours that caused the state to take an interventionist role in the economy and become directly involved in the manufacture of military wares. For security reasons, the state typically encouraged the domestically-owned military manufacturing sector to become technologically independent. It employed many engineers and thus laid the foundation for later technological innovation. From the countryside there also issued a demand for cheap government, which lessened the problem of domestic capital shortage. Finally, politically influential agrarian elements fought for the breakup of old commercial banking systems, oriented towards short-term loans, and the creation of investment banks, oriented towards long-term loans. This had the unintended consequence of making capital more readily available for industrial investment. In Canada, by contrast, farmers were politically weak and disunited. This allowed the French–English conflict so completely to overshadow class-based politics at the turn of this century that the farmers had relatively little influence on public policy. As a result, Canadian farmers could not have the unintended but beneficial effects on the growth of manufacturing that rural classes had elsewhere. In Canada, military manufacturing was mimimal. The state squandered enormous sums of money on the construction of unnecessary transcontinental railway lines. Investment banking developed very late. For these reasons, there was a shortage of domestic capital for investment in manufacturing.

This explanation of why Canada has a weak manufacturing sector neither minimizes the significance of the problem (as the internationalists do) nor locates its origins almost exclusively in external forces (as the dependence theorists do). By analysing the Canadian case in comparative perspective and paying careful attention to domestic economic and political relations, Laxer has offered an innovative explanation of an issue that has galvanized the interest of Canadian social scientists for two decades. This is not to suggest that the Canadian capitalist class is best understood with exclusive reference to domestic political and economic processes. For example, the repatriation of Canadian capital and the greatly increased level of Canadian direct investment in the US that have occurred over the past fifteen years can scarcely be understood apart from the weakening role of the US in the world economy (Carroll 1986: 186–212). Laxer's work does, however, offer a useful counterpoint to the internationalists' important contributions. It serves as a compelling reminder that the political economy of both international and domestic affairs must be examined in order to draw a complete picture of the development and structure of the Canadian capitalist class.

CAPITALIST CLASS RULE

The second major issue that has been investigated by students of the Canadian capitalist class is the nature of capitalist class rule. It was a common theme among researchers in the 1970s that members of the Canadian corporate elite have successfully transformed their continentalist vision into what is widely perceived as the national interest. This was held to be most significantly evident in the behaviour of the two establishment political parties, Liberal and Progressive Conservative. Presumably, these parties have by and large acted to stultify the growth of a vigorous manufacturing sector and reinforce the liaison between indigenous commercial and foreign-controlled comprador elites. Government failure to enact a tough Foreign Investment Review Act limiting US takeovers of Canadian manufacturing and resource companies, and government readiness to introduce laws protecting Canadian banks, insurance companies and transportation companies from foreign competition, are two of the most frequently cited examples of the manner in which governments have acted in the interests of Canadian corporate leaders.

The theoretically important question is: how is it that the class interests of the corporate elite are translated into major government policies? Until the mid-1970s it was commonly argued that the corporate elite controlled government largely in a direct manner, by forging a wide variety of strong social ties to state institutions. These ties ensure that the people who occupy the command posts of economic and political institutions form a ruling class.

The implications of this viewpoint may be more fully appreciated if it is contrasted with the earlier formulation of

John Porter (1965). In the first major sociological work on Canadian elites, Porter discovered that elite members – the chief power-holders in economic, political, media, bureaucratic and intellectual institutions – tend to be recruited from well-to-do families of British and Protestant origin in numbers far greater than the proportion of such families in the population.[5] Moreover, Porter sought to establish that members of the different elites come to share certain values and attitudes as they interact with one another. This cohesion enables them to achieve 'the over-all co-ordination that is necessary for the continuity of the society' (Porter 1965: 523). Cohesion is attained informally by elite members attending private schools together, intermarrying and forming strong friendship ties. In addition, a number of formal mechanisms reinforce cohesion. For example, various commissions and advisory boards are set up by governments, and members of the economic elite are usually the favoured appointees. Similarly, funding for the establishment political parties comes almost exclusively from wealthy corporate patrons. A 'confraternity of power' is thereby established among the various elite groups.

In Porter's opinion this does not, however, amount to saying that Canada's elites form a ruling class: '[T]he elite groups remain separated and never become merged into one effective power group' (Porter 1965: 215). He emphasized that harmony among elites has limits, as is indicated by the fact that various elite groups come into conflict over a wide range of issues.

A decade later, Clement, a student of Porter, acknowledged the existence of such conflict. But he underscored its limits, not the limits of elite harmony. Clement concluded that Canada's major institutional elites do indeed form a cohesive group that represents the country's capitalist class. This cohesion makes the elites a ruling class. The members of this class are presumably united around the goals of protecting private property, preventing the spread of public sovereignty over economic resources, and preserving continentalism as the dominant Canadian way of life. Yet Clement based this argument largely on the same type of data that Porter used to come to the opposite conclusion, data showing the relatively similar class, ethnic, religious and even family origins of members of different elites; and the effective operation of formal and informal mechanisms that bind together corporate and political elites in particular (Clement 1975: 353, 359; cf. Olsen 1980). Even among those scholars inclined to accord the state greater independence of, or autonomy from, the corporate elite, it was common in the mid–1970s to remark on 'a particularly striking characteristic of the Canadian state – its very close personal ties to the bourgeoisie. Whatever the merits of Poulantzas's contention that the most efficient state is that with the least direct ties to the dominant class, it is a rather academic point as applied to Canada' (Panitch 1977: 11).

This line of reasoning was greatly indebted to Miliband's (1973 [1969]) early work. Miliband portrayed the various institutions that the state comprises – the government, legislature, judicial system, military, police and public bureaucracy – as operating more to the advantage of the capitalist class than of other classes. He emphasized that this bias exists because the capitalist class directly controls state institutions. For example, top officials in all state institutions throughout the western world are recruited substantially from the upper reaches of the capitalist class itself. Therefore, said Miliband, they reflect the class's interests. Similarly, state officials tend to rely on members of the capitalist class for advice in policy formulation and, in the case of political parties, for material support in election campaigns. Thanks to the operation of these and other mechanisms the state allegedly serves as an instrument of the capitalist class's will; hence the school's name.

On the whole, the best available Canadian evidence fails to support this theory. In the first place, there are important political and ideological cleavages between corporate leaders and state officials. Thus, the Liberal Party has been in power for most of the postwar era, yet it has rarely been overwhelmingly supported by the corporate elite, which appears to be largely Tory. Accordingly, survey results show that members of the state elite are significantly less right-wing than corporate leaders (Ornstein 1985; 1986). Second, a systematic analysis of people who held both corporate and state positions at some time between 1946 and 1977 shows that the level of interlocking between corporations and the state was not nearly high enough to suggest corporate domination of the state (Fox and Ornstein 1986). Third, critics of instrumentalism have argued that there is insufficient cohesion and unity of purpose within the capitalist class itself to allow direct rule. In this view, many important political conflicts in Canada reflect, at least in part, cleavages within the capitalist class – between, say, its different ethnic or national segments (notably Québécois versus English-Canadian) or between its different regional components (such as Western versus Ontarian).[6] In sum, then, inter- and intra-elite divisions attest to the disunity of the capitalist class and its inability to rule the state directly and with the stability that would promote its overall best interests.

In light of these perceived shortcomings, many Canadian scholars accepted the ideas of Nicos Poulantzas (1975 [1968]) as an alternative to instrumentalism. Poulantzas's theory of the relationship between the capitalist class and the state is usually referred to as 'structuralism'. This term is derived from Poulantzas's insistence that it is the environing system of socio-economic relations that is responsible for the state serving the long-run interests of the capitalist class as a whole. This system (or structure) allegedly places certain restrictions on the state's freedom of operation. For example, state officials are unlikely to take actions that offend capitalist interest too profoundly for fear of provoking an 'investment strike'. It is restrictions like these, not direct ties between the state and the capitalist class, that, according to Poulantzas, make the state act with its characteristic bias. In order to ensure the persistence of capitalist economic relations state officials may even find it necessary to take actions opposed by one or more powerful segments of the capitalist class. In this sense the state must not be closely tied to, but rather 'relatively autonomous' of, the capitalist class; only thus can it perform its functions efficiently.

The work of Tom Traves (1979) illustrates how this theory has been applied to Canada.[7] Traves sought to explain how the Canadian state came to play a more interventionist and regulatory role in the country's economic life during the period 1917–31. He argued that a variety of competing claims were placed on the state – for and against tariff protection, for and against direct financial assistance, and so forth – by different segments of the capitalist class and by industrial workers and farmers as well. The governments of the day did not heed only the demands of the most powerful subgroups in the capitalist class, nor only the demands of the capitalist class as a whole. Rather, they tried to mediate conflicts by working out compromises and maintaining 'a delicate balance of power between contending classes and interest groups' (Traves 1979: 156).

One might well ask how this analysis differs from the pluralist interpretations favoured by political analysts in the 1950s and 1960s, and now widely held in disrepute. Pluralists, too, thought of the state as performing certain 'brokerage functions' and acting as a mediator of conflict between competing classes and other interest groups. But there is one critical difference between structuralism and pluralism. In the structuralist view, government supposedly assumes 'the burden of perpetuating capitalism itself. In this sense it is not a value-free broker, but rather the protector and promoter of a specific set of rules and social relationships founded upon capitalist property relationships' (Traves 1979: 158).

This may seem like functionalist reasoning, and indeed it is. Structuralists like Traves think that, fundamentally, it is the 'needs' of the socio-economic system which compel state officials to adopt policies that appear to satisfy all interests but actually have the effect of perpetuating existing class relations, and therefore benefiting capitalists more than others.

This, however, introduces a number of serious conceptual and empirical problems, some of which have been raised with reference to functionalist reasoning in general. In the first place, imputing needs to socio-economic systems makes it seem as if these systems have human attributes, including the ability to engage in goal-directed behaviour. Of course, people have needs and goals, and powerful people are often able to convince, pay or force others to act in ways that serve the needs and goals of the powerful. But socio-economic systems do not have needs and goals other than those which people, including entire classes of people, impose on them. A capitalist system's 'need' to perpetuate capitalist class relations is no more that a desire on the part of people who benefit from those relations to see things continue pretty much as they are. The teleological and anthropomorphic tendencies of structuralism obscure this fact.

Second, structuralist logic is circular. According to the structuralists, government policies are functional for the capitalist system, i.e. they have certain salutary consequences for existing class relations. How does one know that a given policy is functional? By virtue of the fact that it was adopted: in the structuralist schema all existing state policies are functional. In other words, policies are enacted because they are functional, and they are functional because they are enacted. One is bound to admit this provides little clarification as to why particular state policies are enacted.

Third, structuralists interpret the introduction of unemployment insurance, public health care, laws recognizing the right of workers to form unions, strike and engage in collective bargaining, and all other reforms associated with the growth of the welfare state as 'fundamentally' irrelevant to the long-term well-being of employees since such reforms merely 'legitimize' the existing social order (e.g. Cuneo 1980: 38). What this wholly ignores, however, is that reformist changes may have a cumulative effect on the distribution of income and, more generally, advantages, in society. Thus, there is considerably less economic inequality in Sweden than in Canada, largely because Sweden has a better developed welfare system that provides universal public daycare and other benefits unknown in Canada. This may indeed increase the longevity of capitalism. But one must remember that this more mature capitalism is not the same capitalism that existed in Dickens' England; and that, as Marx and Engels used to argue, it is at least possible that in the most advanced capitalist societies socialism may evolve gradually through electoral politics (Korpi and Shalev 1980; Korpi 1983; Brym 1987; O'Connor and Brym, 1988).

That these reforms are hard-won suggests a fourth and final criticism of the structuralist viewpoint. By claiming that state policies are automatic responses to the needs of the capitalist system, structuralism plays down the fact that workers and farmers had to fight, in many cases bitterly, in order to have these policies implemented. Structuralists also imply that workers and farmers were gullible or irrational to do so since they were 'fundamentally' just contributing to a legitimizing myth that enabled the process of capital accumulation to continue. It is ironic that some Marxists should minimize the significance of class (and other group) conflict and assume a patronizing attitude towards working people, who, after all, may frequently elect to engage in reformist action because that strategy assures them of more certain benefits and fewer likely costs than other possible strategies.

FROM RELATIVE AUTONOMY TO LEVEL OF INTERVENTION

If one strips away these untenable functionalist assumptions, the idea that the state is relatively autonomous of the capitalist class nevertheless amounts to a very useful insight. It overcomes the major weaknesses of instrumentalism and enables one to portray more accurately· the relationship between capitalist classes and states.[8]

The state's relative autonomy derives partly from the mundane fact that state officials want to keep their jobs. State officials thus have an occupational interest in not offending any class or group to such a degree that their re-election or re-appointment is jeopardized. Remaining somewhat removed from the will of the capitalist class is thus a matter of survival for the political elite.

A second and more profound source of relative autonomy derives from the frequently overlooked fact that state policies and institutions are no more than long-lasting legal resolutions of historically specific conflicts among classes and other groups. Said differently, states are socio-legal structures that reflect the distribution of resources, organization and support – in short, of power – among classes and other groups at given points in time. These structures, once created, usually pattern political life for many years – specifically, until power is massively redistributed, at which time newly manifest conflicts may change them. For example, electoral systems are forged out of conflicts over how effectively different categories of the population will be represented in the state. There seems to be an association between the relative historical strength of the working class in the advanced capitalist countries and the openness of electoral systems to working-class representation (Brym 1987). Significantly, however, electoral systems, once in place, are reformed only infrequently and gradually: despite the massive changes undergone by class structures in the advanced capitalist countries in the twentieth century, there have been no major changes in their electoral systems since the 1920s, and in many cases even earlier (Lipset and Rokkan 1967). The enormous influence of electoral rules on how well different classes and other groups get represented is thus relatively autonomous of current class and other group pressures. Anologous arguments can be made for other state institutions and policies.

The view that state institutions and policies reflect contemporary and historical class and other group conflicts suggests that state autonomy is not a fixed quantity but a variable. That is, states may be more or less autonomous of the capitalist class, and there is an association between degree of autonomy and the distribution of power between super-ordinate and subordinate classes: the lower the ratio of superordinate to subordinate class power, the more autono-mous the state from the capitalist class. Nora Hamilton (1981) has thus shown for the Latin American countries that, all else the same, state autonomy increases as dominant classes become more divided. Similarly, as a considerable body of research emanating mainly from Sweden has established (e.g. Korpi and Shaley 1980; Korpi 1983; cf. Rueschemeyer and Evans 1985), states tend to become more autonomous of the capitalist class as subordinate classes increase their capacity to use the state for their own ends.

This association is clearly evident if one examines variations in the degree to which advanced capitalist states undertake interventionist and redistributive policies that benefit subordin-ate classes. One recent study of seventeen advanced capitalist countries (O'Connor and Brym 1988) demonstrates that the more highly organized working classes are in trade unions, the greater the degree to which (a) left parties gain long-term cabinet participation, and (b) corporatist structures are created for societal-level tripartite bargaining among unions, capitalist umbrella organizations, and the state. In turn, the establishment of mechanisms for societal-level bargaining is associated with increased state intervention as reflected in more welfare spending.[9] In other words, taking most of the advanced capitalist countries into account, it appears that the more powerful working classes are relative to capitalist classes, the greater their capacity to cause the state to undertake redistributive initiatives. This capacity is, however, significantly mediated by the structure of state institutions.

The Canadian case illustrates the point well. In 1980 Canada ranked twelfth among seventeen OECD countries in level of welfare spending. This low rank may be attributed to three sets of factors. First, the Canadian capitalist class is relatively powerful: by international standards, the economy is highly oligopolized and corporate interlocking among top capitalists is relatively dense (Ornstein 1989). Second, the Canadian working class is comparatively weak: its level of unionization places it at the low end among OECD countries, and no left party has ever been represented in a Canadian federal cabinet. Third, tripartite societal-level bargaining is minimal in Canada: the country's relatively weak working class and its decentralized federal structure have inhibited unitary state action. For these reasons, the Canadian state is less autonomous of the capitalist class and less interventionist and redistributive than most states in Western Europe (Cameron 1986; Panitch 1986; Banting 1987; Brym 1987; O'Connor and Brym 1988).[10]

Of course, power relations between superordinate and subordinate classes in Canada have fluctuated over time. In concluding, I shall outline how increasing working-class power between 1945 and 1981, and subsequent capitalist class reaction to working-class gains, have influenced Canadian state policy.

The augmentation of working-class power between the end of the Second World War and the 1981–82 recession derived from the increasing unionization, militancy and prosperity of the non-agriculural labour force. During this period the proportion of unionized workers in the non-agricultural labour force doubled, reaching nearly 40 per cent in the early

1980s. Strikes became an increasingly popular means by which workers expressed discontent – to the point where in the 1970s Canada lost more time due to strikes per 1000 workers than any other country in the world. Moreover, this was an era of unprecedented economic expansion. As Canada–US trade and investment grew, Canadians prospered from their close relationship with the world's wealthiest, hegemonic power.

Propitious fiscal conditions, combined with mounting pressure from below, encouraged the expansion of health and education services, unemployment insurance and regional development programmes, and so forth. In the 1970s, state automony and intervention in the economy reached a stage where the Liberal government of Pierre Trudeau began adopting policies aimed at increasing Canadian autarky. The Foreign Investment Review Act set up mechanisms to screen and inhibit takeovers of Canadian companies by foreign multinationals. The National Energy Programme greatly increased Canadian ownership in the important oil and gas industry. An expanded economic role was sought for Crown Corporations.

Not surprisingly, the most powerful Canadian capitalists were increasingly troubled by these developments. In order to help reduce the growing autonomy of the state they formed the Business Council on National Issues in 1976 (Langille 1987). Composed of the chief executive officers of the 150 leading multinational corporations operating in Canada, the BCNI has lobbied diligently and effectively for less government intervention in the economy, a smaller welfare state, free trade with the US and wage restraint.

Heightened international competition in an era of global industrial restructuring rendered BCNI demands more urgent and compelling, and the 1984 election of a Conservative government under Brian Mulroney facilitated the implementation of the BCNI programme. Since 1984, some Crown Corporations have been privatized. The Foreign Investment Review Act and the National Energy Programme have been scrapped. A government assault on the right of public sector workers to strike began as early as 1982 (Panitch and Swartz 1985). But the most momentous development of the decade was the signing of a free trade agreement with the US in January 1988.

Fully 30 per cent of Canada's GNP derives from international trade, and 80 per cent of Canada's international trade is with the US. In the mid-1980s, however, this trade was threatened by US protectionism. Faced with an overvalued dollar, a growing trade deficit and the prospect of increasing unemployment, the US administration restricted imports of Canadian steel, pork, beef, fish, potatoes and softwood lumber. The senior executives of companies that rely on access to US markets – the largest companies in Canada – felt that mounting American economic nationalism could eventually ruin their businesses. As a result, they became the foremost proponents of free trade.

It seems likely that if the 1988 free trade agreement is fully implemented it will help Canadian industry become more efficient and competitive. On the other hand, for Canadian workers, this could very well involve wage concessions and the erosion of welfare state programmes. After all, under free trade, unionized Canadian workers would have to compete against non-unionized workers in the American Sunbelt (who earn less than half the Canadian wage) and in the Maquiladora free trade zone of northern Mexico (who earn one-twentieth the Canadian wage).[11] In that sort of competitive environment, Canadian workers could hardly be expected to maintain the living standards they achieved in the 1970s.

Recent public opinion polls reflect widespread concern over these developments. The free trade issue has become the top public problem worrying Canadians, and while three-quarters of the population thought free trade was a good step for Canada in 1985, fewer than half thought so just before the November 1988 election. Opposition to free trade was insufficient to unseat the ruling Conservatives in 1988. Most commentators agree, however, that the free trade controversy led to more politicized class conflict than Canada has ever seen and modest gains for the country's social democratic party. In 1988 the Canadian capitalist class could claim a series of victories stretching back the better part of a decade and culminating in the free trade deal. None the less, the dimensions that the free trade deal will eventually assume are unclear because of the heightened confrontation between big business and organized labour.

NOTES

* This is a revised version of Brym (1985). The permission of Garamond Press to reprint material is gratefully acknowledged. I would also like to thank Michael Ornstein for helpful comments on a draft of this chapter.
1. An early work in the muckraking style (Myers 1972 [1914]), a Leninist intepretation (Park and Park 1973 [1962]), and a widely acclaimed academic elite study in the tradition of C. Wright Mills (Porter 1965) are especially noteworthy.
2. Jorge Niosi (1978: 14-67; 1981 [1980] 5-10; 1983: 135) argues that this last point cannot be taken to mean that the banks actually control industry. For the contrary view, see Carroll (1986).
3. Ornstein's (1976) finding that the foreign-controlled corporations have fewer directorship ties than Canadian-controlled corporations also casts doubt on the view that foreign-controlled corporations occupy a central position in the Canadian economy. See also Richardson's (1988) analysis of the rise of the Canadian trust industry and its integration into several dominant Canadian conglomerates. Hammer and Gartrell (1986) provide one of the few recent analyses that appear to support dependency theory. They show that American direct investment in Canada has a negative effect on Canadian GNP growth after a nine-year lag. However, they fail to control for a number of important determinants of GNP growth, such as international demand for raw materials and domestic demand for consumer goods and housing. My suspicion is that the posited association would turn out to be spurious if these and other relevant controls were introduced.
4. Canadian multinationals have some unique features. It is often held that multinationals are (a) members of technologically innovative oligopolies in industrialized countries, or (b) large companies in semi-industrialized countries that purchase and improve technological innovations originating in industrialized countries for use in unindustrialized countries. However, Canadian multinationals are not technologically innovative and 80 per cent of their investments are in the most industrialized counties. Niosi (1985: 172) explains the Canadian anomaly as follows: '[B]ecause technology markets are highly imperfect, because Canada is so close geographically, culturally and commercially to the United States and Britain, and because Canadian multinationals enjoy the advantage of large size, considerable resources and oligopoly control of a substantial market, these multinationals are probably among the world's fastest "followers". As soon as innovations are in commercial use elsewhere, Canadian multinationals can get their hands on these innovations. . . .'
5. Porter (1965) and Clement (1975) exaggerated the degree to which members of the corporate elite are recruited from upper- and upper-middle-class origins. Moreover, since their studies were conducted, significant numbers of non-WASPs have entered the ranks of the corporate elite. See Brym (1986: 79-80, 89, 93-4) for an analysis of the evidence.

6. For a general statement linking national disunity to regional fissures in the bourgeoisie, see Stevenson (1982). On the Quebec case, see especially Fournier (1978 [1976]), Niosi (1979) and Sales (1985).
7. See also Craven (1980) and, for a perceptive if harsh critique, from which the following discussion has profited, van den Berg and Smith (1981).
8. The following discussion draws on Alford and Friedland (1985), Esping-Anderson, Friedland and Wright (1976), Evans, Rueschemeyer and Skocpol (1985), and Skocpol (1980).
9. Welfare spending is here broadly defined as total non-military public expenditure. The seventeen countries in this study include Denmark, the Federal Republic of Germany, Austria, Belgium, Ireland, UK, France, Italy, Holland, Norway, Sweden, New Zealand, Australia, Switzerland, Finland, Canada and USA.
10. On the other hand, the openness of the Canadian economy – the relatively high value of exports compared to GNP – has encouraged the expansion of the public sector. Through spending, government has sought to mitigate the consequences of troughs in the business cycle and secular increases in unemployment, both of which are related to Canada's vulnerability to the volatile and deteriorating American economy. Other causes of public sector expansion include the effects of wars (which require increased state coordination and spending), the occurrence of federal elections (governments seek to stimulate the economy before elections) and the identity of the prime minister (although not the identity of the party in power). For a valuable discussion of these factors, see Cameron (1986).
11. Maquiladora industries represent the second largest and fastest-growing economic sector in Mexico. The 1200 US factories in the zone employ 300,000 mainly teenage workers at about 65 cents an hour. About 40 per cent of manufactured goods imported by the US now come from Mexico. As a Texas senator recently stated: 'The progress of the Maquiladora plants keeps the United States competitive with the Far East' (quoted in Saul 1987).

REFERENCES

Alford, Robert R. and Roger Friedland (1985) *Powers of Theory: Capitalism, the State, and Democracy* (Cambridge: Cambridge University Press).

Banting, Keith G. (1987) 'The welfare state and inequality in the 1980s', *Canadian Review of Sociology and Anthropology* (24), 309–38.

Black, Don and John Myles (1986) 'Dependent industrialization and the Canadian class structure: a comparative analysis', *Canadian Review of Sociology and Anthropology* (23), 157–81.

'Border exchanges' (1987) *Toronto Globe and Mail* (21 March), D6.

Britton, John and James Gilmour (1978) *The Weakest Link: a Technological*

Perspective on Canadian Industrial Development (Ottawa: The Science Council of Canada).

Brym, Robert J. (1985) 'The Canadian capitalist class, 1965–85', in R. Brym (ed.) *The Structure of the Canadian Capitalist Class* (Toronto: Garamond), 1–20.

Brym, Robert J. (1986) 'Anglo-Canadian sociology', *Current Sociology* (34, 1), 1–152.

Brym, Robert J. (1987) 'Incoporation versus power models of working class radicalism: with special reference to North America', in W. Outhwaite and M. Mulkay (eds) *Social Theory and Social Criticism: Essays for Tom Bottomore* (Oxford: Basil Blackwell), 204–29.

Cameron, D. R. (1986) 'The growth of government spending: the Canadian experience in comparative perspective', in K. Banting (ed.) *State and Society: Canada in Comparative Perspective* (Toronto: University of Toronto Press), 21–51.

Carroll, William (1982) 'The Canadian corporate elite: financiers or finance capitalists?', *Studies in Political Economy* (8), 89–114.

Carroll, William K., John Fox and Michael D. Ornstein (1982) 'The network of directorate interlocks among the largest Canadian firms', *Canadian Review of Sociology and Anthropology* (19), 44–69.

Carroll, William K. (1984) 'The individual, class, and corporate power in Canada', *Canadian Journal of Sociology* (9), 245–68.

Carroll, William K. (1986) *Corporate Power and Canadian Capitalism* (Vancouver: University of British Columbia Press).

Clement, Wallace (1975) *The Canadian Corporate Elite: An Analysis of Economic Power* (Toronto: McClelland and Stewart).

Clement, Wallace (1977) *Continental Corporate Power: Economic Linkages between Canada and the United States* (Toronto: McClelland and Stewart).

Craven, Paul (1980) '*An Impartial Umpire: Industrial Relations and the Canadian State, 1900–1911* (Toronto: University of Toronto Press).

Cuneo, Carl J. (1980) 'State mediation of class contradictions in Canadian unemployment insurance, 1930–1935', *Studies in Political Economy* (3), 37–65.

Esping-Anderson, Gosta, Roger Friedland and Erik Olin Wright (1976) 'Modes of class struggle and the capitalist state', *Kapitalistate* (4–5), 186–220.

Evans, Peter B., Dietrich Rueschemeyer and Theda Skocpol (eds) (1985) *Bringing the State Back in* (Cambridge: Cambridge University Press).

Fournier, Pierre (1978 [1976]) *The Quebec Establishment: the Ruling Class and the State*, 2nd rev. edn (Montreal: Black Rose).

Fox, John and Michael Ornstein (1986) 'The Canadian state and corporate elites in the post-war period', *Canadian Review of Sociology and Anthropology* (23), 481–506.

Frank, André Gunder (1969) *Latin America: Underdevelopment or Revolution* (New York: Monthly Review).

Friedmann, Harriet and Jack Wayne (1977) 'Dependency theory: a critique', *Canadian Journal of Sociology* (2), 399–416.

204   *The Capitalist Class: An International Study*

Hamilton, Nora (1981) 'State autonomy and dependent capitalism in Latin America', *British Journal of Sociology* (32), 305–29.

Hammer, Heather-Jo and John W. Gartrell (1986) 'American penetration and Canadian development: a case study of mature dependency', *American Sociological Review* (51), 201–13

Kealey, Gregory (1980) *Toronto Workers Respond to Industrialism, 1867–1892* (Toronto: University of Toronto Press).

Korpi, Walter (1983) *The Democratic Class Struggle* (London: Routledge and Kegan Paul).

Korpi, Walter and Michael Shalev (1980) 'Strikes, power, and politics in the Western nations', *Political Power and Social Theory* (1), 301–34.

Langille, David (1987) 'The Business Council on National Issues and the Canadian state', *Studies in Political Economy* (24), 41–85.

Laxer, Gordon (1983) 'Foreign ownership and myths about Canadian development', Working Paper 50, Structural Analysis Programme, Department of Sociology, University of Toronto (Toronto).

Laxer, Gordon (1985a) 'The political economy of aborted development: the Canadian case', in R. Brym (ed.) *The Structure of the Canadian Capitalist Class* (Toronto: Garamond), 67–102.

Laxer, Gordon (1985b) 'Foreign ownership and myths about Canadian development', *Canadian Review of Sociology and Anthropology* (22), 311–45.

Laxer, Jim (1973) 'Introduction to the political economy of Canada', in R. Laxer (ed.) *(Canada) Ltd: The Political Economy of Dependency* (Toronto: McClelland and Stewart), 26–41.

Levitt, Kari (1970) *Silent Surrender: The Multinational Corporation in Canada* (Toronto: Macmillan of Canada).

Lipset, Seymour Martin and Stein Rokkan (1967) 'Cleavage structures, party systems, and voter alignments: an introduction', in S. Lipset and S. Rokkan (eds) *Party Systems and Voter Alignments: Cross-National Perspectives* (New York: Free Press), 1–64.

Macdonald, L. R. (1975) 'Merchants against industry: an idea and its origins', *Canadian Historical Review* (56), 263–81.

Miliband, Ralph (1973 [1969]) *The State in Capitalist Society* (London: Quartet).

Moore, Steve and Debi Wells (1975) *Imperialism and The National Question in Canada* (Toronto: privately published).

Myers, Gustavus (1972 [1914]) *A History of Canadian Wealth* (Toronto: James Lewis & Samuel Ltd).

Naylor, Tom (1972) 'The rise and fall of the third commercial empire of the St. Lawrence', in G. Teeple (ed.) *Capitalism and the National Question in Canada* (Toronto: University of Toronto Press), 1–41.

Naylor, Tom (1975) *The History of Canadian Business, 1867–1914*, 2 vols (Toronto: James Lorimer).

Niosi, Jorge (1978) *The Economy of Canada: A Study of Ownership and Control*, trans. P. Williams and H. Ballem (Montreal: Black Rose Books).

Niosi, Jorge (1979) 'The new French-Canadian bourgeoisie', *Studies in Political Economy* (1), 113–61.

Niosi, Jorge (1981 [1980]) *Canadian Capitalism: A Study of Power in the Canadian Business Establishment*, trans. R. Chodos (Toronto: James Lorimer and Co.).

Niosi, Jorge (1982) 'The Canadian multinationals', *Multinational Business* (2), 24–33.

Niosi, Jorge (1983) 'The Canadian bourgeoisie: towards a synthetical approach', *Canadian Journal of Political and Social Theory* (7), 128–49.

Niosi, Jorge (1985) *Canadian Multinationals*, trans. R. Chodos (Toronto: Garamond).

O'Connor, Julia S. and Robert J. Brym (1988) 'Public welfare expenditure in O.E.C.D. countries: towards a reconciliation of inconsistent findings', *British Journal of Sociology* (39), 47–68.

Olsen, Dennis (1980) *The State Elite* (Toronto: McClelland and Stewart).

Ornstein, Michael D. (1976) 'The boards and executives of the largest Canadian corporations: size, composition, and interlocks', *Canadian Journal of Sociology* (1), 411–36.

Ornstein, Michael (1985) 'Canadian capital and the Canadian state: ideology in an era of crisis', in R. Brym (ed.) *The Structure of the Canadian Capitalist Class* (Toronto: Garamond), 129–66.

Ornstein, Michael (1986) 'The political ideology of the Canadian capitalist class', *Canadian Review of Sociology and Anthropology* (23), 182–209.

Ornstein, Michael (1989) 'The social organization of the Canadian capitalist class in comparative perspective', *Canadian Review of Sociology and Anthropology* (26).

Panitch, Leo (1977) 'The role and nature of the Canadian state', in L. Panitch (ed.) *The Canadian State: Political Economy and Political Power* (Toronto: University of Toronto Press), 3–27.

Panitch, Leo (1986) 'The tripartite experience', in K. Banting (ed.) *The State and Economic Interests* (Toronto: University of Toronto Press), 37–119.

Panitch, Leo and Donald Swartz (1985) *From Consent to Coercion: The Assault on Trade Union Freedoms* (Toronto: Garamond).

Park, Libbie and Frank Park (1973 [1962]) *Anatomy of Big Business* (Toronto: James Lewis & Samuel).

Porter, John (1965) *The Vertical Mosaic: An Analysis of Social Class and Power in Canada* (Toronto: University of Toronto Press).

Portes, Alejandro and John Walton (1981) *Labor, Class, and the International System* (New York: Academic Press).

Poulantzas, Nicos (1975 [1968]) *Political Power and Social Classes*, trans. T. O'Hagan (London: New Left Books).

Richardson, R. J. (1982) ' "Merchants against industry": an empirical study of the Canadian debate', *Canadian Journal of Sociology* (7), 279-95.

Richardson, R. J. (1988) ' "A sacred trust": the trust industry and Canadian economic structure', *Canadian Review of Sociology and Anthropology* (25), 1–22.

Rueschemeyer, Dietrich and Peter B. Evans (1985) 'The state and economic transformation: toward an analysis of the conditions underlying effective intervention', in P. Evans, D. Rueschemeyer and T. Skocpol (eds) *Bringing the State Back in* (Cambridge: Cambridge University Press), 44–77.

Ryerson, Stanley (1973 [1968]) *Unequal Union: Roots of Crisis in the Canadas, 1815–1973* (Toronto: Progress Books).

Ryerson, Stanley (1976) 'Who's looking after business?', *This Magazine* (10, 5), 41-6.

Sales, Arnaud (1985) 'La construction sociale de l'économie québécoise', *Recherches Sociographiques* (26, 3), 319–60.

Saul, John Ralston (1987) 'A gaping hole in free trade', *Toronto Globe and Mail* (25 November), A7.

Skocpol, Theda (1980) 'Political response to capitalist crisis: neo-Marxist theories of the state and the case of the New Deal', *Politics and Society* (10), 155–201.

Stevenson, Garth (1982) *Unfulfilled Union: Canadian Federalism and National Unity*, rev. edn. (Toronto: McClelland and Stewart).

Traves, Tom (1979) *The State and Enterprise: Canadian Manufacturers and the Federal Government, 1917–1931* (Toronto: University of Toronto Press).

Urquhart, John (1984) 'Canada's government proposes easing limits on foreigners' investment in nation', *Wall Street Journal* (10 December), 53.

US Department of Commerce (1986) *Statistical Abstract of the United States*, 107th edn (Washington).

van den Berg, Axel and Michael Smith (1981) 'The Marxist theory of the state in practice', *Canadian Journal of Sociology* (6), 505-19.

Walkom, Thomas (1986) 'G-7 will pull purse strings around globe', *Toronto Globe and Mail* (7 May), A1-A2.

Williams, Glen (1983) *Not for Export: Towards a Political Economy of Canada's Arrested Industrialization* (Toronto: McClelland and Stewart).

8 United States of America

Beth Mintz

Contemporary investigations of the internal structure of the capitalist class in the US typically concentrate on one organizing question: are there mechanisms for cohesion capable of transforming a series of important actors into a unified social class? Beginning with the corporate elite as the defining category, recent work has attempted to evaluate the potential for coordinated action within this group based on shared economic interests and a set of common experiences and value systems. Much evidence has been uncovered in the United States example to demonstrate shared backgrounds and overlapping social and institutional networks. More problematic, however, is the ability to transform these similarities into a coherent strategy of class action.

While the issue of cohesion has taken precedence in recent years, an earlier theoretical development – the separation of ownership and control controversy – laid the foundation for the present research agenda. Formalized most importantly by Berle and Means in their publication *The Modern Corporation and Private Property* (1932), the argument that control of the large corporation had passed from owners to non-propertied managers suggested a fundamental alteration of the contours of capitalism. Subsequent managerialists developed this point, concluding that the ascendance of a hired management stratum would change both the behaviour and the ideology of the business enterprise with more attention to social responsibility and the development of what Kaysen (1957) has referred to as the 'soulful corporation'.

The implications of this argument are important; it suggests that the capitalist class has been replaced. As Bell (1961) asserts, 'family capitalism gave way to social mobility' (p. 43) and 'technical skill rather than property and political position rather than wealth have become the basis on which power is wielded' (p. 45).

Managerialism has inspired a large number of empirical studies designed to test and modify the assumptions of the theory. One strand has attempted to measure the proportion of large American companies with sufficiently dispersed stock ownership to be under management control, and while there is still much controversy about the exact numbers of corporations which can be thus classified, there is general agreement that the trend exists.[1]

The implications for the breakdown of capitalism, however, are much less clear-cut and a major dissenting viewpoint suggests that owners and managers are different segments of the same class. Baran and Sweezy (1966), for example, argue that 'managers are among the biggest owners. And because of the strategic positions they occupy, they function as the protectors and spokesmen for all large-scale property' (p. 35). Similarly, Miliband (1969) suggests that any identifiable differences between owners and managers 'are overshadowed by a basic community of interests' (p. 35).

Evidence consistent with this response falls into three main categories which will be explored below. At present we point out that most studies have followed this lead and the capitalist class is typically defined in terms of both managerial and ownership functions; as an overlapping system based on institutional position and property relations.[2] Recent literature on the structure of the capitalist class in the United States, then, has incorporated the ongoing separation of ownership and control into the analysis while maintaining the importance of the capitalist class. Many, to quote Zeitlin (1980), view corporations as 'units in a class controlled apparatus of private appropriation' (p. 10). This has resulted in the corporate world becoming a more and more common focus of investigations of the capitalist class.

This does not, however, speak to all elements of the managerial challenge to a class analysis of the structure of power in the United States. Continued stock dispersion, and the accompanying concentration of decision-making authority in the hands of inside managers, suggest the development of a system of autonomous corporations impervious to inter-organizational coordination. While class-based analyses had assumed coordinated action based on the stock ownership of multiple firms by dominant capitalist families or overt intervention by the financial community, the separation of ownership and control undermined these mechanisms.[3] And given the various dimensions along which capitalist interest might diverge, the issue of cohesion has become pivotal. This chapter reflects this emphasis. Implicit in our analysis of the organization of the capitalist class in the United States is the question of cleavage versus cohesion; of mechanisms capable of transforming autonomous actors into a unified social class. We begin with an investigation of the social composition of this grouping and we trace the link between this literature and the question of elite cohesion.

PATTERNS OF RECRUITMENT: THE SOCIAL COMPOSITION OF THE CAPITALIST CLASS

E. Digby Baltzell captured both the social composition of the upper class of the United States and their positional importance in the title of his book, *The Protestant Establishment* (1964). Consistent with the sketch drawn by C. Wright Mills (1956), Baltzell identified a narrow, homo-geneous grouping as major power-wielders. Domhoff (1967; 1970; 1983) fills in the details with the most developed portrait of the upper class to date. Drawing on this literature, we see that typical members are very wealthy, white, male Protestants who are listed in the *Social Register*, attended elite prep schools and Ivy League universities, belong to at least one and often several elite social clubs and share a life-style and value-system learned in these exclusive schools and shared environments. Characterized by a tendency towards inter-marriage, the group reproduces itself and seems to be self-perpetuating. although one of the areas not well studied is the role of kinship networks in solidifying these relationships (Zeitlin 1974; Zeitlin et al. 1974; Useem 1980). Further, the wealth of the contemporary upper class is rooted in the corporate world making the modern corporation an important component in investigations of elite cohesion.

Although women comprise approximately half of the upper class, their participation within the capitalist class is severely limited. And while the literature on their precise role is quite sparse, two conclusions may be drawn. First, the typical role of women in this grouping is integrative: both within the family and within the larger community women contribute to the maintenance of the position of the larger class (Ostrander 1979–80). Second, when women participate in the management of major coporations, they are usually in secondary roles. And, unlike their male counterparts, women are rarely recruited into the capitalist class from the corporate community (Ghiloni 1984).

At the same time the American upper class *does* assimilate new members, admitting recruits into the social institutions which facilitate cohesion and the income brackets which serve to transform an elite stratum into a capitalist class. Recruitment is typically via the corporate community where bright, young, male executives with proper educational credentials are groomed for membership and invited to participate in the world of elite social clubs. Ascension is solidified as these entrants acquire the financial resources which place them among the propertied and as they marry into the upper class, sending their children to the right schools where appropriate contact networks and value systems are developed. Although evidence suggest that the group remains extremely homogeneous in regard to ethnicity, recent work has found some broadening as illustrated by the slow, but ongoing, integration of Jews into the highest reaches (Zweigenhaft 1979–1980; Zweigenhaft and Domhoff 1982).

Although data on the approximate distribution of old versus new members at a given time are very sketchy, the typical method for evaluating the degree of mobility into the upper echelon is through investigations of the social backgrounds of high level corporate executives. Domhoff (1983: 68) summarizes this literature with an approximate figure of 30 per cent of the corporate elite with upper-class origins. This can be interpreted in various ways. On the one hand, these figures underscore the disproportionate participation of the upper class in corporate affairs. Given that this stratum is estimated at about ½ per cent of the population, the 30 per cent is quite striking (Domhoff 1983: 18). On the other hand, these figures also point to the limitations implicit in a definition which equates the capitalist class with the corporate elite. That 70 per cent of corporate executives are not upper class in origin emphasizes the differences between a corporate elite and an upper class. This problem is consistent with the point made by Allen (1976: 893) when he argued that the aggregation of managers and stockholders into an amorphous capitalist class may well obscure many crucial questions about elite organizations.

To address this problem, research into the internal differentiation of the capitalist class has become more and more important. The concept of the power elite has been used by Domhoff (1970; 1983) – and of course by C. Wright Mills (1956) – to explore the leadership arm of the upper class. Useem focuses on the 'inner circle' in this regard. Thus, while the emphasis on the social composition of the capitalist class addresses a fundamental issue by arguing that cohesion is generated through shared value-systems maintained and reinforced by an interrelated set of social and institutional relationships, this literature feeds directly into a related set of questions: What are the major lines of cleavage within the group, and do some or all of these cleavages generate differences in interests which ultimately remain too broad to be bridged by shared values and overlapping networks?

COHESION AND CLEAVAGE

Over the years a wide assortment of potential lines of division within the elite have been suggested and while some of these have not been supported by systematic evidence, others raise serious questions about the possibility of transforming individual members into a unified capitalist class. Important splits have been posited along many dimensions: liberal vs. conservative elements (Weinstein 1968); finance vs. industrial capitalists (Hilferding 1910; Fitch and Oppenheimer 1970);

national vs. regional orientations (Bearden and Mintz 1984; Palmer et al. 1986); elite vs. non-elite segments (Domhoff 1970, 1983; Soref 1976; Useem 1984); Yankees vs. cowboys (Sale 1975); steel vs. auto (Mintz and Schwartz 1981); large vs. medium firms (Useem 1980) and managers vs. major stockholders (Berle and Means 1932) to identify a few. And while some of these divisions are based on social criteria, others suggest divergent economic interest. Still others, of course, merge the two.

When potential differences are located in the corporate community and revolve around sectoral competition – conflicts of interest among different industries – or disagreements over strategy of maximizing profits, for example, one important mechanism for mediation is the policy planning process. Discussed in detail by Domhoff (1970, 1979, 1983), this included a small number of policy planning groups which function as a debating ground for airing differences and outlining strategy options. Included among the most important are the Council on Foreign Relations, The Committee for Economic Development, and The Conference Board, all of which provide a vehicle for conflict resolution. And while compromise is not found on all issues, research has suggested that these organizations often are an effective vehicle for cohesion formation.

Not all differences are rooted in sector conflicts, of course. A particularly fundamental split within the elite is the presumed divergence between corporate owners and hired managers discussed above in relation to the separation of ownership and control controversy. In response to the managerial argument that non-propertied executives are guiding the modern corporation in directions inconsistent with the interests of the ownership class, much data have been collected which demonstrate that managers are, in fact, large stockholders (Mills 1956; Villarejo 1961; Domhoff 1967, 1970, 1983) and therefore members of the capitalist class. And in addition to the shared value-systems discussed above, managers and owners have been found to pursue similar profit-seeking strategies (Kamerschen 1968; Hindley 1970; Larner 1970; Norich 1976; Zeitlin and Norich 1979) suggesting that the behavioural implications of the separation of ownership and control are overstated.[4]

Nevertheless, while this evidence addresses some of the possible differences between the two groups, questions about the degree of cohesion remain and a particularly interesting approach to the issue is presented by Useem (1982, 1984). Arguing for the primacy of neither corporate credentials nor upper-class origins, he suggests the merging of interests into a broader class-wide principle based on the overarching needs of both segments (1984: 14). Termed the inner circle, and including only a small subset of business leaders, this vanguard plays a crucial integrating role by supplying coherence and direction to the business world, emphasizing the interests of the larger corporate community (Useem, 1984: 3).

Note that inner circle members incorporate many of the characteristics emphasized in the social background literature of Baltzell (1964) and others: they belong to the same circle of elite social clubs; many have attended the most prestigious prep schools; and they are enmeshed in a system of friendship and acquaintance networks which lend coherence to the group. At the same time, corporate prominence is key. These individuals sit on the boards of directors of two or more major corporations; they are typically large stockholders and are members of the most important business associations. When these threads are merged, inner circle members embody both class and organizational concerns, and the class-wide perspective which emerges is an effective organizing element within the elite.

Useem's argument, then, speaks to potential splits between owners and managers by identifying the most active segment of the group and demonstrating their place as both owners and managers. More important than their individual characteristics, however, Useem sees an overlapping set of networks and organizations as the institutional apparatus of the inner circle. And in addition to differences between owners and managers, these individuals can mediate between company or industry differences, regional loyalties and other splits argued to prevent the consolidation of the corporate elite into a unified capitalist class.

The Network of Interlocking Directorates

While Useem addressed class and organizational variables simultaneously, a complementary theme in the investigation of the capitalist class has emphasized the corporation as the unit of analysis. Central to many of these studies is the same question of cohesion: what are the identifiable divisions within the corporate community and what are the potential mechanisms for mediating among different segments?

Most popular in this regard are investigations of interlocking directorates, a field which has a long history and a literature which has expanded greatly within the last decade.[5] Rooted in government investigations dating back to the early part of the twentieth century, the study of corporate interlocks has developed from a focus on dyadic relations – which types of relationship between two corporations are reflected by a shared director? – to an emphasis on corporate structure – what do the patterns of corporate interlocks reveal about the overall dynamics of corporate interaction? And while two traditions have developed – resource dependency theory which views interlocks as mechanisms through which organizations attempt to control uncertainties in their environments (Allen 1974; Burt 1979; 1980; 1983; Pennings 1980) and a power structure perspective, which uses the corporate community to investigate the organization of the the capitalist class (Koenig et al. 1979; Ratcliff 1979–80; 1980a; 1980b; Gogel and Koenig 1981; Mintz and Schwartz 1981b; Mizruchi 1982; Roy 1983a; 1983b; Palmer 1983a), two consistent results have been identified: commercial banks play a very particular role within the system (Allen 1974; Bearden et al. 1975; Mariolis 1975; Mintz and Schwartz 1985) and the business world contains pockets characterized by regional organization (Dooley 1969; Songquist and Koenig 1975; Allen 1978; Bearden and Mintz 1984). We begin with a discussion of financial prominence within the system.

The unique position of commercial banks has gained much attention because it speaks to a theoretical debate about capitalist fragmentation dating back to the arguments of Hilferding (1910) and Lenin (1917) about the structure of financial–industrial relations. Lenin, in particular, posited bank domination of industrial corporations and over the years this argument developed into a theory of bank control.[6] This asserts that through such mechanisms as stock ownership, long-term and short-term debt instruments, control of pension funds and trust accounts, financial institutions have the power to control non-financial corporations (Fitch and Oppenheimer 1970; Kotz 1978). Moreover this theory, especially in its earlier days, viewed the corporate community as organized into a number of competing interest groups, the internal structure of which were dominated by the financial institution at the centre. Group vs. individual profits were maximized, this emphasizing the interests of the financial at the expense of the other companies.

Baran and Sweezy (1966) describe these groups as a 'number of corporations under common control, the locus of power being normally an investment or commercial bank or a great family fortune' (p. 17). Note that while this definition includes capitalist families as coordinating mechanisms, research on interest groups usually concentrates on bank-centred groupings since this is most consistent with Lenin's position; it also points to the success of the managerial paradigm in defining family stockholding as unimportant in corporate affairs. Note also that implicit in the interest-group notion are two lines of potential cleavage. In addition to the coercion thought to be practised over industrial corporations by banks, different interest groups are seen as in competition. Thus, fragmentation within the business world parallels financial–industrial divisions as well as interest-group formation and potentially reflects both inter-group and intra-group conflict.

Over the years a handful of investigations of corporate structure have studied the interest-group idea and, while initially a good deal of support was generated for the notion of financial-centred groupings, disagreement emerged over the extent to which these collections were characterized by internal conflict and coercion.[7] More recently, the structure of inter-corporate relations appears to have changed and, today, little evidence remains in support of the interest group idea (Mintz and Schwartz 1983; Mariolis 1984; Bearden and Mintz 1984). However, one feature still points to the possibility of financial–non-financial cleavages: the continued prominence of financial institutions within the interlock network. And while this result is consistent with bank control theory, a more recent perspective – financial hegemony – has developed to address these findings.

Building on Gramsci's (1971) work on ideological hegemony and applied to the structure of class relations by Koenig et al. (1979), Michael Schwartz and I (Mintz and Schwartz, 1985) argue that a financial–non-financial cleavage characterizes the corporate world; that this cleavage is based on an indirect domination of non-financial corporations by a unified financial sector; that this is the most important line of division within the system; and that, at the same time, this long-term dominance lends an order to inter-corporate relations unavailable through any other mechanism. The theory of financial hegemony, then, posits both cleavage and cohesion and attributes both to the role of financial institutions which simultaneously dominate and unify.

The source of power is control over capital flows, a control resulting from the concentration of capital in the hands of a limited number of major commercial banks and insurance companies whose structural position within the system produces a commonality of interest. The source of unity is identical; the need for capital is so important to contemporary industry that its availability often determines the future of a company or a sector. Rather than the direct intervention into the decision-making process of the modern corporation posited by bank control theory, finance hegemony views capital flow decisions as affecting the environment within which the firm operates, and thus these decisions constrain the actions of corporations producing a broad coordination within the business community. The looseness of the process does not undermine the overall result of inter-corporate unity although individual corporate response to capital constraint may be disruptive to the larger system. In the long run, however, capital flow decisions provide centralized planning, and this planning mediates among different interests thus providing an overriding source of unity within the system.

Thus, the theory of financial hegemony argues that bank prominence within the system of interlocking directorates reflects the centralized role of financial institutions within the business world, and that this role serves to unify rather than divide. At the same time, finance hegemony incorporates the second set of consistent findings found in the interlock literature: traces of regional organization.

Dooley's (1969) work on the structure of interlocking directorates identified a change in the composition of corporate interaction patterns. Rather than the interest groups found in earlier studies, the more recent network of director exchanges exhibited a marked tendency for corporations to interlock with firms located in the same geographical area. While these groups were still characterized by financial prominence – commercial banks or life insurance companies occupied central positions within each grouping – the regional character suggested a different set of divisions within the system. Regional organization joined financial–non-financial differences as potential cleavage points within the system. Subsequent work confirmed this pattern. Sonquist and Koenig (1975) found a series of geographically-defined cliques in their interlock analysis; Allen's (1978) study of interest group formation underscored the regional character of the groupings.

These regional groups did contain suggestions of coordination, however, and it is again financial institutions which play a role in this capacity. Sonquist and Koenig (1975) identified a series of corporations which functioned as liaisons between cliques and more that half of these firms were financial institutions. Schwartz and I (Mintz and Schwartz, 1985) found a similar structure in our interlock analysis and indentified a division of labour within the system. Distinguishing between New York money market commercial banks, regional banks and national insurance companies, this again posits a system in which financial institutions simultaneously divide and unite. At the local level the largest regional banks are in the centre of dense pockets of interlocking. These densely interlocked groups are connected to the larger money market banks by a series of bridging links created by the country's largest insurance companies. The regional orientation is thus organized by the local banks whose interests are rooted in the local economic environment and whose position in the interlock network reflects its role in local capital allocation. The financial–non-financial fragmentation of the larger system is replicated locally and the same dynamic conditions the relationship: control of capital flows enables banks to constrain the actions of non-financial corporations. The unity which results from centralized decision-making is also present. Local orientations are transcended by the bridging function of the major insurance companies which link the regions into a coherent whole. As the largest industrial corporations in the regions outgrow the capital capabilities of their banks, they go directly to the money market centres and thus also serve in uniting the system.

Thus, at the same time, regional interests are organized around financial institutions and this suggests division, both between financials and non-financials within the region as well as between regions. However, intra-regional differences are mediated by the force of capital flow direction. At the same time, the individual locales are united into a coherent whole by another segment of the financial community and, hence, we find what we interpret as an important mechanism for unity.

Class vs. Organizational Variables
The regional character of intercorporate relations parallels an identified feature of intra-class formation and returns us to the research on upper-class cohesion of Domhoff and Useem. Investigations of the structure of the upper class have found regional organization overlaid by a series of national ties. Elite social clubs serve as mechanisms for cohesion in this regard; members belonging to clubs in several cities integrate regional groupings into a coherent whole producing the set of interrelated social institutions described by Domhoff (1983: 17). Structural investigation of the system of overlapping memberships confirms this idea: Bonacich and Domhoff (1981) found regional clusters of elite social clubs connected by an additional club of boundary spanners.[8]

These findings suggest that the structures of class and corporate relations are characterized by some very interesing parallels, the regional similarities among the most apparent. This leads in two, perhaps contradictory, directions. On the one hand, these results underscore Useem (1984) and Domhoff's (1983) emphasis on the meshing of class and organizational networks. On the other hand, attempts to separate the impact of each system are beginning to appear.

Palmer et al. (1986), for example, explored the impact of regional contact on the formation of the interlock network. They found that corporations headquartered in the same locale are less likely to reconstitute a broken director tie than firms in different areas.[9] They interpret these results to suggest that at the regional level, class-based organization may substitute for corporate-based organizational mechanisms (p. 794).

Galaskiewicz et al. (1985), exploring the internal structure within a particular region, found that both class and organizational variables contribute to director recruitment patterns. And Mizruchi (1984), approaching the problem from a different direction, has proposed an intercorporate theory of class cohesion.

James Bearden and I (Bearden and Mintz 1988) investigated the different role structures of corporate vs. class organization through an analysis of the network of relations among directors. Using directors rather than corporations as the unit of analysis, the person or director network provides the opportunity to explore sources of cohesion within the capitalist class. Termed the dual of the corporate network, this system is expected to produce results different than analyses of corporate interaction patterns (Breiger 1974).

Investigation of the person network uncovered the same types of regional pockets discussed above. Using a component analysis – the identification of distinct groupings within a larger system – we (Bearden and Mintz 1988) found 13 groups of size four or more, 11 of which were geographically based. The remaining two were national and semi-national in orientation as defined by the location of individual members. While the regional components contained directors who lived in a specific locale, the national and semi-national groups were composed of individuals from a variety of locations. We interpreted this result to suggest a two-stage process of cohesion formation: a local consensus-forming process tied into a national network of class relations. This conclusion was buttressed by an analysis of the class backgrounds of component members. Directors in the national and semi-national groups were more likely than their regional counterparts to be members of Useem's (1984) inner circle.

They tended to belong to elite social clubs and policy groups, to hold more directorships than their regional counterparts, and to hold an executive position in one of the largest corporations in the United States. These inner circle members, then, were organized differently from non-members, and the structure of these relations underscores the integrative role suggested by Useem.

One additional finding is of interest here. Members of the national and semi-national components were more likely to be bank directors than their regional counterparts. This parallels the result of investigations of the interlock network which found banks to be particularly prominent in intercorporate affairs. The analysis of the organization of the capitalist class returns us to the role of financial institutions in cohesion formation since those directors most important in integrating a regionally organized elite into a national whole are also those most involved in bank affairs. This suggests that class organization and corporate organization are both attuned to the same dynamic; capital flows regulate relations within the corporate community and serve as a major mechanism for cohesion formation. Findings from this investigation of intra-class relations suggest that those individuals most important in the formation of a national network of class relations tend to be the same directors who participate in the orchestration of capital flow direction. This lends support to the argument on the integration of class and corporate networks and suggests that both the organizational and class components of cohesion formation are crucial to the process. It also calls for further study in isolating the role of each.[10]

Political Action Committees

A recent development in the literature on capitalist class cohesion considers the corporation as the unit of analysis and uses political campaign contributions to explore the question of unity within the corporate world. While companies are prohibited by law from donating funds to national political campaigns, Political Action Committees (PACs) are a legal device for such activity. Soliciting voluntary contributions from managerial employees, corporate PACs are an increasingly important vehicle for campaign financing. And since contributions are organized by employers, these funds have been viewed as a proxy for corporate political preferences.

Political Action Committees are not the first political financing techniques studied in the context of capitalist class cohesion. Whitt's investigation of a series of transportation proposals appearing on ballots in California elections speaks to this issue: was the business community able to resolve its differences on the very important infrastructural question of urban transportation when individual interests were in conflict (Whitt 1981, 1982)? Analysing patterns of corporate contributions to each campaign, Whitt found a striking similarity in corporate donations: little evidence of business community segmentation was displayed with a marked tendency away from internal differentiation.

The systematic data on federal campaign contributions now available with the creation of the Political Action Committee as a formal mechanism for federal campaign contributions have formalized this approach to the question of elite cohesion. Using similarity of contributions to Congressional candidates in the 1980 election as a measure of cohesion within the business world, Mizruchi and Koenig (1986) found economic leverage between industries to be associated with similarity of donations. They interpreted these results to suggest leverage as a source of conflict resolution within the corporate world. Clawson, Neustadtl and Bearden (1986), also investigating corporate PACs in the 1980 congressional election, asked a similar question: what is the extent of business unity as measured by similarity of candidates selected for donations? They found that while corporate PACs followed different strategies – some were strongly ideological while others were best described as strongly pragmatic – this seldom translated into direct confrontations. In fact, when measured by candidate selection for individual races, they found that in about three-quarters of the cases one candidate received at least nine times as much money as his or her opponent, suggesting a remarkable degree of business unification. From this they suggest that the mechanisms of cohesion formation identified by earlier research receive empirical validation in the sense that unity is indeed demonstrated within the corporate community.[11]

The Nature of Capitalist Class Rule: The Role of the State
Thus far we have emphasized both the barriers which impede and the mechanisms which facilitate unified class action but we have not considered the process through which shared economic interest is translated into social policy. In the literature we can tease out at least three distinct answers to this question, two of which revolve around business–government relations.

Since the 1950s, the literature on the capitalist class has been marked by a heated debate about the location of ultimate power in the United States. Rooted in the work of Floyd Hunter (1953) and C. Wright Mills (1956), who asserted the concentration of decision-making in the hands of a small number of institutional leaders – political, business and military in Mills' version – the power structure debate emerged as different theoretical perspectives attempted to make sense of this argument. The three paradigms most relevant to the discussion include pluralism, elitism and ruling-class theory and while the details of each have been explored in detail elsewhere, here we concentrate on the parts of the debate most crucial to understanding current trends in the literature.[12]

The elitist position of Hunter (1953) and Mills (1956)[13] was answered by the pluralist response of dispersed decision-making and competition for resources. And although there are several variations of pluralist thought,[14] the key distinctions between elitism and pluralism turn on unity of elites and the arena of decision-making. Elitism assumes a unified elite who make decisions of major consequence; pluralism assumes a divided elite who compete for policy preferences in the governmental arena, the identified site of decision-making. Although most observers agree that elites are potentially quite powerful, the pluralist assertion of division undermines that power base. Ruling-class theory, a Marxist view of power-wielding, also assumes a unified elite, although there is disagreement about the actual location of decision-making.

While these themes established the parameters of the power structure debate, in recent years emphasis has shifted from the pluralist-defined question of whether unity occurs to the Marxist question of how it occurs or, to use the more current language of the debate, how capitalists organize. This, of course, returns us directly to the issue of cohesion considered in detail above and adds one more reason – and a particularly important one – for the current emphasis on sources of unity.

In addition, we note the convergence of two threads crucial to any consideration of the structure of a capitalist class. While our discussion of mechanisms of cohesion concentrated on the process through which individual actors are transformed into a unified social class – an economic question – the power structure debate explores the nature of democracy in the United States and is, thus, basically, a political question. Hence while we can identify two fairly distinct threads to the literature on capitalist class structure, these converge in the question of the nature of class rule.[15]

Turning to this, two approaches have rooted capitalist domination in governmental power, a tradition derived from Marx's famous comments about the state functioning as an arm of the ruling class. The first assumes that, over the years, the business community has developed mechanisms for both resolving the types of conflict discussed above and for delivering a unified stance to government for implementation. In this view, the typical method for communicating policy preferences is through personnel interchange and this is the motivation for many of the studies of government recruitment of business leaders so popular in the late 1970s (e.g. Domhoff 1970; Dye and Pickering 1974; Freitag 1975; Mintz 1975; Salzman and Domhoff 1979–80).

Despite some very strong evidence demonstrating that high-level government officials are often drawn from the business community, the relationship between the capitalist class and the governmental policy planning process remained controversial. Drawing on Poulantzas's argument about the relative autonomy of the state and distinguishing between the state as an instrument of capitalist rule vs. the state as an institution which acts on its own in the interests of capital in general, Mollenkopf (1975) outlined two opposing theories of class rule. Formalized into the instrumentalist vs. structuralist view of the state, this disagreement developed into a sub-debate within power structure research. While instrumentalists argued that business presence in government indicated routes for preference transfer, structuralists suggested that the divisions within the capitalist class inhibited the formulation of joint preference; that individual interest outweighed collective interest; and that internal mechanisms were incapable of mediating among fractions. Thus, the state performed this function.[16]

In this view, then, the business presence documented so carefully by empirical research was a result, rather than a cause, of state action. Policy formation was the purview of an autonomous state whose major function was to facilitate capital accumulation and preserve legitimacy, two necessities for capitalist survival. To the extent that the policies developed by the state to ensure this were consistent with the needs of capitalist fractions, then those fractions might be represented in a particular administration. As Poulantzas (1969) argues, however, this may be viewed as coincidental: 'if the function of the state in a determinate social formation and the *interests* of the dominant class in this formation *coincide*, it is by reason of the system itself; the direct participation of members of the ruling class in the State apparatus is not the *cause* but the *effect*' (p. 73).

Thus, both structuralists and instrumentalists view the state as the force for implementation of policy developed in the interest of the capitalist class, while disagreeing about the location of the development of that policy. Both schools also agree that governmental policy is the vehicle for the implementation of decisions, even though the ability to carry through on particular items may be limited by class struggle.[17] These agreements and disagreements have translated into different research agendas. Structuralists moved away from the confines of this particular debate in an attempt to develop a broader theory of the state (see Wright 1978; Skocpol 1979; 1981; Evans et al. 1985; Alford and Friedland 1985), while power structure researchers returned to the question of mechanisms for cohesion within the capitalist class with renewed vigour, now addressing managerialist, pluralist and structuralist criticism (see Domhoff 1979–80).

And while many of the forces for cohesion identified above are consistent with the emphasis on the state as actor, one theory – finance hegemony – roots both decision-making and implementation in the corporate community and in this way differs from the typical explanation of the state as the location of policy formation, either in the instrumental or structural version.

Instead, the power derived from the centralized control over capital flows is viewed as broad but primary; decisions made in the boardrooms of major financial institutions create policy without state intervention. Although this power cannot be translated into direct dictation to government of specific corporations in the normal course of events, decisions about the direction of capital flows have profound implications for US policy decisions, both on the national and international levels. Loans to specific sectors – nuclear power for example – at the expense of other sectors – solar energy, perhaps – set national agenda for energy development. Loans to Third World countries tie the US economy to the health of the Third World in ways which have crucial political implications. And when taken as a whole, 'collective decision-making within the business world directs capital flows that commit the resources of the country as a whole to the projects selected by financial institutions. This form of ... decision-making is ... the primary decision-making apparatus in American society' (Mintz and Schwartz 1985: 252). Hence, 'capital allocation decisions set the agendas ... for collective political action' (p. 252).

From this discussion, it is clear that capitalist class rule is multi-faceted and multi-layered. While the location – government or corporate – of ultimate power is still in dispute, and the major decision-makers – the state, capitalist or financial institutions – are still in contention, virtually all analyses of the structure of the capitalist class in the United States identify the same major actors and locations. While different theories emphasize a different order of import, study after study has identified one or several of these dimensions as primary. Thus, while the exact nature of capitalist rule is still controversial, current research trends emphasize the role of the state, the role of capitalists and the role of financial institutions. And while the next question which must be addressed is the ways in which these three pieces fit together, case studies are beginning to appear which offer in-depth investigations of this process (Glasberg 1983; 1987a; 1987b).

CONCLUSION

Work on the structure of the capitalist class in the United States has developed nicely in recent years and although we have not yet formulated the definitive model for understanding the process through which united action is solidified, we have identified the major actors and the major processes at issue. We have found that the class is characterized by an entangled web of conflicts overlaid by multiple sources of cohesion. We have also found that despite the many opportunities for conflict development, cohesion seems to be the point of equilibrium.

Nevertheless, rich areas for continued study remain. Most importantly, we do not understand the relationship between class and organization in advanced capitalism. While much of contemporary social thought emphasizes the role of institutional power in the modern world, studies of the capitalist class continue to document the importance of capitalist participation in inter-organizational affairs. This raises some very specific questions about the implications of ownership versus institutional power; about the consequences of unified action based on shared interests. Put more forcefully, although research on the structure of the capitalist class rule is coordinated, the implications of this rule – both nationally and internationally – have remained unexplored.

On the national level, for example, how does the possibility of unified class action impact on the way that work is organized? What is the role of the capitalist class in the process of industrial decline, and what can we predict about the possibilities of reindustrialization? What is the impact of capitalist unity on the contours of class structure, in general?

Internationally, what are the implications for the future of Third World development? The consequences for militarism or imperialism? How do international alliances of capital impact on internal relations within the United States? In what ways would incorporating these pieces redefine the boundaries and functions of the United States capitalist class?

While these questions remain uninvestigated, our knowledge of the structure of the United States capitalist class allows us, at least, to speculate on some of these issues. For example, consider the consequences of the organization of class relations on the nature of economic development around the world. It is clear that in the past the investment decisions of US capital, both in terms of the development strategies of multinational corporations as well as direct bank loans to Third World countries, have had enormous influence on the direction of international industrial development. What can our understanding of the structure of the capitalist class tell us about the direction of future development, especially with the continuing decline of US hegemony?

To address this question, we emphasize several points. First, the *raison d'être* of class organization is class profit-maximization and the underlying point of unified action is to realize this goal. Second, while American capitalists have been extremely successful in generating mechanisms for unified action, this has taken place in a national, rather than international, arena. The sources of cohesion which have been documented on the national level are largely absent from international relations. Work on interlocking directorates, for example, has demonstrated that the most central United States corporations are not well integrated into transnational networks of director exchanges (Fennema and Schijf 1984). This suggest that even as the US becomes weaker as a world power, they face the world with a unified agenda for profit-maximization. The structure of class relations further suggests that the multinational corporation is part of this process. Therefore, from the contours of capitalist class organization in the United States, we conclude that capital accumulation remains a national question organized around the interests of a potentially unified national capitalist class.

Given the domestic nature of class relations, let us consider the available strategies for restoring growth to the industrialized world. Recently we have seen attempts at establishing international alliances for the pursuit of common interests. What, then, are the implications of the organization of class relations within the United States for the possibility of a successful alliance of international capital? While the history of transnational relations within the West has varied from aggressive competition to shared strategies for profit-seeking, most eras of cooperation have been based on the ability of the

United States to emphasize its interests at the expense of its allies. With the decline of US hegemony and failed attempts at recapturing world dominance, the US is no longer able to play this role. Instead, faced with excess manufacturing capacity on the global level, increased competition among capitalist countries, as well as decreasing investment opportunities in the Third World, successful strategies for economic cooperation have not yet been developed. From our reading of the research on the structure of the capitalist class of the United States, we conclude that the likelihood of such an alliance is minimal. The sources of cohesion contributing to unified action on the part of American capitalists suggest that, even as the United States gets weaker as a world power, they maintain the strength that comes with the ability to generate a unified agenda. We suggest, therefore, that rather than cooperating in an alliance which they are no longer able to craft, we should expect an autonomous US economic strategy.

Two separate scenarios come to mind. The reindustrialization of the United States is a possibility, with investment capital channelled back into domestic projects. Given continued multinational expansion abroad, coupled with few attempts to modernize plants and equipment at the national level, this does not seem to be the chosen strategy. Instead, we expect the United States to retain its international orientation. And given the persistence of bank centrality in economic affairs, we expect the continuation of economic planning by the financial sector with no indication of a centralized governmental role in regulating or coordinating foreign economic policy.

This suggests that in addition to the external industrial investment organized by multinationals which should not be ignored, we might expect the continuation of an international economic agenda based on the export of capital. We should also expect the trend away from the developing world as the primary site of investment – either industrial or financial – to continue; as competition among the advanced industrial nations for investment outlets in the Third World intensifies, and as solutions to the debt crisis remain illusive, Europe and Japan will continue to attract US capital.

This strategy of capital accumulation spells continued crisis for world economic development. To the extent that the United States concentrates on foreign investment, markets for imported goods within the US continue to shrink and as this occurs, Third World exports face even fewer market outlets. Debt-servicing, therefore, will be still harder to maintain and the outcome will be a continued decline in the standard of living in large parts of the Third World.

Finally, it is important to add that an economic policy based on capital export will continue to need buttressing by a stable military capacity. Therefore, we expect the United States to maintain its position as a world leader in the development of military technology. And while certainly this will provide an export commodity of interest on the world market, it is clear that this will not solve the problems associated with outdated plants and equipment in other sectors; instead militarism, rather than industrial development, will still be used to address the structural weakness in the US economy. For the position of the United States in world affairs, then, military influence has replace economic influence and current trends indicate that this will not change in the foreseeable future.

NOTES

1. Studies in this tradition include the original work of Berle and Means (1932), Gordon (1938), TNEC (1940), Gordon (1945), Villarejo (1961), Larner (1966: 1970), Chevalier (1970), Vernon (1970) and Burch (1972). For an excellent critique of this type of investigation, see Zeitlin (1974).
2. Domhoff (1983), for example, notes that 'the ruling class is socially cohesive' and 'has its basis in the large corporations and banks' (p. 1). And Useem's (1984) inner circle – the leading edge of class-wide organization – is 'rooted in intercorporate networks through shared ownership and directorship of large companies' (p. 3). See Allen (1974) for a dissenting view.
3. For a more detailed discussion of this type of coordination, see Mintz and Schwartz (1987).
4. See Useem (1980) and Glasberg and Schwartz (1983) for extensive reviews of this issue.
5. For recent work see Allen (1974), Bearden et al. (1975), Berkowitz et al. (1979), Bunting (1976; 1977), Galaskiewicz and Wasserman (1981), Gogel and Koenig (1981), Levine (1972), Mariolis (1975), Mintz and Schwartz (1981a; 1981b; 1985), Mizruchi (1982; 1983), Palmer (1983a;

1983b), Pennings (1980), Sonquist and Koenig (1975). For reviews of the interlock literature, see Fennema and Schijf (1979), Glasberg and Schwartz (1983), DiDonato et al. (1988).

6. Hilferding (1910) viewed finance capital as the coalescence of bank and industrial capital and rather than the domination of one group by the other, he argued that the two would meld into a single group of finance capitalists.

7. Sweezy's (1939) early work identified eight interest groups assumed to be under financial control. Perlo (1957) also identified eight groups but argued the merger of industrial and financial interests rather than antagonism as did Menshikov (1969) and Knowles (1973).

8. Domhoff (1983: 21) suggests that an additional indicator of the national scope of the capitalist class is the consolidation of 12 local volumes of the *Social Register* into one merged directory.

9. For analyses of broken ties of interlocking directorates on the national level, see Palmer (1983a).

10. Work in this area is continuing. Johnsen and Mintz (1986; 1988), for example, examine the extent to which shared social characteristics pattern shared intercorporate ties in a series of regional networks.

11. See also Clawson, Kaufman and Neustadtl (1985), Kouzi and Ratcliff (1985), Jenkins and Shumate (1985), and Burris (1987).

12. For discussions of these paradigms see Mankoff (1970) and Whitt (1979). See also Kerbo and Della Fave (1979).

13. Elitism did not develop in the 1950s but dates back to the work of Plato and in the twentieth century is most often associated with Pareto and Mosca (Bachrach 1966).

14. The major distinction is between interest-group pluralism which assumes a competition among different interest groups for policy preferences, and elite pluralism which argues that competition occurs within the elite itself. Both assume that a particular group or a particular elite wins only occasionally and, thus, even when it is only the elite who are active, democracy is ensured by the divisions within the group.

15. The literature on power structure typically includes the economic since most theories of power distribution turn on the ability of the business community to dominate state policy. While the political implications of the parameters of capitalist class structure are crucial, this literature has a tendency to make these questions implicit, rather than explicit.

16. Structuralists who address the power structure debate include Gold, Lo and Wright (1975), Esping-Anderson, Friedland and Wright (1976) and Block (1977).

17. Both agree, at least theoretically, that the state is limited in its ability to implement policy by class struggle, although the degree to which this limitation has been incorporated into research agendas has been the subject of controversy. See Balbus (1971), Mollenkoph (1975) and Freitag (1981; 1983).

REFERENCES

Alford, Robert and Roger Friedland (1985) *Powers of Theory* (New York: Cambridge University Press).

Allen, Michael (1974) 'Interorganizational elite cooptation', *American Sociological Review* 39: 393-406.

Allen Michael (1976) 'Management control in the large corporation', *American Journal of Sociology* 81: 885-94.

Allen, Michael (1978) 'Economic interest groups and the corporate elite structures', *Social Science Quarterly* 58: 597-615.

Bachrach, Peter (1966) *The Theory of Democratic Elitism* (Boston: Little, Brown).

Balbus, Issac (1971) 'Power elite theory vs. Marxist class analysis', *Monthly Review* 22 (May): 36-46.

Baltzell, E. Digby (1964) *The Protestant Establishment* (New York: Random House).

Baran, Paul and Paul Sweezy (1966) *Monopoly Capital* (New York: Monthly Review Press).

Bearden, James and Beth Mintz (1984) 'Regionality and integration in the US Corporate Network', in Stokman, Frans, Rolf Ziegler and John Scott (eds), *Networks of Corporate Power* (Cambridge: Polity Press).

Bearden, James and Beth Mintz (1988) 'The structure of class cohesion: The corporate network and its dual', in Mizruchi and Schwartz (eds) *Structural Analysis* (Cambridge: Cambridge University Press).

Bearden, James, William Atwood, Peter Freitag, Carol Hendricks, Beth Mintz and Michael Schwartz (1975) 'The nature and extent of bank centrality in corporate networks'. Paper presented at the Meetings of the American Sociological Association.

Bell, Daniel (1961) 'The breakup of family capitalism', in *The End of Ideology* (New York: Collier).

Berkowitz, S. D., Peter Carrington, Yehuda Kotowitz and Leonard Wavarman (1979) 'The determination of enterprise groupings through combined ownership and directorship ties'. *Social Networks* 1: 415–35.

Berle, Adolph Jr and Gardiner Means (1932) *The Modern Corporation and Private Property* (New York: Harcourt, Brace and World).

Block, Fred (1977) 'The ruling class does not rule: Notes on the Marxist theory of the state', *Socialist Revolution* 7: 6–28.

Bonacich, Phillip and G. William Domhoff (1981) 'Latent classes and group membership', *Social Networks* 3: 175–196.

Breiger, Ronald (1974) 'The duality of persons and groups', *Social Forces* 53: 181–190.

Bunting, David (1976) 'Corporate interlocking', *The Journal of Corporate Action* 1: 6–15.

Bunting, David (1977) 'Corporate interlocking', *The Journal of Corporate Action* 2: 27–37.

Burch, Phillip (1972) *The Managerial Revolution Reassessed* (Lexington, Mass.: D. C. Heath).

Burris, Val (1987) 'Business support for the New Right: A consumers' guide to the most reactionary American corporations', *Socialist Review* 91: 33–64.

Burt, Ronald (1979) 'A structural theory of interlocking corporate directorates', *Social Networks* 1: 415–35.

Burt, Ronald (1980) 'Cooptive corporate actor networks: a reconsideration of interlocking directorates involving American manufacturing', *Administrative Science Quarterly* 25: 557–82.

Burt, Ronald (1983) *Corporate Profits and Cooptation* (New York: Academic Press).

Chevalier, J. M. (1970) *La Structure Financière de L'Industrie Américaine* (Paris: Editions Cujas).

Clawson, Dan, Allen Kaufman and Alan Neustadtl (1985) 'Corporate PACs for a New Pax Americana', *Insurgent Sociologist* 13 (1,2): 63–77.

Clawson, Dan, Alan Neustadtl and James Bearden (1986) 'The logic of business unity', *American Sociological Review* 51: 797–811.

DiDonato, Donna, Davida Glasberg, Beth Mintz and Michael Schwartz (1988) 'Theories of corporate interlocks: a social history', *Perspectives in Organizational Sociology*, ed. Sam Bacharach.

Domhoff, G. W. (1967) *Who Rules America?* (Englewood Cliffs, NJ: Prentice-Hall).

Domhoff, G. W. (1970) *The Higher Circles* (New York: Random House).

Domhoff, G. W. (1979) *The Powers that Be* (New York: Random House).

Domhoff, G. W. (1983) *Who Rules America Now?* (Englewood Cliffs, NJ: Prentice-Hall).

Dooley, Peter (1969) 'The interlocking directorate', *American Economic Review* 59: 314–323.

Dye, Thomas and J. Pickering (1974) 'Government and corporate elites', *Journal of Politics* 36: 900–925.

Esping-Anderson, Gosta, Roger Friedland and Erik Wright (1976) 'Modes of class struggle and the capitalist state', *Kapitalistate* 4–5: 186–220.

Evans, Peter, D. Rueschemeyer and Theda Skocpol (1985) *Bringing the State Back In* (New York: Cambridge University Press).

Fennema, Meindert and B. Schijf (1979) 'Analyzing interlocking directorates: theory and methods', *Social Network* 1: 297–332.

Fennema, Meindert and B. Schijf (1984) 'The transnational network', in Stokman, Frans, Rolf Ziegler and John Scott (eds) *Networks of Corporate Power* (Cambridge: Polity Press).

Fitch, Robert and Mary Oppenheimer (1970) 'Who rules the corporations?' *Socialist Review* 1,4: 73–108.

Freitag, Peter (1975) 'The cabinet and big business', *Social Problems* 23: 137–52.

Freitag, Peter (1981) 'Class struggle and the rise of government regulation', PhD dissertation. SUNY at Stony Brook.

Freitag, Peter (1983) 'The myth of corporate capture', *Social Problems* 30: 480–91.

Galakiewicz, Joseph and Stanley Wasserman (1981) 'Change in a regional corporate network', *American Sociological Review* 46: 475–84.

Galaskiewicz, Joseph, Stanley Wasserman, Barbara Rauschenback, Wolfgang Bielefeld and Patti Mullaney (1985) 'The influence of corporate power, social status, and market position on corporate interlocks in a regional network', *Social Forces* 64: 403–31.

Ghiloni, Beth (1984) 'Women, power and the corporation', *Power and Elites* 1: 37–50.

Glasberg, Davida (1983) 'Corporations in crisis: Institutional decision-making and the role of finance capital', Ph.D Dissertation. SUNY at Stony Brook.

Glasberg, Davida (1987a) 'Control of capital flows and class relations', *Social Science Quarterly* 68: 51–69.

Glasberg, Davida (1987b) 'The ties that bind? Case studies in the significance of corporate board interlocks with financial institutions', *Sociological Perspectives* 30: 19–48.

Glasberg, Davida and Michael Schwartz (1983) 'Ownership and control of corporations', *Annual Review of Sociology* 9: 311–32.

Gogel, Robert and Thomas Koenig (1981) 'Commercial banks, interlocking directorates on economic power: an analysis of the primary metals industry', *Social Problems* 29: 117–28.

Gold, David, Clarence Lo and Erik Wright (1975) 'Recent developments in Marxist theories of the state', *Monthly Review* 27: 29–43.

Gordon, Robert (1938) 'Ownership by management and control groups in the large corporation', *Quarterly Journal of Economics* 52: 367–400.

Gordon, Robert (1945) *Business Leadership in the Large Corporation* (Washington, DC: The Brookings Institution).

Gramsci, Antonio (1971) *Selections From the Prison Notebooks* (New York: International Publishers).

Hilferding, R. (1910) *Finance Capital* (London: Routledge and Kegan Paul).

Hindley, Brian (1970) 'Separation of ownership and control in the modern corporation'. *Journal of Law and Economics* 13: 185–221.

Hunter, Floyd (1983) *Community Power Structure* (Chapel Hill: University of North Carolina Press).

Jenkins, J. Craig and Teri Shumate (1985) 'Cowboy capitalists and the rise of the "New Right" ', *Social Problems* 33: 130–45.

Johnsen, Gene and Beth Mintz (1986) 'Corporate directors: Organizational vs. class components of recruitment'. Annual meeting of the American Sociological Association, New York.

Johnsen, Gene and Beth Mintz (1988) 'Organizational and class components of interlocking director networks', in Perucci, Robert and Harry Potter (eds) *Networks of Power: Organizational Actors at the National, Corporate and Community Levels* (New York: Aldine).

Johnson, S. (1976) 'How the West was won: Last shootout for the yankee-cowboy theory', *Insurgent Sociologist* 4: 15–26.

Kamerschen, David (1968) 'The influence of ownership and control on profit rates', *American Economic Review* 58: 432–47.

Kaysen, Carl (1957) 'The social significance of the modern corporation', *American Economic Review* 47: 311–19.

Kerbo, Harold and L. Richard Della Fave (1979) 'The empirical side of the power elite debate', *Sociological Quarterly* 20: 5–22.

Knowles, James C. (1973) 'The Rockefeller Financial Group'. Warner Modular Publications, Module 343: 1–59.

Koenig, Thomas, Robert Gogel and John Sonquist (1979) 'Models of the significance of interlocking corporate directorates', *American Journal of Economics and Sociology* 38: 173–83.

Kotz, David (1978) *Bank Control of Large Corporations in the United States* (Berkeley: University of California Press).

Kouzi, Anthony and Richard Ratcliff (1985) 'Political contributions and corporate influence'. Annual Meeting of the American Sociological Association, Washington, D.C.

Larner, Robert (1966) 'Ownership and control in the 200 largest nonfinancial corporations, 1929 and 1963', *American Economic Review* 56: 777–87.

Larner, Robert (1970) *Management Control and the Large Corporations* (New York: Dunellen).

Lenin, V. I. (1917) *Imperialism: The Highest State of Capitalism* (New York: International Publishers (published 1969)).

Levine, Joel (1972) 'The sphere of influence', *American Sociological Review* 37: 14–27.

Mankoff, Milton (1970) 'Power in advanced capitalist society: a review essay on recent elitist and Marxist criticism of pluralist theory', *Social Problems* 17: 418–30.

Mariolis, Peter (1975) 'Interlocking directorates and the control of corporations', *Social Science Quarterly* 56: 425–39.

Mariolis, Peter (1984) 'Interlocking directorates and financial groups: A peak analysis', *Sociological Spectrum*.

Menshikov, S. (1969) *Millionaires and Managers* (Moscow: Progress Publishers).

Miliband, Ralph (1969) *The State in Capitalist Society* (New York: Basic Books).

Mills, C. Wright (1956) *The Power Elite* (New York: Oxford University Press).

Mintz, Beth (1975) 'The President's Cabinet, 1897–1972', *Insurgent Sociologist* 5: 131–48.

Mintz, Beth and Michael Schwartz (1981a) 'Interlocking directorates and interest group formation', *American Sociological Review* 46: 851–69.

Mintz, Beth and Michael Schwartz (1981b) 'The structure of intercorporate unity in American business', *Social Problems* 29: 87–103.

Mintz, Beth and Michael Schwartz (1983) 'Financial interest groups and interlocking directorates', *Social Science History* 7: 183–204.

Mintz, Beth and Michael Schwartz (1985) *The Power Structure of American Business* (Chicago: The University of Chicago Press).

Mintz, Beth and Michael Schwartz (1987) 'Sources of intercorporate unity', in M. Schwartz (ed.) *The Structure of Power in America* (New York: Holmes and Meier).

Mizruchi, Mark (1982) *The American Corporate Network: 1904–1974* (Beverly Hills: Sage).

Mizruchi, Mark (1983) 'The structure of relations among large American

corporations', *Social Science History* 7: 165–82.
Mizruchi, Mark (1984) 'An interorganizational model of class cohesion', *Power and Elites* 1: 23–36.
Mizruchi, Mark and Thomas Koenig (1986) 'Corporate political consensus', *American Sociological Review* 51: 482–91.
Mollenkoph, John (1975) 'Theories of the state and power structure research', *Insurgent Sociologist* 5(3): 245–64.
Norich, Samuel (1976) 'Managerial theory and the profit performance of the leading United States industrial corporations', ASA Convention, September 1976.
Ostrander, Susan (1979–80) 'Class consciousness as conduct and meaning: the case of upper class women', *Insurgent Sociologist* 9(2–3): 38–50.
Palmer, Donald (1983a) 'Broken ties: Interlocking directorates and intercorporate coordination', *Administrative Science Quarterly* 28: 40–55.
Palmer, Donald (1983b) 'On the significance of interlocking directorates', *Social Science History* 7: 217–31.
Palmer, Donald, Roger Friedland and Jitendra Singh (1986) 'The ties that bind: Organizational and class bases of stability in a corporate interlock network', *American Sociological Review* 51: 781–96.
Pelton, Richard (1970) *Who Really Rules America* (Somerville, Mass: New England Free Press).
Pennings, Johannes (1980) *Interlocking Directorates* (San Francisco: Joss wey Bass).
Perlo, Victor (1957) *The Empire of High Finance* (New York: International Publishers).
Poulantzas, N. (1969) 'The problem of the capitalist state', *New Left Review* 58: 67–78.
Ratcliff, Richard (1979–80) 'Capitalist class structure and the decline of older industrial cities', *The Insurgent Sociologist* 9(2–3): 60–74.
Ratcliff, Richard (1980a) 'Banks and the command of capital flows', in M. Zeitlin (ed.) *Classes, Conflict and the State* (Cambridge, Mass.: Winthrop Publishers), pp. 107–32.
Ratcliff, Richard (1980b) 'Banks and corporate lending', *American Sociological Review* 45: 553–70.
Roy, William (1983a) 'Interlocking directorates and the corporate revolution', *Social Science History* 7: 143–64.
Roy, William (1983b) 'The interlocking directorate structure of the United States', *American Sociological Review* 48: 243–57.
Sale, Kirkpatrick (1975) *The Power Shift* (New York: Random House).
Salzman, Harold and G. W. Domhoff (1979–80) 'Corporations, non-profit groups and government', *Insurgent Sociologist* 9(2–3): 121–35.
Skocpol, Theda (1979) *States and Social Revolutions* (Cambridge: Cambridge University Press).
Skocpol, Theda (1981) 'Political response to Capitalist Crisis: Neo-Marxist theories of the state and the case of the New Deal', *Politics and Society* 10: 155–211.
Sonquist, John and Thomas Koenig (1975) 'Interlocking directorates in the

top U.S. corporations: a graph theory approach', *Insurgent Sociologist* 5: 196–230.

Soref, Michael (1976) 'Social class and a division of labour within the corporate elite', *Sociological Quarterly* 17: 360–8.

Sweezy, Paul (1939) 'Interest groups in the American economy', in the *Structure of the American Economy*, National Resources Committee (Washington, DC: US Government Printing Office).

Temporary National Economic Committee (TNEC); Goldsmith, Raymond and Parmelee, Rexford (1940) 'The Distribution of Ownership in 200 Largest Non-Financial Corporations', Washington, DC: Government Printing Office, Monograph 29.

Useem, Michael (1980) 'Corporations and the corporate elite', *Annual Review of Sociology* 6: 41–77.

Useem, Michael (1982) 'Classwide rationality in the politics of managers and directors of large corporations in the United States and Great Britain', *Administrative Science Quarterly* 27: 199–226.

Useem, Michael (1984) *The Inner Circle* (New York: Oxford University Press).

Vernon, Jack (1970) 'Ownership and control among large member banks', *Journal of Finance* 25: 651–7.

Villarejo, Don (1961) 'Stock ownership and the control of corporations', (Somerville, Mass.: New England Free Press).

Weinstein, James (1968) *The Corporate Ideal and the Liberal State: 1900–1918* (Boston: Beacon).

Whitt, J. Allen (1979) 'Toward a class-dialectical model of power: An empirical assessment of three competing models of political power', *American Sociological Review* 44: 81–99.

Whitt, J. Allen (1981) 'Is oil different? A comparison of the social background and organizational affiliations of oil and non-oil directors', *Social Problems* 29: 142–55.

Whitt, J. Allen (1982) *Means of Motion* (Princeton, NJ: Princeton University Press).

Wright, Erik (1978) *Class, Crisis and the State* (London: New Left Books).

Zeitlin, Maurice (1974) 'Corporate ownership and control: The large corporation and the capitalist class', *American Journal of Sociology* 79: 1073–119.

Zeitlin, Maurice (1980) *Classes, Class Conflict and the State* (Cambridge, Mass.: Winthrop).

Zeitlin, Maurice, Lynda Ewen and Richard Ratcliff (1974) 'New princes for old? The large corporation and the capitalist class in Chile', *American Journal of Sociology* 80: 87–123.

Zeitlin, Maurice and Samuel Norich (1979) 'Management control, exploitation and profit maximization in the large corporation', *Research in Political Economy* 2.

Zweigenhaft, Richard (1979–80) 'American Jews: In or out of the upper class?', *Insurgent Sociologist* 9,2: 24–37.

Zweigenhaft, Richard and G. William Domhoff (1982) *Jews in the Protestant Establishment* (New York: Praeger).

9   The International Level[1]

Kees van der Pijl

THE PROBLEM STATED

Introduction

This chapter deals with the capitalist class as a social force operating not merely within each state, but also in the wider setting of the totality of capitalist states. Our argument will be that while there have always been cosmopolitan elements in the bourgeoisie (as, of course, in its historical antagonist, the working class), this cosmopolitanism was transformed into a conscious deployment of a world bourgeoisie only with the explosion of a potentially *global* revolutionary challenge in the Bolshevik Revolution and with the internationalization of actual *production* in the twentieth century.

The existence of an international capitalist class can be approached from two angles. On the one hand, the existence of multinational corporations has fostered the idea that somehow a distinct set of people specifically associated with this business system must exist as well. In a sociological sense, this idea is brought out in the following quote from a business magazine: 'The global manager begins to emerge as a new class. ... The cultural barriers that separate world markets from each other can be formidable obstacles to business growth. But a new class of global executive – with many personal traits in common – is clearly taking shape' (*International Management*, September 1985). Putting the matter in more analytical terms, Stephen Hymer writes that due to the continuing internationalization of capital, 'an international capitalist class is emerging whose interests lie in the world economy as a whole and a system of international property which allows free movement of capital between countries. ... There is a strong tendency for the most powerful segments of the capitalist class increasingly to see their future in the further growth of the world market rather than its curtailment' (Hymer 1978: 23).

The actual identification of some sort of power-centre is the logical next step in this type of analysis. Again, the business press often joins in speculation on this score: 'The hard financial core of capitalism in the free world', *Fortune* estimated in a 1968 article, 'is composed of not more than sixty firms, partnerships, and corporations, owned or controlled by some 1,000 men' (*Fortune*, August 1968: 101). Meindert Fennema has tried to map this 'core' in his analysis of the international network of interlocking directorates linking 176 major industrial firms and banks. While concluding that 'there exists a cohesive international network of interlocking directorates', he warns that at the same time, given the nature of the network, it 'should be considered primarily a communication network rather than a network of domination and control' (Fennema 1982: 201). In Table 9.1 the centre of this network is shown for 1970 and 1976.

Table 9.1   Nodal points in the network of joint directorates ranked by number of adjacent firms and belonging to the 10 per cent most densely interlocked firms

1970		1976	
1. JP Morgan	b, US	1. Chase Manhattan	b, US
2. Chemical Bank	b, US	2. Deutsche Bank	b, FRG
3. Chase Manhattan	b, US	3. Canadian Imperial	b, CAN
4. Royal Dutch/Shell	i, Nl/GB	4. Chemical Bank	b, US
5. Deutsche Bank	b, FRG	5. Dresdner Bank	b, FRG
6. International Nickel	i, Can	6. Ford	i, US
7. AKZO	i, Nl	7. JP Morgan	b, US
8. Gen. Electric	i, US	8. Swiss Bank Corp.	b, Swi
		9. Volkswagen	i, FRG
		10. Royal Dutch/Shell	i, Nl/GB

Source: M. Fennema, *International Networks of Banks and Industry*, The Hague/Boston/London, 1982), Table 5.6, p. 117; compiled from tables 8.8 and 8.9, p. 191. b=bank; i=industrial firm.

From Table 9.1, the increased centrality of European firms, and of banks among the firms, can be seen. Power-brokers or 'big linkers' do exist in this network. These men are 'often engaged in formulating broad business strategies for handling economic and political problems. Rather than representing specific business interests ... they are the promoters of sections of the business community, or even the business community as a whole ... it is the big linkers ... who tackle such problems as how to handle the oil crisis, how to influence governments, how to enhance or oppose trilateralism, and the like' (Fennema 1982: 208).

The idea of policy planning bodies bringing together such pivotal figures is implied in the analysis of interlocks, and the fact that changing patterns of them are reflected in specific features of such international forums as the Bilderberg Group and, later, the Trilateral Commission, is significant in this respect (Fennema and Van der Pijl 1987: 47-8).

In contrast to this economic approach to the existence of an international capitalist class, a second strand of thinking that has crystallized on this topic sees the problem in terms of the loss of national political cohesion. Thus political scientists have recorded their awareness of so-called 'penetrated political systems', defined by James Rosenau as a system 'in which nonmembers of a national society participate directly and authoritatively, through actions taken jointly with the society's members, in either the allocation of its values or the mobilization of support on behalf of its goals' (Rosenau 1966: 65). This idea has been elaborated by the 'transnational' school in international relations, but its application to class relations has mainly been the work of Marxists. Kurt Gossweiler (1975 [1971]), who analyses the existence in Weimar Germany of an 'American fraction' in the German bourgeoisie; the authors of the Club Turati (1975) who did the same for contemporary Italy (an 'American party in Italy'); and Nicos Poulantzas in his seminal essay on the internationalization of capitalist relations (1974), in which he takes issue both with the idea of Mandel that a European bourgeoisie is confronting the American one, and with the French Communist Party thesis of a 'national bourgeoisie' withstanding the impact of Americanization (and hence a potential ally for the Left), should be mentioned in this respect (see also Granou 1977). This approach has the advantage of clearly locating 'international' classes in 'national' contexts, of tackling the issue of class structure and national state cohesion where the economic approach tends to skip this problem and looks for an imaginary extraterritoriality not unlike the champions of full 'multinationalization' themselves. On the other hand, the second tendency tends to confine its analysis to class relations in dependent societies, identifying comprador classes after the Latin American (originally Chinese) pattern. This leaves the dominant international class unidentified as a force in its own right. As De Brunhoff writes, the United States remains a black box in analyses (like Poulantzas's) which take the dominance of US capital as their point of departure. American capital, she concludes, 'is presented as an unalterable force, i.e., in an abstract and static way', whereas instead, this capital, too, should be analysed 'according to its evolution in time and also to the relation between domestic development and external expansion' (De Brunhoff 1976: 97-8).

In my view, the limits of these two approaches are not removed if we simply combine them. The failure of the business elite approach to take into account the continuous, *active* challenge posed by social forces hampering capital accumulation (whether in actual production or politically) would only be compounded by the failure of the comprador approach to see the likewise active, *strategic* dimension of the inclusion of the national class fractions in a transnational deployment. Only if we analyse class dialectically, that is, as the crystallization of antagonistic social positions (themselves subject to continuous drift) reflecting conflicting tendencies in the mode of production and the quest for control, can we hope to grasp the process of its tendential internationalization in capitalism.

Class and Class Consciousness

To begin with, a few terminological clarifications are in order. By *class* we mean the division of society into groups of people differently related to the production and distribution of wealth and participating, on this basis, in historically determined social power struggles. This applies both to 'polar opposites' like the bourgeoisie and the working class in capitalism, whose antagonism ultimately involves the nature of the mode of production and social organization as such; and to fractional interests whose differences and aspirations remain within one mode of production, or, by historical circumstance, are marginal to the struggle over the dominant mode of production (say, financial versus industrial interests within the capitalist class; or the landowning aristocracy in capitalism). The articulation of economic interests and political aspirations is essential to this understanding of class, and presupposes a degree of *class consciousness* – a quality most highly developed among a ruling class. In other classes, revolutionary situtations apart, class consciousness is mostly rudimentary, atavistic or otherwise limited, even if the awareness of social status may be high.

Class consciousness is not a fixed quantity. It is subject to continuous change and development, just like class itself; even within the coordinates of one mode of production. Class positions, while remaining within a magnetic field of fundamental polarities centring on production relations, are subject to continuous diversification and redefinition in the course of the development of the mode of production, and so is class consciousness.

In its most developed form, that is, in the ruling class, class consciousness takes the form of particular *concepts of control*. Concepts of control are integrated programmes of class rule phrased in terms of the general interest to secure their legitimacy, but are related to functional roles in the economy. In capitalism, a concept of control may crystallize either from the vantage-point of 'the market', or from that of production properly speaking, depending on the aspect that objectively needs to be reaffirmed if the system (which by necessity includes both) is to 'work'. As a market economy, capitalism requires order. In a concrete situation, the need for either quality may be felt along a broad front, objectively; but clearly those who stand to gain immediately from its application will be particularly prominent now that their particular interest seems to be a timely approximation of the general interest, and hence will add a subjective *class* ingredient to the emerging consensus.

'Market economy' and 'social planning', then, are inherent propensities of different segments or *fractions* of the capitalist class, imparting an objective rationality to their desire to 'stay on top'. The forms of the interrelation of the two aspects, and indeed the ability to think of them as independent realities at all, have varied in the history of capitalism. Planning, which is intrinsic to production from its most simple forms, has long remained confined to the workshop, plant or at least the *local* level, while markets, ultimately linking different production sites, were to some extent intercontinental already at the outset of the capitalist era. Those associated with trade, finance, transport, etc. have therefore historically been the protagonists, not just of liberalism, but more specifically, of the abstract, *general* capitalist interest. To the extent that a single functional fraction of capital can be designated as such, the most concentrated expression of this interest, however, is *money capital*. As a liquid mass, money capital, controlled by the financial sector in the broadest sense, comes closest to what Marx calls 'social capital' (Marx 1973 [1939]: 449; *MEW* 25: 382).

The productive capitalists, on the other hand, have tended to represent not just the planning moment of capitalism, but also its individuality and particularity, tied as they are to existing men and machines (cf. Shortall 1986). 'Planning' here refers to the technical equations between x men and y machines, the 'visible hand' against the 'invisible' one of the market. The *strategic* planning at the level of the capitalist class, which takes place in its highest echelons and is functionally related to money capital (but may take its clue as to the concrete direction of strategy from either the productive or the circulating-capital vantage point), will be expressly denoted as such.

Traditionally, productive interests have manifested themselves locally and nationally, seeking to combine into, or add to, a national interest *from within*; while the 'laws of the market' rather made themselves felt *from outside*. But, as we shall see, the actual development of capitalism has entwined the two aspects ever more closely to the point where planning may become mandatory for the system as a whole, and productive capital the protagonist of an international interest.

Before discussing the process and patterns of internationaliz-ation of capital, however, we have to establish that class formation in real life is always historical and concrete. This means that it takes place within given geographical and ethnic surroundings, in which previous productive arrangements have already developed and have moulded a primordial awareness of such geographical, ethnic and other circum-stances into forms of consciousness to which contemporary class consciousness attaches itself, which it modifies and redefines, but never completely replaces.

The Internationalization of Class in Capitalism

Nationally, the capitalist ruling class is structured between some sort of 'national' economy and state power. The subordination of labour to capital, crystallizing in an emerging or pre-existing territorial unit of social cohesion, defines a national bourgeoisie interested in subordinating the national economy as such (the fact that its capacity to do so may be derived from foreign operations is secondary here). To achieve this, the bourgeoisie has to gain control over the state in a political power struggle. In this struggle, the bourgeoisie sharpens its awareness of its historical tasks, learns to protect the conditions of its reproduction, and develops its elementary class consciousness into a concept of control. But in the process, its class consciousness also diversifies along functional lines, for beyond the subordination of labour, a concrete economic policy will inevitably have to be patterned either after a productive-capital or a money-capital concept, which in turn will determine the concrete form of labour relations. 'Economic policy' here refers to managing national markets and infrastructure outside the jurisdiction of corporations (in which planning prevails and labour is directly socialized) but still potentially controlled. I shall use Mandel's (1972: 215) distinction between planning and programming to categorize the conscious direction of the two spheres.

Class struggle and fractional strife thus determine the formation of a capitalist ruling class, *given* the existence of a state functioning along capitalist lines in key areas like labour legislation and monetary and financial matters, and demarcat-ing a space subject to programming along planning or market lines. The relative *socialization of labour* in the national economy (distinct from the direct socialization of labour inside the corporation) provides the basis for this. Socialization refers to the process of the individual worker becoming part of an imaginary 'collective worker' as a consequence of the division of labour and to a corresponding dialectic of standardization and differentiation of social roles and mental outlooks. In the form of joint-stock companies replacing the owner-managed archetypical firm and comparable effects of the expanding scale of production, socialization spills over to capital and, ultimately, tends to isolate pure property from ongoing production.

What would be the determinants of an *international* ruling class? Three determinants are suggested by the discussion thus far: (a) the bourgeoisie develops an 'elementary' class consciousness pertaining to the international sphere; (b) this class consciousness takes the form of a concept of control through international class struggle, which presupposes a state-like structure at the international level; (c) an international economic space is demarcated by the relative socialization of labour, to which programming along either market or plan lines can be applied.

In the next section, I shall try to locate these separate 'moments' of the development of an international capitalist ruling class in the historical setting in which they originated.

THE PREHISTORY OF INTERNATIONAL CLASS FORMATION

The Development of an 'Elementary' Class Consciousness Pertaining to the International Sphere: Grotius and Kant

As indicated above, production historically developed locally, while the market economy ('circulation') was already international at the outset of the capitalist era. As long as production remained overwhelmingly concentrated within national states, the international sphere was the preserve of independent commerce and finance, i.e. of circulating capital representing the general capitalist, liberal point of view. Bourgeois class consciousness pertaining to the international sphere under these conditions tended to remain both elementary and negative, enumerating the negative conditions for the circulation of capital; or at most, sought to synthesize this freedom with the plurality of national interests.

Thus Grotius, as a representative of the Dutch commercial bourgeoisie in the early seventeenth century, developed the theory of the freedom of the seas, first as a lawyer for the Dutch East Indian Company challenging the papal decrees that divided the newly discovered world between the Portuguese and Spanish empires, later as a political theorist of the commercial bourgeoisie as such. The essence of Grotius's argument, and a standard tenet of bourgeois orthodoxy since, was the claim that the international sphere should remain free of state claims. In fact, this noble ideal was by necessity an ornament of more down-to-earth ambitions, freedom being a medium of establishing order rather than a goal in itself. Yet as a doctrine and expression of bourgeois class consciousness, liberalism in the international sphere remained committed to a general idea that no political interference with the freedom of capital was allowed.

Later, Immanuel Kant devised a political philosophy of world peace (in conjunction with an outline for a general theory of history) in which he tried to reconcile the multiplicity of states and their inevitable conflicts with their necessary conciliation. Kant developed the idea that inherent (and wholesome) conflict between men had nevertheless produced a state of law. By analogy, the international sphere, which likewise was characterized by perennial conflict, would eventually produce a peaceful international order. 'Just as nature wisely separates the peoples', Kant wrote, '...so on the other hand, it unites the peoples ... by reciprocal self-interest. It is the commercial spirit, which cannot co-exist with war, and which, sooner or later, every people adopts' (Kant 1953 [1795]: 49). Since international law as developed by Grotius and others lacked an enforcement mechanism, Kant postulated the need for a world state, conceding however that it might remain a negative *league* of states (with all the inherent dangers of its falling apart) instead of a true world republic (Kant 1953 [1795]: 34-5, cf. 32).

Although remarkable as an expression of the bourgeois

interest at the international level, Kant's pamphlet could not solve, on account of both its philosophical limitations and the actual level of development of such a bourgeois interest, the contradiction between nature's tendency to generate conflict and its capacity to provide peace. Its recommendations, as one critic put it, seemed to 'guarantee perpetual war rather than perpetual peace', and its inherent contradiction could only be solved on the methodological basis of the dialectic, and practically, by the actual unfolding of class struggle on a world scale (Timm 1969: 219; cf. 220). Indeed the step taken by the bourgeoisie to rise above its mutual antagonisms and adopt a common posture, which Kant could not convincingly theorize at the close of the eighteenth century, could only be taken when its historic antagonist, the working class, manifested itself on the international plane. For Kant, peace among republican/democratic states was still a moral need; with the rise of an international working class, it became a necessity.

The Internationalization of Class Struggle and the World State: Wilson and the League

The Bolshevik Revolution forced the bourgeoisie to end its internecine struggle and redeploy on the level where the challenge posed itself, that is, the international plane. By the logic of events, this attitude was most difficult to adopt by the ruling classes actually engaged in the fighting. Therefore, the task of formulating a comprehensive answer by which the Bolshevik challenge could be met fell to the American President, Woodrow Wilson. American initiative in response to Lenin's revolution thus served as the *deus ex machina* that solved the contradiction between national conflict and international conciliation which Kant, and bourgeois politics until 1917, had failed to solve.

Wilson had developed a pragmatic, reformist approach to socialism from an early date, and the Bolshevik Revolution offered the occasion for its application as a concept of control to which the bourgeoisie of the West could rally. On the one hand, by championing the 'Open Door' principle as the foundation of international economic relations, Wilson renewed the liberal capitalist claim to freedom – simul-taneously expressing the American interest in expansion as previous ideologues had done in respect of their 'empires' (e.g. Grotius, the Cobdenites). But more important was his proposed League of Nations, based on the principle of collective security. While the League itself remained an inter-governmental institution, a 'superstructure' was created that transcended the traditional intergovernmental pattern of international relations by projecting functional bodies to deal with class relations at the international level. Thus, a new space was demarcated in which such international class relations could be formed – under the auspices of the bourgeoisie. The spark that ignited the process was the threat of world revolution; the need to formulate immediate alternatives to the Bolshevik call was therefore mandatory. In the case of the International Labour Organization, this aspect of duplication was evident. As Hass writes, 'The origin of the ILO retains few mysteries. In a very real sense, the organization is the result of the political commitments undertaken by the Allied governments during World War I, commitments that were later endorsed by Imperial Germany and given the quality of an urgent political necessity by the success of the Bolshevik Revolution and the imminence of kindred outbreaks in the West' (Hass 1964: 140).

For the Social Democratic parties in Europe opposed to the revolution, Wilson's proposals, contained in the Fourteen Points, corroborated their 'ultra-imperialist' predilections, explored by Kautsky's 1914 article on the possible future reconciliation of the imperialist powers. Their statements of support for Wilson were considered 'almost pathetic' by Wilson's confidant, Colonel House, who was present at their conference in Berne in Februry 1919 (Radosh 1969: 291). In a sense, the new framework that the ILO held out to compromising labour leaders was a straight extension of their 1914 willingness to compromise on a *national* level, and built on compromises arrived at in the context of war production.

The British Empire, evolving into the Commonwealth as far as the white or white-ruled colonies were concerned, in several respects prefigured the League system. The League bureau-cracy, for one thing, owed its basic structure to the British Committee on Imperial Defence (Jordan 1971). Also, the transnational private body created at Versailles to deal with foreign affairs, the Institute of International Affairs, represented an attempt on the part of the British imperial elite to enlist US support for Cecil Rhodes' concept of 'the furtherance of the British Empire, the bringing of the whole uncivilised world under its rule, the recovery of the United States of America, the making of the Anglo-Saxon race into one Empire' (quoted in Shoup and Minter 1977: 12-13).

American non-participation in the League of Nations eventually killed this project, too, and the interest of British imperialists in the League turned into a clear rejection. Related to this was the problem, insoluble without formal US involvement of providing the international quasi-state with effective police power. At a later juncture, the advocates of Anglo-Saxon unity in the British ruling class, organized in the Round Table Society, directly appealed to the United States to enter into a durable alliance with Britain; Clarence Streit's mission to the USA in 1937 under the auspices of the Rhodes Trustees and Churchill's 1946 Fulton speech were both inspired by a wish to subordinate universal world organization to Atlantic unity.

Harnessing American power as the 'strong arm' of a quasi-world state, whether it was projected on the world or the 'bloc' level, remained the essential political problem. In a world of multiple sovereignties, enforcing an international interest can be achieved only by creating an identity between the strongest national power and the general interest. But if the strongest power is indeed to act in the general interest, the international interest has to be hegemonic in all capitalist countries including the USA. Therefore, it is preferable to use the term 'hegemony' for class relations (for which it was actually developed by Gramsci) and not for American supremacy in the capitalist orbit or the world at large. The formation and hegemony of the international fraction of the bourgeoisie over national fractions was crucially determined by developments within the United States, but it depended primarily on the existence of quasi-state structures on the international level by which American power could be applied in the interest of all, against equally *international* challenges.

Class struggles were not mechanically transposed to the international level by 1917 and by Wilson. Rather, competing contexts of national and international class formation were created, in which challenges to capitalism were met depending on the scope of their impact. Yet, if always mediated by the state system of multiple sovereignties, a tendential shift to internationalization of class formation was noticeable, reflecting the secular trend towards global socialization of labour.

Socialization of Labour and Integration in the Interwar Years
The socialization of labour, which is absolute within the plant (in the sense that there is a technical division of labour subject to unified control), almost so in the company, and still relatively complete within a distinct financial group, also extends beyond the corporate sphere. But here control is subject to competition, and a division of labour can only be programmed, remaining subject to the vagaries of the competitive accumulation of capital. The national state provides the obvious mechanism by which programming is attempted, and accordingly, the socialization of labour will tend to cluster around the infrastructure of the national economy. But circulation of productive capital, socialization of labour and the demarcation of a space subject to programming do not stop at the border.

The League, as a quasi-state on the international level, was not itself fit to serve as a channel through which an international bourgeoisie could attempt to programme an economic space in line with a particular concept of control. It did, however, demarcate an internationalized space in which various official and semi-official bodies like the ILO and the International Chamber of Commerce could come into existence. These bodies were meant to eliminate politically dangerous imbalances between national economies, while facilitating the internationalization of production. The work of the ICC and the League's Fiscal Committee, in laying the groundwork for a variable system of international business taxation, was crucial in this respect (Picciotto 1987). Simultaneously, the organs of the League system served as transmission-belts for diverse interests to crystallize outside the national context, as 'pressure groups' surrounding an imaginary world state, contributing to the shaping of international concepts of control in addition to 'pressures' exerted through national channels. In these bodies (as in their national counterparts), disagreements between national, fractional and conjunctural viewpoints were thrashed out and synthesized in one direction or another. Again, the Commonwealth showed the way by operating 'as a system of interlinked groups, organizations and societies within the greater community' that simultaneously 'was able to avoid in very large measure the growth of rigidities and compartmentalization in its political, economic and social structure' (Hall 1971: 106).

In the perspective of an informal, transnational capitalist class able to operate in such a way, the 'national' then becomes simply an additional set of 'interests' to be accommodated. Simultaneously, the productive complex represented by each state becomes part of a global productive grid, and the circulation function turns into an aspect of production as a totality. As Marx put it in his notebooks for *Capital*, 'Commerce no longer appears here as a function taking place between independent productions for the exchange of their excess, but rather as an essentially all-embracing presupposition and moment of production itself' (Marx 1973 [1939]: 408).

To the degree that the socialization of labour spills over into the international sphere, the concept of control of an international capitalist class therefore cannot remain confined to Grotian liberalism and has to incorporate elements of the productive-capital perspective as well. In this sense the internationalization of production should have been the material counterpoint to Wilson's idealism. But in the situation following World War I, international economic links were still overwhelmingly commercial and financial. The war had even reinforced industrial capital within states, re-emphasizing the national context of the socialization of labour. For the bourgeoisie engaged in the internationalization of production, it was mandatory to decouple the redistribution of spheres-of-influence, inherent to imperialism, from the state-war system. The term *integration* captures this undertaking. Integration implied that of the two trajectories along which the socialization of labour progresses, the international one had to be encouraged while the national-state one had to be constrained. In pursuing this strategy, the traditional representatives of the internationalist interest, the bankers (whose concern was mainly in restoring the Atlantic circuit of money capital) were joined by representatives of internationalizing productive capital.

Indeed, one key project, aimed at creating a fully internationalized structure of production in Europe, was that of Walter Rathenau, president of the German electrical engineering trust, AEG, and successively Minister of Reconstruction and of Foreign Affairs in 1921–2. A visionary internationalist active in a country that was crucial both in the international financial context and in the defence line against the spread of revolution, Rathenau was the foremost representative of the enlightened and cosmopolitan bourgoisie in Germany. Working out an elaborate set of plans that linked Franco-German cooperation in reconstruction and reparations payments with an ambitious plan for joint western exploitation of Russian raw materials (the *Europa Consortium*), Rathenau hoped to disentangle the fate of the German bourgeoisie from its national situation and redeploy along a 'Wilsonian' battle-line from which concessions to the working class could be made from a position of economic strength and political self-confidence. After having been rebuffed by the French and Belgians, the participants at the Genoa Conference, and the nationalist ultras in his own country, his assassination pre-ordained the failure of the formation of an international bourgeoisie at this juncture.

In the absence of formal US backing, the efforts of the internationalists remained confined to trying to restore international trade and payments on a liberal basis. The Dawes Plan of 1924, which restructured the Atlantic circuit of money capital, launched a brief period in which internationalism seemed to be triumphant. Various spokesmen of the internationalist interest at this juncture argued for extending the American system of mass production of durable consumer goods to Europe; Count Coudenhove-Kalergi, who with the aid of bankers prominent in the Atlantic cirucit of money capital recruited a cross-section of the internationalist bourgeoisie in Europe into his *Paneuropa Union*, thought this new industrialism would be critical in deciding Europe's choice for either Wilson or Lenin (Coudenhove-Kalergi 1958: 88, 107. But US investment in Europe hardly corroborated these views and remained either speculative or oriented to bolstering German heavy industry, and with it the identity between industrial capital and nationalism. After the explosion of the Atlantic circuit of money capital in 1929 and the subsequent crisis of the international banking system, the liberal method of programming the prospective Euro-Atlantic economic area lost out to a rival method that sought to organise it as an extension of state–industry collusion, building on cartels spanning the Atlantic, on domestic corporatism, and on state monopolism generally. Ultimately, Hitler would perform the feat of uniting Europe against Bolshevism by dictatorial means.

THE FORMATION OF AN ATLANTIC BOURGEOISIE

Socialization of Labour in the Atlantic Economy

Faced with a complex set of challenges to liberal capitalism, the formation of an international bourgeoisie was resumed in the course of World War II. I shall discuss the different 'moments' of this process distinguished above, turning first to the problem of economic integration.

The re-establishment of a 'free world' in the economic sense was a key dimension of the war. The need to terminate German autarkic policies and the reintegration of German production into an international circuit of finance capital (i.e. the integrated internationalization of financial and commodity flows linking productive operations in different countries; 'multinational corporations'), was prominent in this respect. Opening up the colonial empires of Britain, France and Holland had been a major concern of the Roosevelt administration throughout the war, and Wilson's Fourteen Points were in essence reproduced in the Atlantic Charter and the subsequent United Nations Declaration.

Only with the Marshall Plan could a comprehensive attempt be made to extrapolate the mode of capital accumulation based on mass production of consumer durables ('Fordism') from the United States to Western Europe. Previously,

American insistence on liberalization (through Lend-Lease, and in the British loans preceding the Plan) had remained confined to re-establishing a free international sphere of circulation. Now, American credits and US control of counterpart funds provided by recipient countries were used to introduce technologies designed for mass-producing all the elements of the automotive complex from steel to oil, alongside infrastructural investments and emergency aid. The introduction of continuous strip mills in the steel industry, a technology in which Europe lagged twenty years behind the US, fostered not only actual capital interpenetration (Armco, the inventor company, was thus linked with Thyssen in Germany) but also generated an Atlantic division of labour in which mass-produced flat steeel could alternatively be delivered to US or European automobile firms. Thus the first output of the new Dutch wide-strip mill at Ijmuiden went straight to Detroit. The Schuman Plan for a European Coal and Steel Community, launched in 1950, was meant among other things to guarantee that increased steel output would remain low-priced for use in the Atlantic car and packaging industries, while being separated from European national interests (Van der Pijl 1978).

The Atlantic economy in the period from 1947 to the early 1970s developed on this basis into a system in which the socialization of labour, the productive economy as such, could expand on the international level. At the same time, the relative weight of exchanges with the rest of the world diminished dramatically as Atlantic integration developed. 'In the "old" imperialist division of labour, the "outside world" appeared as a giant thermostat regulating capitalist growth,' Lipietz writes. '... But the question of markets was solved on an *internal* basis through the post-1945 development of mass consumption in the metropolises.' Exports of manufactures to developing countries in the mid-1960s reached a low of 2 per cent of GDP for the EEC, 0.8 per cent for the USA, and 3.2 per cent for Japan (Lipietz 1982: 36-7).

This process received a major spur when the Kennedy administration, in an attempt to adjust to the ongoing processes of European integration and US direct investment in Western Europe, launched a proposal to eliminate all tariffs on

. agricultural products and on products in which at least 80 per cent of trade among capitalist countries was accounted for by exports of the USA and the EEC combined (assuming British membership then applied for) (Evans 1967: 7-9). This would have further deepened the division of labour, partly already engulfed in corporate structures, and hence, *socialization* of labour, in an integrated Atlantic economy. In that sense it went beyond mere liberalization. However, the French veto against British EC membership torpedoed this proposal too. Gaullist France did not at this juncture want to be absorbed into the Atlantic economy directly. This has to be seen against the background of the difficult transition through which the French economy and class structure were then passing, involving the decolonization of its African empire and the shift to Fordism in the mother country. It was certainly no autarkic policy as such; as Clarke writes, ' "nationalist" policies with respect to particular capitals tend to improve the terms on which "national" capitals are integrated into the circuit of world capital rather than to resist that integration' (Clarke 1978: 62). Later developments have fully vindicated this judgement, although the French bourgeoisie has maintained its integrity as a distinct fraction of world capital to a greater extent than any other European bourgeoisie.

The Atlantic Concept in the Formation of an International Bourgeoisie

At the time of Lend-Lease, a movement in the American bourgeoisie developed, reciprocating the cry for help coming from Britain, and more specifically from the British bourgeoisie united in the Round Table society. For this segment of the British ruling class, US support was necessary to maintain the integrity of the British Empire, but the American supporters of aid to Britain set their sights on a *Pax Americana*. The foreign correspondent, Edgar Snow, wrote in 1941 that supporting Britain would only be useful if the British were induced 'to make a joint statement defining our whole struggle as a revolutionary war of democracy having for one of its prime political aims the emancipation of the advanced colonial countries and their entry into a federation of democratic nations at the conclusion of the war' (*Fortune*, June 1941: 177-8).

Such views, of which many more could be cited, gradually added up to a concept of control formulated in terms of transcendent capitalist interests ('the Free World') rather than national or narrow class interests. The first context in which such an international concept was developed was wartime London. Adopting the US interpretation of the Atlantic Charter, which combined the Open Door with national self-determination, European exile governments animated by the Pole, Joseph Retinger, devised various schemes meant to reinforce bourgeois hegemony on the basis of an extension of the American ideas. Often, 'exile' allowed a degree of 'automony' from national class structures and compromises to these arrangements. Thus, early in the war, economic statesmen from Holland and Belgium had already concluded that a customs union between the two countries (the eventual Benelux, with Luxemburg's participation) would best be concluded while still in London so as to prevent a veto from smaller interests in the occupied countries (Van der Pijl 1984: 119-20).

After the war, Wilsonianism again inspired the liberal bourgeoisie to project a flexible, informal pattern of association. As Atlantic banker James Warburg estimated in a 1947 book on Germany, 'the Westward thrusting of Communism will not be stopped by any physical frontier. It can be stopped only by a planned, US-aided reconstruction so liberal and even revolutionary as to meet the challenge on its own grounds, and to strike the meaning from the accusation of American "dollar diplomacy"' (Warburg 1947: 247). National differences were adjusted to, rather than confronted by, the quest for a concept of Atlantic integration. In each national setting, the new format of class relations that was required by the Fordist mode of accumulation was adorned by different labels. In Germany, where 'liberalism' had a favourable ring after National Socialism, it was extolled by Erhard, but Mendès France, who was committed to the same policy, wryly commented that German recovery rested on a synthesis with state intervention, a form of economic order much needed in

France (Van der Pijl 1984: 172). But then, as Gramsci noted, 'A class that is international in character has – in as much as it guides social strata which are narrowly national (intellectuals), and indeed frequently even less than national: particularistic and municipalistic (the peasants) – to "nationalise" itself in a certain sense' (Gramsci 1978: 241).

On the political plane, various concepts of Atlantic unity were hegemonic at different points. Elsewhere, I have distinguished between an Atlantic Union and the Atlantic Partnership concept. Atlantic Union expressed the overwhelming supremacy of the United States at the time of the Marshall Plan, matched by a still largely parasitic interest on the part of the European bourgeoisie in the spread of the American empire; the partnership concept signalled the resurrection of European capitalism on a Fordist basis following the establishment of the EC. In their study of 'Atlanticist' elite opinion, Lerner and Gorden also distinguished a 'Euronational' scenario to denote Gaullism and its counterparts in other European countries (Lerner and Gorden 1967; Van der Pijl 1984). In these different concepts, the relative weight of the perspective of circulating or productive capital tended to reflect the liberal or planning preferences of the nationally ascendant capital fractions involved *and* the prevailing international configuration of capitalism. For, as Gossweiler writes, 'it is certainly not always the strongest group that emerges as the winner in the struggle between tendencies and groups within the ruling class, but ... in general those groups carry the day whose specific group interests at a given point in time correspond most to the general interest of the respective imperialism and whose individual situation reflects most closely that of the respective imperialism' (Gossweiler 1975 [1971]: 56, emphasis deleted).

Quasi-State Forms in Atlantic Integration

Atlantic integration was particularly rich in actual quasi-state bodies at the international level, some intergovernmental, some supranational, but all of them providing contexts of bourgeois class formation on the corresponding international plane. The task of subordinating labour in the context of the Cold War was embedded in confrontation with the Soviet

Union, and the discussions in 1948 that eventually led to NATO were primarily motivated by the fear of Communist Parties inside the Treaty countries ('indirect aggression'), and the inclusion of Italy particularly was seen in this perspective (Wiebes and Zeeman 1983: 205). But the European Coal and Steel Community was also meant to provide mechanisms for counterbalancing national working-class militancy, which had exploded in the wake of the Marshall Plan and the expulsion of Communist ministers in Latin Europe. Conferring with US Senators in 1953, Monnet, the President of the ECSC High Authority, 'pointed to [ECSC] success in incorporating the trade union leadership, particularly in Germany, in the authority's decision making. This had the utilitarian effect of preventing strikes in France, since they could simply step up production in Germany' (Kolko and Kolko 1972: 468).

In addition, programming the integrated area in a liberal or planning sense was realized through quasi-state structures spanning the North Atlantic area, sometimes as a subset of world organizations like the UN, or global capitalist institutions like the IMF and the World Bank. Rather than merely listing the institutions that together formed this state system (again with informal bodies, like the Bilderberg Conferences, the European Movement, etc. operating in their shadow), we should point to the fact that their establishment as such reflected the process of internationalization of capital, its stages and direction. The key role of the ECSC in monitoring the restructuring of the European steel industry to the Fordist pattern has been mentioned already, and accordingly, the international bourgeoisie was actively engaged in its functioning at this stage. The first EEC Commissions were likewise manned by 'heavy' candidates and were capable of pressing the international interest against national ones voiced in the Council of Ministers. 'In the middle of 1962', Anthony Sampson writes, 'the prestige of the Commission, and of [President Walter] Hallstein, was probably at its peak' (Sampson 1968: 36).

Once the institutions were operating on a more or less routine basis, and the jurisdiction of the supranational level *vis-à-vis* the member-states had been demarcated, manning them was left to lesser figures, not only because the actual supranational institutions had only limited powers, but also because the bourgeoisie cannot abandon the historical power base that is provided by national sovereignty. Its internationalization is confined to the *class* dimension, for which it needs an informal, internationalized space rather than the formal institutions, although these are important to legitimize the outcomes of transnational collusion. As Calleo writes:

Contrary to widespread theory about the evolution of the [European] Communities, their significance, which is very great, rests neither upon those few supranational functions which the Commission performs, nor upon their lingering pretensions to become a European central government. Rather, the Communities have come to play their crucial role as the central locus for continual, organized consultation and bargaining among the national governments and bureaucracies of Europe. (Calleo 1976: 20)

With the changing of the coordinates of internationalization of capital and integration, the quasi-state structures on the international level tend to change as well. Thus the organization of the countries that received Marshall Aid, OEEC, which was devoted to trade liberalization, was transformed in 1959 into the OECD, of which the US was also a member. This reflected the shift from the initial commercial nature of Atlantic integration to productive integration and the need for mutual adjustments of economic policy in the light of European industrial parity (Beloff 1963: 135–7).

It should be borne in mind, however, that one very fundamental brake on the internationalization of state structures is the complex role of the national state in keeping the national working class separated from other working classes (Fennema 1975: 89; Farhi 1976: 83). Thus, on the one hand, the international socialization of labour requires a deepening of integration and close collaboration between ruling classes; on the other, the working classes have to remain a passive element in this process of internationalization and are not supposed to organize international quasi-state structures. This may explain why the bourgeoisie is wary of allowing these structures to acquire too much authority and why it prefers to use informal channels of communication surrounding them.

TRILATERALISM AND THE NEO-LIBERAL OFFENSIVE

Trilateralism and Planned Interdependence
The prime vehicle of the internationalization of capital in the era of Atlantic integration had been the multinational corporation. Its expansion from the United States coincided with the projection of a global *Pax Americana*. But this two-pronged expansion of the US economy became a major source of international and domestic tensions. Finally, in 1971, the United States resorted to unilateral defensive measures in the monetary and trade fields, jeopardizing the postwar monetary system and multilateralism in order to bolster the position of American capital *vis-à-vis* its rivals. By sacrificing the transcendent class interest in American expansion, Nixon inadvertently deserted the European Atlanticists and the Japanese pro-US comprador fraction, exposing them in their domestic settings. The unilateral way out of the dilemmas of American capitalism, mediated by the system of floating exchange rates and the oil price hike of 1973, provoked reciprocal reactions in Europe and Japan; while the Lockheed scandal publicly humiliated prominent protagonists of the Atlantic ruling class like the Chairman of the Bilderberg Conferences, Holland's Prince Bernhard, as well as tainting politicians in Italy and Japan.

Trilateralism, launched by a transnational informal planning body of unprecedented standing, and organizational and ideological sophistication – the Trilateral Commission was founded by David Rockefeller and Zbigniew Brzezinski – aimed at restoring the international unity of the bourgeoisie, partly through new international quasi-state structures like the European Council of 1973 and the annual world summits initiated by Giscard in 1974 (Gill 1987). The idea that only a united capitalism could survive the current crisis was essential in the Trilateral concept, and in the context of a projected 'world domestic politics' for the capitalist orbit, a first common task was demarcated: the dismantling of the democratic welfare states, which were judged to enhance the structural power of the working class, and thus to be incompatible with the long-term aims of capitalism.

Otherwise cautious, the Trilateral Commission sought to overcome the crisis of a Cold War approach to socialism by redefining the ideological conflict with the Soviet Union. The first Trilateral US government under President Carter accepted the Helsinki Agreement as a point of departure but in that context concentrated on human rights, subtly linking the idea of world unity of bourgeois individualism. However, the challenges facing capitalism were too acute to be met by the flexible, 'organic' approach favoured by the Trilateral Commission. The oil crisis exposed European dependence on predominantly US-controlled raw material supplies, and with the Atlantic interest at its lowest ebb, a marked willingness to conclude direct agreements with OPEC states and with the Soviet Union made the European bourgeoisie gravitate towards a loose coalition that also included the ruling classes in the newly industrializing Third World.

This array of forces, sharing a distaste for US economic unilateralism and military interventionism, threatened to supplant the postwar liberal capitalist order by a system of *planned interdependence*, in which the socialization of labour between the areas involved was made subject to planning in the sense of the productive-capital concept. The role of the state and international quasi-state institutions ought, in this view, to be dramatically enhanced at the expense of direct world market-oriented internationalization of capital. Supporting such instances of international, UN-monitored regulation of private capital as the project for a Code of Conduct for multinational companies, the mass of interests behind the idea of a New International Economic Order exposed the regulatory and, hence, democratic potential of existing state and international quasi-state structures (cf. Krasner 1985: 124).

The anti-capitalist thrust of these developments was enhanced by the defeats of the US in Indo-China, the collapse of Portuguese imperialism, the revolution in Ethiopia, and the growth of Soviet military power to parity proportions. Moreover, the increased structural power of the working class in capitalism, expressed in Europe in Social Democracy and 'Eurocommunism', added a critical internal dimension. Economic problems and the waverings of the Carter administration in the face of revolution in Central America and Iran, effectively terminated the first instalment of Trilateral rule by 1979.

Money Capital and Monetarism

The temporary prominence of a reformist coalition in world politics, challenging US-led multinational capitalism, was paradoxically aided by western finance. Bank capital, awash with funds once the dollar was no longer tied to the gold standard and the proceeds of the oil price hike were recycled into the Atlantic financial system, became the financiers not only of deficitary metropolitan countries but also of the long-term industrialization plans of Arab, Latin American, East Asian and socialist states. Operating from a fractional rentier perspective negligent of the long-term interests of the capitalist class, the banks were in fact instrumentalized by the newly industrializing states of the capitalist periphery in their struggle against the multinationals, and unwittingly financed the planned interdependence system, the contours of which became visible in the second half of the 1970s (cf. Frieden 1981).

In this situation, the *coup* in Chile, with hindsight, has to be judged a major turning-point. In 1973, the generals' *coup* still seemed an isolated action, and abroad, the implication of ITT and the US government further added fuel to the anti-multinational and anti-American movement then still ascendant. In Chile, however, a concept of control was developed which in due course would spread to the capitalist world at large. As Alex Fernández Jilberto has shown, the generals aimed at recasting the entire development model away from domestic industrialization and towards selective, world market-oriented growth so as to destroy the structural setting in which the forces favouring socialism had developed (Fernández Jilberto 1985). This solution, applied to a society which had earlier been in the forefront of the NIEO movement, proved to be effective also for dealing with the process behind this movement on a global level. More particularly, the economic policy chosen, that of *monetarism*, was soon elevated to the principal instrument for bringing debt-financed 'autonomous' industrialization under private control.

Monetarism holds that by making money scarce, inflation can be combatted effectively and sound microeconomic reasoning can be forced on the state and society as a whole. It represents an instance of the money-capital concept against the encroachment by planning from the productive-capital point of view. It became the popular label of a neo-liberal concept of control that was tried out in Chile by a team headed by Finance Minister Jorge Cauas (a former World Bank official) with IMF people and academic advisers such as Milton Friedman looking over his shoulder (Sampson 1982: 334-5).

Interest in monetarism, and in the Chilean experiment, now spread, notably through the *Mont Pelerin Society*, founded in 1947 by the Austrian economist Hayek, and interlocked through its treasurer Ed Feulner Jr, with the American *Heritage Foundation* (of which Feulner is president). The Mont Pelerin Society, which has approximately 600 members recruited from the business community and the economics profession, acts as a transnational neo-liberal think-tank and pressure group (*Hoy*, 25 November 1981). Here too, the quasi-state structure – in this case the IMF – spawns informal bodies operating on the international plane and elaborating class strategies applicable on this level.

After their adoption in Chile and (in a diluted form at first) in Argentina, monetarist principles spread, through IMF conditions and the activities of informal channels of capitalist class collusion, to Britain. Labour Chancellor of the Exchequer Denis Healey in fact outlined the monetarist strategy already in his letter of intent to the IMF in 1976, but as Overbeek notes, 'it would take a new Tory government ... to broaden the scope of the new liberalism and transform it into a explicitly political strategy' (Overbeek 1986: 22).

In 1979, the monetarist strategy was adopted by the United States to terminate the expansive policy of planned interdependence. The new head of the Federal Reserve, Paul Volcker, saw his job as correcting 'twenty years of government policies promoting inflation' (*Newsweek*, 15 June, 1987). At the same time, his nomination marked the point at which the monetarist approach, hitherto propagated by a neo-liberal pressure group overlapping with the Mont Pelerin Society and call the *Shadow Open Market Committee* (Milton Friedman,

Chicago banker Beryl Sprinkel, and others), was plugged into the Trilateral network, of which Volcker was a member. In 1981, Pinochet himself could boast that while seven years earlier, he and his fellows had been all on their own in combating Soviet imperialism and 'socializing Etatism', they were now part of 'a global categoric tendency' (quoted in Müller-Plantenberg 1981: 24).

In 1981–2, the contradictory collusion between the growth of world bank capital and the crystallization of an NIEO was finally terminated by the confrontationist policy of the new Reagan administration. Regan and Sprinkel at the Treasury used international monetarism to throttle the industrialization strategies of the Third World states. By then, all capitalist states were again oriented or reorienting to the US war economy as the pivot, not only of the world circuit of money capital but also in terms of industrial exports (Fennema and Van der Pijl 1987: 59, 68). In this sense, a certain unity of the global bourgeoisie was restored, albeit on a very unstable basis fraught with future problems.

Neo-liberalism has tried to stem the socialization of labour by reactivating market forces and clearly demarcating capitalism from socialism by rekindling the Cold War, attacking planning and state intervention, and dismantling the class compromises of the previous Fordist era (notably by attacking the power positions of organized labour). But neo-liberalism has not by itself been able to reverse the underlying trend towards greater socialization of labour on a world scale. As Krasner concludes at the end of his study of the challenge to liberal capitalism posed by the Third World: 'The kind of demands embodied in the call for a New International Economic Order will not disappear, because the structural conditions that prompted them are enduring characteristics of the international system' (Krasner 1985: 295).

The strategies by which this enduring challenge (compounded even more by the emergence of a new, imaginative leadership in the USSR) will have to be met, must be international in character. The channels through which they can be worked out by an international capitalist ruling class (in which the Trilateral Commission holds a place of honour) will no doubt play a crucial, if essentially private, role in the process.

NOTE

1. I owe a debt to colleagues in the Department of International Relations of the University of Amsterdam for comments on an earlier version of this chapter.

REFERENCES

Beloff, M. (1963) *The United States and the Unity of Europe* (New York: Vintage).

Calleo, D. (1976) 'The Postwar Atlantic System and its Future', in E. O. Czempiel and D. A. Rustow (eds) *The Euro-American System* (Frankfurt: Campus/Boulder, Col.: Westview Press).

Clarke, S. (1978) 'Capital, fractions of capital and the state: "Neo-Marxist" analysis of the South African state', *Capital & Class 5*.

Coudenhove-Kalergi, R. (1958) *Eine Idee erobert Europe. Meine Lebenserinnerungen* (Wien etc.: Desch).

De Brunhoff, S. (1976) *Etat et Capital: recherches sur la politique économique* (Grenoble: Presses Universitaires de Grenoble/Maspero).

Evans, J. B. (1967) *U.S. Trade Policy. New Legislation for the Next Round* (New York/Evanston: Harper & Row).

Farhi, A. (1976) 'Europe: Behind the Myths', in T. Nairn (ed.) *Atlantic Europe? The Radical View* (Amsterdam: Transnational Institute).

Fennema, M. (1975) *De multinationale onderneming en de nationale staat* (Amsterdam: SUA).

Fennema, M. (1982) *International Networks of Banks and Industry* (The Hague/Boston/London: Nijhoff).

Fennema, M. and Van der Pijl, K. (1987) *El triunfo del neoliberalismo* (Santo Domingo: Taller).

Fernández Jilberto, A. E. (1985) *Dictadura Militar y Oposición en Chile 1973-1981* (Dordrecht/Cinnaminson, NJ: Foris).

Frieden, J. (1981) 'Third World indebted industrialization: international finance and state capitalism in Mexico, Brazil, Algeria, and South Korea', *International Organization*, 35, 3.

Gill, S. (1987) *American Hegemony and the Trilateral Commission*, PhD dissertation, University of Birmingham.

Gossweiler, K. (1975 [1971]) *Großbanken, Industriemonopole, Staat. Ökonomie und Politik des staatsmonopolistischen Kapitalismus in Deutschland 1914-1932* (Berlin: DEB).

Gramsci, A. (1978) *Selections from the Prison Notebooks*, ed. Q. Hoare and G. N. Smith (New York: International Publishers).

Granou, A. (1977) *La Bourgeoisie financière au pouvoir et les luttes de classe en France* (Paris: Maspéro).

Hass, E. B. (1964) *Beyond the Nation-State. Functionalism and International Organization* (Stanford: Stanford University Press).

Hall, H. D. (1971) *Commonwealth. A History of the British Commonwealth of Nations* (London, etc.: Van Nostrand Reinhold).

Hymer, S. (1978) 'International Politics and International Economics: A Radical Approach', in *Monthly Review*, 29, 10.

Jordan, R. S. (1971) 'The Influence of the British Secretariat Tradition on the Formation of the League of Nations', in Jordan (ed.) *International Administration* (New York/London/Toronto: Oxford University Press).

Kant, I. (1953 [1795]) *Zum ewigen Frieden* (Stuttgart: Reclam).

Kolko, G. and Kolko, J. (1972) *The Limits of Power. The World and United States Foreign Policy, 1945-1954* (New York, etc.: Harper & Row).

Krasner, S. D. (1985) *Structural Conflict. The Third World Against Global Liberalism* (Berkeley, etc.: California University Press).

Lerner, D. and Gorden, M. (1967) *Euratlantica. Changing Perspectives of the European Elites* (Cambridge, Mass./London: MIT Press).

Lipietz, A. (1982) 'Towards Global Fordism?', *New Left Review* 132.

Mandel, E. (1972) *Der Spätkapitalismus* (Frankfurt: Suhrkamp).

Marx, K. (1973 [1939]) *Grundrisse*, translated by M. Nicolaus (Harmondsworth: Pelican Books).

MEW. Marx-Engels Werke, ed. Dietz (Berlin/DDR): vols. 23-25 of this edition are *Capital* vols. 1-3.

Müller-Plantenberg, U. (1981) 'Die mögliche historisch-politische Bedeutung der dritten großen Depression', *Prokla* 44.

Overbeek, H. (1986) 'The Westland Affair: Collision over the future of British capitalism', *Capital & Class*, 29.

Picciotto, S. (1987) *Slicing a Shadow - Business Taxation in an International Framework*, manuscript, University of Warwick.

Poulantzas, N. (1974) 'L'internationalisation des rapports capitalistes et l'Etat-Nation', in *Les Classes sociales dans le capitalisme d'aujourd'hui* (Paris: Seuil).

Van der Pijl, K. (1981) 'De EEG als kader voor controle', *Tijdschrift voor Diplomatie*, 7, 10.

Van der Pijl, K. (1978) *Een Amerikaans Plan voor Europa* (Amsterdam: SUA).

Van der Pijl, K. (1984) *The Making of an Atlantic Ruling Class* (London: Verso).

Radosh, R. (1969) *American Labor and United States Foreign Policy* (New York: Random House).

Rosenau, J. N. (1966) 'Pre-theories and Theories of Foreign Policy', in R. B. Farrell, *Approaches to Comparative and International Politics* (Evanston, Ill.: Harper & Row).

Sampson, A. (1968) *Anatomy of Europe* (New York/Evanston, Ill.: Harper & Row).

Sampson, A. (1982) *The Money Lenders. Bankers in a Dangerous World* (London: Coronet).

Shortall, F. (1986) 'Fixed and Circulating Capital', *Capital and Class* 28.

Shoup, L. H. and Minter, W. (1977) *Imperial Brain Trust. The Council of Foreign Relations and United States Foreign Policy* (New York/London: Monthly Review Press).

Timm, H. (1969) 'Wer garantiert den Frieden? Über Kants Schrift "Zum ewigen Frieden"', in G. Picht and H. E. Tödt (eds) *Studien zur Friedensforsschung*, Band I (Stuttgart: Keltt).

Warburg, J. P. (1947) *Germany - Bridge or Battleground* (New York: Harcourt , Brace).

Wiebes, C. and Zeeman, B. (1983) '*A Star is Born*'. *Militaire Alliantievorming in de Atlantische regio, 1945-1948*, Amsterdam (Mededelingen van de Subfaculteit Algemene Politieke en Sociale Wetenschappen 31).

Contributors

Y. Michal BODEMANN teaches sociology at the University of Toronto and is currently a visiting professor at the Freie Universität, Berlin. For many years he has conducted research in Sardinia, and his major interests include southern Italian society, ethnicity, new social movements, and theoretical issues within Marxism. His recent publications deal with the role of Jews in pre- and postwar Germany, Marx's conception of class, and the German Green Party.

Tom BOTTOMORE is Emeritus Professor of Sociology at the University of Sussex. His publications include *Elites and Society* (1964), *Political Sociology* (1979), *A Dictionary of Marxist Thought* (ed., 1983), *Sociology* (3rd edn., 1987), and *The Socialist Economy: Theory and Practice* (forthcoming 1989).

Robert J. BRYM is Professor of Sociology at the University of Toronto, and sociology editor of the *Canadian Review of Sociology and Anthropology*. His recent publications include *From Culture to Power: The Sociology of English Canada* (with Bonnie J. Fox, 1989), *Soviet-Jewish Emigration and Soviet Nationality Policy* (with Victor Zaslavsky, 2nd edn., 1989), and he has edited and contributed to *The Structure of the Canadian Capitalist Class* (1985). His current research deals with class voting in the advanced capitalist countries.

Antonio CHIESI is Assistant Professor at the University of Trieste. His publications include 'Property, capital and network structure in Italy', in F. N. Stokman, R. Ziegler and J. Scott (eds), *Networks of Corporate Power* (1985), and *The Organization of Time in Society: Determining Factors, Interactions and Consequences* (1985). His research interests are the substantive and methodological problems concerning financial elites, and the social organization of time.

David COATES is Senior Lecturer in Politics at the University of Leeds. His publications include *The Labour Party and the Struggle for Socialism* (1975), *Labour in Power?* (1980), and *The Context of British Politics* (1984). His current research deals with the politics of industrial relations in contemporary Britain.

Jane MARCEAU is Professor of Public Policy at the Australian National University. She has published numerous papers on French society, notably on education and the class structure, and her books include *Class and Status in France: Economic Change and Social Immobility, 1945–1975* (1977), *Masters of Business?* (with R. Whitley and A. Thomas, 1981), and *A Family Business? The Making of an International Business Elite* (in press, 1988).

Alberto MARTINELLI is Dean of the Faculty of Political Sciences at the University of Milan, where he teaches sociology and political science. His publications include 'Organized business and Italian politics', in P. Lange and S. Tarrow (eds), *Italy in Transition* (1980), 'The Italian experience', in R. Vernon and Y. Aharoni (eds), *State-Owned Enterprise in the Western Economies* (1981), *The New International Economy* (ed. with H. Makler and N. Smelser, 1983), and *Economia e Società* (1986). His current research interests are complex organizations, the political representation of business interests, industrial relations, and social policies.

Beth MINTZ is Associate Professor of Sociology at the University of Vermont. Her recent publications include 'The power structure of American business' (with Michael Schwartz), 'Capital flows and the process of financial hegemony' (with Michael Schwartz), in *Theory and Society*, and 'Class vs. organizational components of director networks', in Perrucci and Potter (eds), *Networks of Power*. Her major research areas include elite studies, corporate structure and labour market participation.

Koji MORIOKA is Professor of Economics at Kansai University. His most recent publication is *An Elucidation of Theories of Monopoly Capitalism* (revised and enlarged edn., 1987). His current research interests concern the problems of accumulation under monopoly capitalism.

Kees VAN DER PIJL is a staff member in the Department of International Relations and International Law at the University of Amsterdam. His publications include *The Making of an Atlantic Ruling Class* (1984), and *El Triunfo del Neoliberalismo* (with Meindert Fennema, 1987). His current research deals with the struggle over world order in the 1970s, and with the history of international relations theory.

Willfried SPOHN teaches sociology at the Freie Universität in Berlin, and is currently a member of the Institute for Advanced Study at Princeton. His major publications deal with the industrialization of Germany 1870–1914, the historical sociology of working class formation in Germany, the controversy between E. P. Thompson and P. Anderson, and theoretical issues within Marxism. He is working at present on the religious attitudes of workers in Imperial Germany in a comparative perspective.